# EMPIRE AND POLITICA?
## THE ROMAN WUKLD

This book evaluates a hundred years of scholarship on how empire transformed the Roman world and advances a new theory of how the empire worked and was experienced. It engages extensively with Rome's Republican empire as well as the "Empire of the Caesars," examines a broad range of ancient evidence (material, documentary, and literary) that illuminates multiple perspectives, and emphasizes the much longer history of imperial rule within which the Roman empire emerged. Steering a course between overemphasis on resistance and overemphasis on consensus, it highlights the political, social, religious, and cultural consequences of an imperial system within which functions of state were substantially delegated to, or more often simply assumed by, local agencies and institutions. The book is accessible and of value to a wide range of undergraduate and graduate students as well as of interest to all scholars concerned with the rise and fall of the Roman empire.

EMMA DENCH is McLean Professor of Ancient and Modern History and of the Classics at Harvard University. Her publications include *Romulus' Asylum: Roman Identities from the Age of Alexander to the Age of Hadrian* (2005) and *From Barbarians to New Men: Greek, Roman, and Modern Perceptions of Peoples of the Central Apennines* (1995), as well as numerous articles and chapters on ethnicity, race, empire, and historiography in the ancient world.

# KEY THEMES IN ANCIENT HISTORY

EDITORS

P. A. Cartledge
*Clare College, Cambridge*
P. D. A. Garnsey
*Jesus College, Cambridge*

Key Themes in Ancient History aims to provide readable, informed and original studies of various basic topics, designed in the first instance for students and teachers of Classics and Ancient History, but also for those engaged in related disciplines. Each volume is devoted to a general theme in Greek, Roman, or where appropriate, Graeco-Roman history, or to some salient aspect or aspects of it. Besides indicating the state of current research in the relevant area, authors seek to show how the theme is significant for our own as well as ancient culture and society. It is hoped that these original, thematic volumes will encourage and stimulate promising new developments in teaching and research in ancient history.

## Other books in the series

*Death-Ritual and Social Structure in Classical Antiquity*, by Ian Morris
978 0 521 37465 1 (hardback) 978 0 521 37611 2 (paperback)
*Literacy and Orality in Ancient Greece*, by Rosalind Thomas
978 0 521 37346 3 (hardback) 978 0 521 37742 3 (paperback)
*Slavery and Society at Rome*, by Keith Bradley
978 0 521 37287 9 (hardback) 978 0 521 37887 1 (paperback)
*Law, Violence, and Community in Classical Athens*, by David Cohen
978 0 521 38167 3 (hardback) 978 0 521 38837 5 (paperback)
*Public Order in Ancient Rome*, by Wilfried Nippel
978 0 521 38327 1 (hardback) 978 0 521 38749 1 (paperback)
*Friendship in the Classical World*, by David Konstan
978 0 521 45402 5 (hardback) 978 0 521 45998 3 (paperback)
*Sport and Society in Ancient Greece*, by Mark Golden
978 0 521 49698 8 (hardback) 978 0 521 49790 9 (paperback)
*Food and Society in Classical Antiquity*, by Peter Garnsey
978 0 521 64182 1 (hardback) 978 0 521 64588 1 (paperback)
*Banking and Business in the Roman World*, by Jean Andreau
978 0 521 38031 7 (hardback) 978 0 521 38932 7 (paperback)
*Roman Law in Context*, by David Johnston
978 0 521 63046 7 (hardback) 978 0 521 63961 3 (paperback)

*Religions of the Ancient Greeks*, by Simon Price
978 0 521 38201 4 (hardback) 978 0 521 38867 2 (paperback)
*Christianity and Roman Society*, by Gillian Clark
978 0 521 63310 9 (hardback) 978 0 521 63386 4 (paperback)
*Trade in Classical Antiquity*, by Neville Morley
978 0 521 63279 9 (hardback) 978 0 521 63416 8 (paperback)
*Technology and Culture in Greek and Roman Antiquity*, by Serafina Cuomo
978 0 521 81073 9 (hardback) 978 0 521 00903 4 (paperback)
*Law and Crime in the Roman World*, by Jill Harries
978 0 521 82820 8 (hardback) 978 0 521 53532 8 (paperback)
*The Social History of Roman Art*, by Peter Stewart
978 0 521 81632 8 (hardback) 978 0 52101659 9 (paperback)
*Ancient Greek Political Thought in Practice*, by Paul Cartledge
978 0 521 45455 1 (hardback) 978 0 521 45595 4 (paperback)
*Asceticism in the Graeco-Roman World*, by Richard Finn OP
978 0 521 86281 3 (hardback) 978 0 521 68154 4 (paperback)
*Domestic Space and Social Organisation in Classical Antiquity*, by Lisa C. Nevett
978 0 521 78336 1 (hardback) 978 0 521 78945 5 (paperback)
*Money in Classical Antiquity*, by Sitta von Reden
978 0 521 45337 0 (hardback) 978 0 521 45952 5 (paperback)
*Geography in Classical Antiquity*, by Daniela Dueck and Kai Brodersen
978 0 521 19788 5 (hardback) 978 0 521 12025 8 (paperback)
*Space and Society in the Greek and Roman Worlds*, by Michael Scott
978 1 107 00915 8 (hardback) 978 1 107 40150 1 (paperback)
*Studying Gender in Classical Antiquity*, by Lin Foxhall
978 0 521 55318 6 (hardback) 978 0 521 55739 9 (paperback)
*The Ancient Jews from Alexander to Muhammad*, by Seth Schwartz
978 1 107 04127 1 (hardback) 978 1 107 66929 1 (paperback)
*Language and Society in the Greek and Roman Worlds*, by James Clackson
978 0 521 19235 4 (hardback) 978 0 521 14066 9 (paperback)
*The Ancient City*, by Arjan Zuiderhoek
978 0 521 19835 6 (hardback) 978 0 521 16601 0 (paperback)
*Science Writing in Greco-Roman Antiquity*, by Liba Taub
978 0 521 11370 0 (hardback) 978 0 521 13063 9 (paperback)
*Politics in the Roman Republic*, by Henrik Mouritsen
978 1 107 03188 3 (hardback) 978 1 107 65133 3 (paperback)
*Roman Political Thought*, by Jed W. Atkins
978 1 107 10700 7 (hardback) 9781107514553 (paperback)

# EMPIRE AND POLITICAL CULTURES IN THE ROMAN WORLD

EMMA DENCH

*Harvard University*

# CAMBRIDGE
## UNIVERSITY PRESS

University Printing House, Cambridge CB2 8BS, United Kingdom

One Liberty Plaza, 20th Floor, New York, NY 10006, USA

477 Williamstown Road, Port Melbourne, VIC 3207, Australia

314–321, 3rd Floor, Plot 3, Splendor Forum, Jasola District Centre, New Delhi – 110025, India

79 Anson Road, #06–04/06, Singapore 079906

Cambridge University Press is part of the University of Cambridge.

It furthers the University's mission by disseminating knowledge in the pursuit of education, learning, and research at the highest international levels of excellence.

www.cambridge.org
Information on this title: www.cambridge.org/9780521810722
DOI: 10.1017/9781139028776

© Cambridge University Press 2018

First published 2018

Printed and bound in Great Britain by Clays Ltd, Elcograf S.p.A.

A catalogue record for this publication is available from the British Library.

ISBN 978-0-521-81072-2 Hardback
ISBN 978-0-521-00901-0 Paperback

# Contents

# Figures

# Acknowledgments

Huge thanks first and foremost to Paul Cartledge, Peter Garnsey, and Michael Sharp for issuing me the challenge all those years ago, for not giving up on me, and for their incisive criticisms and suggestions. For hundreds of conversations over far too many years with colleagues, friends, and former and current graduate students in and out of the classroom, I especially thank Dimiter Angelov, Valentina Arena, Nate Aschenbrenner, Charlie Bartlett, Sahar Bazzaz, Anna Bonnell-Freidin, Glen Bowersock, Kathleen Coleman, Coleman Connelly, the late Patricia Crone, Tiziana D'Angelo, Rowan Dorin, Susanne Ebbinghaus, Carrie Elkins, Stephanie Frampton, Eliza Gettel, Christopher Gilbert, Henry Gruber, Danny Jacobs, Maya Jasanoff, Andrew Johnston, Christopher Jones, Julia Judge, Cemal Kafadar, Rebecca Katz, Paul Kosmin, Nino Luraghi, Duncan MacRae, Patrick Meehan, Lizzie Mitchell, John Mulhall, Greg Nagy, Monica Park, Nicolas Prevelakis, Michael Puett, Christopher Smith, Katie van Schaik, Brent Shaw, Andrew Wallace-Hadrill, and Shiaoxiang Yan. I am enormously grateful to Eliza Gettel, Paul Kosmin, and Carlos Noreña for their generosity in sharing forthcoming work with me. Audiences, participants, students, and collaborators in many venues over the years have indulged me while I developed my ideas, especially during the Harvard Summer Program in Greece, my Gray Lectures at Cambridge University in May 2016, my lectures at Capital Normal University, Beijing, in October 2016, and my Magie Lecture at Princeton University in November 2016. During my visit to the Harvard Business School in 2015–2016, huge thanks to Frances Frei and our MBA and Executive Education students for the inspiring search for leadership lessons in the Roman empire. In the course of my year as Interim Dean of the Graduate School of Arts and Sciences (2017–2018), my colleagues in University Hall and the geniuses of the 3rd floor of the Smith Center and Dudley House patiently supported my efforts to put my scholarly enquiry into ancient imperial structures, systems, and cultures to practical use. The eagle-eyed Nadav Asraf put in many hours of highly skilled, meticulous, and patient work to get my mess of a bibliography into shape, for which I am extremely grateful. And most of all, love and thanks to Jonathan and Jacob for making me laugh and supplying my horror movie habit when the going got tough.

# Chronology

**BCE**

| | |
|---|---|
| ca. 560–ca. 547 | Croesus rules Lydia |
| 559–530 | Cyrus II traditional founder of Achaemenid Empire |
| 522–486 | Darius I rules Achaemenid Empire |
| 509 | Traditionally first year of Roman Republic |
| 486–464 | Xerxes rules Achaemenid Empire |
| 490 | Battle of Marathon (Persian Wars) |
| 480 | Battles of Thermopylae and Artemision (Persian Wars) |
| 479 | Battles of Plataea and Mycale (Persian Wars) |
| 478–404 | Delian League/Athenian Empire |
| 447–432 | Building of Parthenon on Athenian Acropolis |
| 431–404 | Peloponnesian War (Athenians vs. Spartans) |
| 404 | Spartans defeat Athenians in Peloponnesian War |
| 378–338 | Second Athenian Confederacy |
| 338 | Battle of Chaeronea (Philip II of Macedon vs. Athenians, Thebans, and other Greek forces) |
| 338 | Rome assigns statuses to ethnically Latin towns in Latin settlement |
| 334–323 | Campaigns of Alexander III ("the Great") of Macedon, defeating Achaemenid Empire in 330 |
| 323–168 | Antigonid kingdom (Successor kingdom) |
| 312–64 | Seleucid kingdom (Successor kingdom) |
| 323–330 | Ptolemaic kingdom (Successor kingdom) |
| 273 | Rome sends out colonists to Cosa and Paestum |
| 268 | Rome sends out colonists to Beneventum and Ariminum; end of Rome's Italian wars |
| 264–241 | First Punic War |
| 247–224 CE | Parthian Empire |
| 218–201 | Second Punic War |

| | |
|---|---|
| 168 | Day of Eleusis (Antiochus IV Epiphanes obeys Roman ultimatum) |
| 167 | Roman settlement of Macedonia |
| 149–146 | Third Punic War |
| 146 | Roman Destruction of Carthage and Corinth |
| 142–63 | Hasmonaean dynasty rules Judaea |
| 135–32 | First Sicilian Slave War |
| 133 | Tribunate of Tiberius Graccchus; Attalus III bequeathes his kingdom to the Roman people |
| 123–2 | Tribunate of Gaius Gracchus |
| 107 | Marius' first consulship |
| 104–100 | Second Sicilian Slave War |
| 91–89 | Social War |
| 89–85 | First Mithradatic War |
| ca. 83–81 | Second Mithradatic War |
| 82–81 | Dictatorship of Sulla |
| 73–66 | Third Mithradatic War |
| 63–62 | Pompey's settlement of the east |
| 63 | Cicero's consulship |
| 58–51 | Julius Caesar's campaigns in Gaul |
| 55–54 | Julius Caesar's expeditions to Britain |
| 44 | Foundation of colony of Urso (Colonia Iulia Genetiva); murder of Julius Caesar |
| 43 | Triumvirate created (Antony, Octavian, and Crassus) |
| 27–14 CE | Principate of Augustus |
| 41–54 | Claudius emperor |
| 66–70 | Great Jewish Revolt |
| 98–117 | Trajan emperor |
| 132–35 | Bar Kokhba Revolt |
| 212 | Edict of Caracalla on (near) universal citizenship of free persons in the Roman Empire |
| 224–642 | Sasanian Empire |
| ca. 239–70 | Shapur I "King of Kings" |
| 250 | Edict of Decius on universal sacrifice |
| 272–74 | Palmyrene Empire of Vaballathus and Zenobia |
| 284–305 | Diocletian emperor |
| 476 | Fall of Roman Empire in the west |
| 1453 | Fall of Byzantine Empire (self-conscious continuation of the Roman Empire) to the Ottomans |

# Abbreviations

Abbreviations of names and works of Greek and Latin authors follow *Oxford Classical Dictionary* conventions. Other editions/collections/translations of inscriptions, papyri, and documents on other materials are indicated by name of editor/translator and date and can be followed up in the main bibliography.

| | |
|---|---|
| *AE* | *L'Année Épigraphique* |
| *CIL* | *Corpus Inscriptionum Latinarum* |
| *CPJ* | V. Tcherikover, A. Fuks, M. Stern and D. M. Lewis, *Corpus Papyrorum Judaicarum*, 3 vols., Cambridge, MA (1957–1964) |
| *FIRA* | S. Riccobono, *Fontes Iuris Romani Antelustiniani*, Florence (1941) |
| *IG* | *Inscriptiones Graecae*, Berlin (1873– ) |
| *IGBulg* | G. Mihailov, *Inscriptiones Graecae in Bulgaria repertae*, Sofia (1958–1970) |
| *ILLRP* | A. Degrassi, *Inscriptiones Latinae Liberae Rei Republicae*, Florence, vol.1 (1965), vol. 2 (1963) |
| *ILS* | H. Dessau, *Inscriptiones Latinae Selectae*, Berlin (1892) |
| *P. Lond.* | *Greek Papyri in the British Museum*, London (1893– ) |
| *P. Oxy.* | *The Oxyrhynchus Papyri*, London (1898– ) |
| *P. Yadin* | N. Lewis, Y. Yadin, and J. C. Greenfield, J. C. (eds.), *The Documents from the Bar Kokhba Period in the Cave of Letters: Greek Papyri; Aramaic and Nabatean Signatures and Subscriptions*, Jerusalem (1989) |
| | Y. Yadin, J. C. Greenfield, A. Yardeni, and B. A. Levine (eds.), *The Documents from the Bar-Kokhba Period in the Cave of Letters: Hebrew, Aramaic and Nabatean-Aramaic Papyri*, 2 vols., Jerusalem (2002) |

RDGE        R. K. Sherk, *Roman Documents from the Greek East: Senatus*
            *consulta and Epistulae to the Age of Augustus, Baltimore* (1984)
Sel. Pap.   A. S. Hunt, C. C. Edgar, and D. L. Page, *Select Papyri*, 3
            vols., London (1932–1950; reprinted 1970–1977)
Syll. ³     W. Dittenberger, *Sylloge Inscriptionum Graecarum*, 3rd edn.,
            Leipzig (1924)
VA          R. D. Van Arsdell, *Celtic Coinage of Britain* (London, 1989)

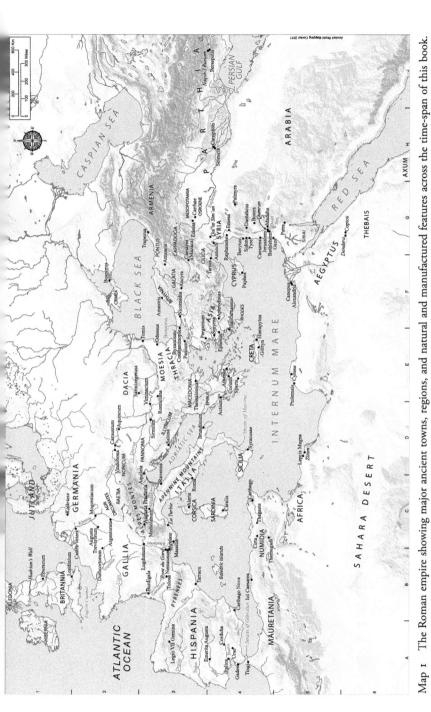

Map 1   The Roman empire showing major ancient towns, regions, and natural and manufactured features across the time-span of this book. Ancient World Mapping Center © 2018 (awmc.unc.edu). Used by permission.

# Introduction

But suicides have a special language.
Like carpenters they want to know which tools.
They never ask why build. [1]

Anne Sexton, "Wanting to Die"

How can we understand the local experience of change attendant on empire in the Roman world? Where should we look, and how do we begin to understand the processes involved? For much of the twentieth century, the end result that required explanation seemed self-evident, its manifestations all around in the landscapes (Roman roads, villas with mosaics, Hadrian's Wall), townscapes (urban grids, baths, theaters, and amphitheaters) and place-names of northern and western Europe (e.g., Aosta = Augusta [Praetoria], Köln/Cologne = Colonia [Claudia Ara Agrippinensium], Zaragoza = Caesaraugusta), its identification with "civilization," and, in more sophisticated accounts, its "blending" of distinctive regional and international features. Giving it a pseudo-technical name, most often "Romanization" or "Romanitas" (a term that appears in antiquity as a one-off with obscure meaning in Tertullian's *De Pallio* (4, 1, 1), and that has been hopelessly generalized in modern scholarship), has only strengthened the sense that we are talking about a readily identifiable phenomenon, and that we are all talking about the *same* phenomenon.

The assumption that the end-result is self-evident persists in many accounts of the Roman empire, along with a blurriness about the processes involved in such change that shows up in the impersonal and imprecise

---

language used to describe it: the "spread of Roman culture" is a well-used phrase. Meanwhile, every aspect of the process has been bitterly contested in a vast scholarly literature increasingly atomized by field of enquiry (disciplinary, theoretical, chronological, and regional). At least some of these contests are political: the Roman empire, insofar as it has been *the* iconic empire for much of the history of the western world, invites us to toggle backward and forward between "our" world and that of classical antiquity, not so much because of an inert "legacy," but because of a fraught reception history. Intellectual enquiry is inexorably tangled up in the politics of the real world through both the historical self-identification of formal and informal modern empires with Rome, and the appeal of its subjects' identities as entities (within, before, and beyond the Roman empire) for both emergent nation-states in the nineteenth century and newly independent, decolonized states in the second half of the twentieth century.[2]

In the first two sections of this chapter, I will map the major contours of these debates about change accompanying empire. I will start by considering Francis Haverfield's analysis of the scope and processes of change attendant on empire in Latin-speaking, northern provinces, in his *The Romanization of Roman Britain*, first delivered in 1905 as a British Academy lecture, and revised and republished several times in rapid succession in the early years of the twentieth century. This foundational text, and the debates within which it situates itself, usefully introduces many of the major contests of the twentieth century, the subject of the second section of this introduction. Finally, I will trace the path taken by this book and each of its chapters, with occasional glances at disciplinary, theoretical, and chronological roads not taken.

### Talking to Haverfield

Francis Haverfield's *The Romanization of Roman Britain* is remarkable for its sophistication. With its engagement in the newly scientific fields of anthropology and archaeology, its overtly comparative approach, and polemical insistence on the interpretative opportunities offered by non-textual material culture (especially art, ceramics, housing, town planning, and representations of the gods), it is an excellent vantage-point from

---

[2] For nation-building in Britain, see Vance 1997; Hingley 2000; Bradley 2010; Butler 2012; for the Maghreb: Mattingly 2011, chapter 2.

which to consider the debates that would vex scholarship for much of the twentieth century, some of which are ongoing.[3]

*The Romanization of Roman Britain* is a small book on a grand scale: Haverfield's magisterial opening paragraphs answer the implied question of what was the greatest Roman achievement, judged by the criterion of what the Romans did for "us." Pride of place among Roman achievements is the process that Haverfield calls "Romanization," following precedents in German and French scholarship,[4] a process restricted to what will become the Latin-speaking west. The end-result is the erasure of local difference and substantial homogeneity "in speech, in material culture, in political feeling and religion." Haverfield insists that the process can accurately be described as "becoming Roman." For some time, and in certain places more than others, there are "traces of tribal or national sentiments or fashions" (22). These remain largely inert rather than signaling "national sentiment," although it is possible to activate them under certain conditions, notably the invasion of new groups such as the Irish, among whom such "national sentiments" are still alive (chapter 9).

If these are the end-results of "Romanization," one remarkable passage encapsulates Haverfield's conceptualization of its processes:

> When the Romans spread their dominion over the island, it ["native" art] almost wholly vanished. For that we are not to blame any evil influence of this particular Empire. All native arts, however beautiful, tend to disappear before the more even technique and the neater finish of town manufactures. The process is merely part of the honour which a coherent civilization enjoys in the eyes of country folk. Disraeli somewhere describes a Syrian lady preferring the French polish of a western boot to the jewels of an eastern slipper. With a similar preference the British Celt abandoned his national art and adopted the Roman provincial fashion. (48)

This passage takes us to the heart of contemporary debates about the interplay between Roman expansion and change within the Roman imperial world, debates to which Haverfield alludes through the course of the book. The perceived relevance and urgency of the case of the Roman empire for questions and arguments about contemporary empires and nations are signaled in this passage particularly by Haverfield's intriguing vignette of the Victorian Prime Minister Benjamin Disraeli's "Syrian lady,"

---

[3] Haverfield 1905; 1912; 1915; 1923. I cite the 1915 edition (the last version revised by Haverfield himself) throughout; for detailed examination of Haverfield and his intellectual contexts, see Freeman 1997; 2007. Gettel (2018) is an important discussion of the late nineteenth- and early twentieth-century context for Haverfield's concept of 'culture.'

[4] Notably Mommsen 1885.

which turns out to be an allusion to a minor character in his novel *Tancred, or the New Crusade* (1847) (Book 5, chapter 7). When Haverfield refuses to attribute the near disappearance of "native art" in Britain to the "evil influence" of the Roman empire, we think of models of empires as politically and economically exploitative that sometimes predate the "evil empire" of early twentieth-century Marxist-Leninist writings by centuries. When he writes of the natural attraction of "country folk" toward a "coherent civilization," we think of Mommsen's Hegelian inevitability of nations and their centripetal draw.[5]

As this passage suggests, Haverfield's *Romanization of Roman Britain* effectively carves out a field by its choices of material on which to focus, the questions it asks, the answers it gives, and its silences. Power dynamics are glimpsed only at the margins of the account, even while they hang uncomfortably in the air via the vignette attributed to Disraeli in this passage. The attractions of French polish on western boots hint at military and institutional dimensions of empire that are otherwise barely seen. In the same passage, "Roman dominion" indicates the temporal and causal framework of the scene, but conquest and force are periodized out, belonging to the time before the narrative begins, and the text focuses squarely on a quotidian world of Roman Britain rather than crises, revolt, and rebellion. Political structures and institutions of imperial government (including the citizenship) are explicitly "passed over" at the beginning of the book as the monumental achievement of Mommsen (10), but the physical structures that mark Roman presence, such as Hadrian's Wall and army camps, are likewise largely omitted, as are "imperial cult" sites and other accommodations and naturalizations of Roman imperial power.[6]

This passage also illustrates beautifully Haverfield's conceptualization of how change happens in the process of "Romanization," and the status of that change. For the "Syrian lady," it is a comprehensive, bottom-up, cognitive, rational change that involves recognizing the truth of "coherence." Elsewhere in the work, Haverfield contrasts the degree to which change and assimilation are achieved in the western Roman empire with the incomplete mission of European empires. In the western Roman empire, he argues, there were no racial barriers to obstruct a process that involves not just stylistic and aesthetic change, but a total realignment of

---

[5] 'Evil empires' before Marxist-Leninist traditions: succinctly Armitage 2000; cf. Hobson 1902; Lenin 1939. Mommsen and the centripetal draw of nations: Mouritsen 1998.
[6] The major exception is urbanization, which functions as an index of 'Romanization' in Haverfield 1915, chapter 6.

hearts and minds. The "Asiatic" or "African" of Haverfield's contemporary world may put on western clothes temporarily and instrumentally, for "profit or pleasure," but the Roman provincial equivalent puts on the clothes, consciously recognizes the value of civilization that they represent, and simultaneously switches his loyalty to Rome (20). While in the passage quoted above the "native" element does not wholly disappear, all that is left is a tiny bit of its aesthetic that comes out in Romano-British representations of animals and monsters, a touch of liveliness and vigor amidst what Haverfield sees as the conformist and imitative downside of the process of "Romanization" (chapter 5). This liveliness and vigor are a reflex rather than an indicator of the identity and allegiance of the ancient Britons: any remaining "national" sentiment lies dormant, a silent genetic trait that will reemerge only when the arrival of new, unaltered native peoples stimulate it.

Haverfield distinguishes these processes of secular change from the pragmatic polytheism that he imagines in the pre-Christian ancient world, where a man who changed his town or province "could change his gods as easily as his washerwoman," while "Roman" and "native" were "harmoniously intertwined" in a "blending-vat of worships." This easy religious boundary crossing, or functional god-changing that involved no inner crisis, could not be more different from the modern world, where, Haverfield says, "no man can be in any real sense Mahometan and Jew at once" (67). The distinction that he draws between secular and religious processes of change in the pre-Christian Roman empire interestingly maps rather neatly on to the distinction that A. D. Nock would draw several decades later between conversion to a "prophetic" religion (Judaism, Christianity, or Islam) and the experience of religious change in the "pagan" world. Haverfield's vision of the ease of changing and combining gods sounds very much like Nock's notion of being outside of "prophetic religion", where individuals experience unexciting, functional, gradual change including "borrowing," "fusion," and "adhesion" rather than "any definite crossing of religious frontiers" (1933, 6–7). Haverfield's vision of secular change, of "becoming Roman," will be mirrored by Nock's characterization of conversion to a "prophetic" religion as typically involving a profound, conscious, and rational recognition of truth and an identity shift from one state of being to another, with no going back (1933, esp. 1–16).

I am of course not arguing for a specific connection between Haverfield's model of secular change in the Roman empire and Nock's of religious conversion: that would be a chronological impossibility. But I do want to highlight the degree to which notions of cultural assimilation and Christianization were broadly interlinked in the nineteenth and early twentieth centuries because of the particular expectations of empire at that time. In this context, it is well worth wondering what baggage early usage of the noun "Romanization" by Haverfield and others carried with it, before it became narrowly the specialist (if very problematic) term that it is for us today. Among historical (and, in the twenty-first century, largely obsolete) usages of the English verb "to Romanize," "Romanization," "Romanized," and "Romanizing," it is easy to forget the importance from the seventeenth century of the heavily pejorative sense of "going Catholic" on the part of Protestants. The noun "Romanization" was historically used of the transliteration process into "Roman" letters that was associated primarily with Jesuit missions to East and South Asia.[7]

Haverfield's engagement with contemporary debates that envisaged religious change at the center of an imperial project of assimilation is implicit in his allusion to Disraeli's "Syrian lady." Within the context of Disraeli's novel *Tancred: or the New Crusade,* the "Syrian lady," one Thérèse de Laurella, has learned through her education in Marseilles to despise Syria and be ashamed of her own Jewish origins (Book 5, chapter 7). The novel is a parody of misguided colonialism and assimilation tendencies, which one would not guess from Haverfield's allusion. It is, however, telling that a novel of this kind, one that directly confronts European colonialism, missionary activities, and political intervention in the "Holy Land" in the course of its protagonist's quest for a spiritual purity lost in the travesties of established religion in contemporary England, was very much on Haverfield's mind while he was writing *The Romanization of Roman Britain.*

Haverfield's *The Romanization of Roman Britain,* then, represents a particular fusion of the comparative study of empire with contemporary ideas about nationalism, colonialism, and religious conversion that would underlie fundamental notions of change attendant on the Roman empire for much of the twentieth century. It is worth emphasizing that textual sources of the earlier and "high" Roman empires rarely ethnicize change attendant on empire, in ancient equivalents of "becoming Roman."[8] Strabo, the early first-century CE Augustan geographer, is the major exception, when he characterizes the Spanish Turdetani as having

---

[7] See *Oxford English Dictionary* for historical usage of 'Romanize,' 'Romanization,' 'Romanizing,' and 'Romanized'; problematizing 'Romanization': e.g., Barrett 1997; Freeman 1997.
[8] For reservations about the ethnicization of change in the Roman empire, see Vanacker and Zuiderhoek 2017.

"completely changed over to the way of the Romans." But even for Strabo this is unusual: he elsewhere introduces qualifiers when characterizing change (3, 2, 15; cf. 4, 1, 12; 5, 4, 7). In Tacitus *Agricola* 21, the ancient literary source most frequently cited as evidence in discussions of "Romanization," Agricola's encouragement of the ancient Britons to succumb to quiet and peace is characterized in the traditional moralizing terms of imperial discourse, while the "real" end-point of the process (as opposed to the *humanitas*, usually translated as "civilization," that the Britons perceive it to be) is the equally traditional servitude. The political/ethnic vocabulary of "becoming Roman" does not appear here at all.[9]

This should not surprise us. Roman identity meant something quite specific in the early Empire. Roman citizenship had long been extended to the freed slaves of Roman citizens, remarkably to Greek eyes, and, from the middle Republic, to the inhabitants of certain communities in Italy, including some of Rome's former enemies. The traditional assumption was that Roman citizenship would entail direct participation in the obligations and privileges of the Roman state, including the political institutions of the city of Rome. It is significant that our best ancient evidence for peoples said to "become" or "be made" Romans before late antiquity comes from Republican-period texts or from narrative accounts of Republican-period history.[10] This assumption of direct participation in the Roman state's and city of Rome's political institutions was progressively challenged by the extension of the citizenship in the decades following the Social War of 91–89 BCE to all communities of peninsular Italy, and to the communities of Cisalpine Gaul in 49 BCE, by the increasing diaspora of Roman citizens outside Italy (particularly military veterans settled in Roman colonies overseas), and by the growing expectation in the last decades of the Republic that the citizenship was *de facto* in the gift of individuals. In discursive contexts of the late Republic and early Empire, we find intense engagement with myths of Roman ethnic hybridity and legal and social mobility, in addition to Cicero's famous reflection on dual citizenship (*Laws* 2, 5), that of Rome and that of one's local Italian town. In terms of more general experience, Roman citizenship in the Empire was regularly inflected as a privilege or honor claimed and enjoyed within the context of one's local community. The argument that it substantially remained as

---

[9] For a fuller discussion of ancient intellectual modes of conceptualizing behavioral change attendant on empire, see Dench 2005, 80–91, with bibliography.

[10] E.g., "nos sumus Romani qui fuimus ante Rudini," "We are Romans, who were once Rudini" (Ennius *Ann.* 524–5 Skutsch); Sherwin-White 1973, chapter 2.

such until the Edict of Caracalla in 212 CE, which extended citizenship to almost the whole free population of the Roman Empire, is reinforced by Myles Lavan's recent estimate of the percentage of Roman citizens at the beginning of the third century CE, somewhere between 15 percent and 33 percent. He has also emphasized the unaccelerated rhythm of extensions in the later first and second centuries CE. Traditional arguments about a "flood tide" of extensions diminishing the value of the Roman citizenship before the Edict are now untenable.[11]

As Michael Maas and Neil McLynn have eloquently shown, late antique characterizations of the process of conquest, change, and rule can be significantly and strikingly different from Tacitus' depiction of Agricola in Britain, the most interventionist of early imperial texts. While Agricola works on the sidelines by cheering the Britons on, giving a helping hand, rewarding and scolding them, and working on their competitive spirit, early Byzantine emperors are not just in the thick of it but on top of it, abolishing "bestial" and "barbarous" practices such as inheritance practices and castration. While Tacitus' hoodwinked Britons think they are getting *humanitas*, but are actually succumbing to slavery, the addressees of early Byzantine decrees and characters in early Byzantine ethnographical passages are left in no doubt that they are being given *Roman* laws and lifestyles in place of "bestial" or "barbarous" ones. Perhaps the most striking difference is that top-down, imposed religious change goes hand-in-hand with changing to Roman laws and practices: "barbarians" in these accounts change their *diaita*, "lifestyle," for the gentler, and change their *doxa*, their belief system, to Christianity. This is a very significant development within an ethnographical discourse that is generally quite conservative. This development involves importing and adapting a new vocabulary: the noun *doxa* is borrowed from disputes about the borderlines between orthodoxy and heresy among groups claiming to be Christians. These representations still do much more than merely describe the complicated world in which they were produced, but suggest both the increased, assertive ideal of Romans verus "barbarians" in the particular conditions of late antiquity and the paradigm-shifting character of monotheism.[12] The specific conditions of the late antique/early Medieval world arguably formed a striking alliance with the specific conditions of the nineteenth- and early twentieth-century west to persuade us of a very particular

---

[11] Mouritsen 1998; Dench 2005, chapter 2; Purcell 2005a; Lavan 2016; "flood tide": Sherwin-White 1973, chapter 10.
[12] Maas 2003; McLynn 2003.

understanding of the nature of change attendant on Roman imperial conquest and rule.

## One Hundred Years of Imperial Change

The broad lines in the sand that Haverfield both observed and drew largely continued to demarcate territories of enquiry for much of the twentieth century, with expertise and an ever-increasing volume of evidence encouraging further splintering and atomization along chronological, methodological, disciplinary, and regional lines. The largest rift was between "politics," almost universally the domain of "the Romans," and "culture," almost universally that of "natives." However, much we might regret the splintering and atomization of discussions, this process also encouraged considerable refinement of source bases, questions, and argument.

Among the subfields within which the broad study of the Roman empire and its impact was divided, one of the largest focused on the "formative" processes of conquest and imperial coming of age between the middle Republic and the early first century BCE. This was a subfield with almost exclusive focus on "the Romans" as political and military actors, whether conquest and expansion were viewed primarily as defensive or as aggressive, and even if "the Romans" were considered on location, within a sphere of military action. One major exception that challenged this close focus on "the Romans" was the emerging subfield of Greek perspectives on and engagement with the Roman empire. Examples of this emerging subfield include Erich Gruen's important *The Hellenistic World and the Coming of Rome* (1984), as well as Polybian studies, and the extraordinary epigraphic contributions of Louis Robert and others. It was characterized by serious enquiry into Greek political ideas within the Roman empire, long before this was fashionable, and without assigning Greek activity to a category of "culture" that tended to exclude "politics."[13] Ernst Badian's *Foreign Clientelae (264–70 BC)*, first published in 1958, exaggerates the prevalence of patronage (in the formalized, Roman sense rather than the more general modern sociological concept of enduring, unequal, reciprocal relationships) in Roman Republican imperial contexts.

---

[13] For a sample of approaches to "the Romans" as military and political actors, see Champion 2004b, chs. 1–2; for a superior treatment of 'the Romans' on location, see Richardson 1986; formative Polybian studies include Walbank 1957–1979; 1972; Derow 1979; Champion 2004b; cf. Smith and Yarrow 2012; Gibson and Harrison 2013; Greek political ideas: for Louis Robert, see, succinctly, Rousset 2012; serious early treatments of Greek political ideas include Millar 1964; Bowersock 1965; 1969; Bowie 1970; Jones 1971; 1978; Crawford 1978.

However, the book is path-breaking in its vision of imperial sway as a network of complex, competing asymmetrical relationships, as opposed to a narrower view of exclusively Roman political and military action.[14]

Thinking of Rome's Republican empire as primarily a problem that concerned the Roman state, its principal actors, its army, and its institutions of government might not have left much space for considering the agency and contexts of peoples within spheres of engagement, but it undoubtedly had broader implications for the ways in which scholarship framed and judged the imperial project. The acquisition of empire, its early steps elided with the dynastic escalations of the late Republic, continued to function implicitly as a prelude and backdrop to a focus on "culture" within individual provinces, as it had in Haverfield's account. Judgment on whether imperial acquisition was Rome's fault rather than an accident, necessary self-defense or an act of benevolence to posterity would substantially inform understanding of the imperial project. Rome's acquisition and management of empire was generally reckoned to fall somewhere along a scale running between enslavement and the bringing of civilization. The representation of Roman imperial processes as a story in two distinct parts (with a rough divide at the Augustan principate), the politics and warfare of conquest and the cultural effects, viewed at and from the provincial level, to a considerable extent continues in the arrangement of overviews and sourcebooks, particularly those aimed at students. A third distinct area, "Roman government of the empire," might be added, including institutions, law and taxation, and regional or province-based enquiries rooted in specific kinds of evidence: the epigraphy of the "Greek city"; the papyrology of (especially) Egypt; the archaeology of northern and western provinces.[15]

In the later decades of the twentieth century, amidst the very different politics of decolonization and postcolonialism, much energy was invested in shifting focus away from Romanocentric approaches and onto the agency and distinct agenda of local peoples of empire, building narratives of resistance and, to quote from the title of David Mattingly's important edited volume, "discrepant experience." Even if they tended ultimately to enforce the binary distinction between "Romans" and "natives," and to

---

[14] For recent reappraisals, see Eilers 2002; Jehne and Pina Polo 2015.

[15] Thinking of provinces as a distinct topic separable from the politics of imperial acquisition is arguably in part a legacy of Mommsen's *Römische Geschichte* (vols. 1–3: 1854–1856; vol. 5: 1885), its overall program distorted by the fact that Mommsen himself never completed the fourth volume, on the Empire (of the Caesars); recent overviews and sourcebooks that substantially maintain this division include Champion 2004b; Erskine 2010; Hoyos 2013.

conceptualize the role of "natives" as primarily a reaction to Roman rule, these studies valuably developed and took in different directions a number of the premises and lines of enquiry that are apparent already in Haverfield's *The Romanization of Roman Britain*. These include approaches to and expectations of material culture informed by the archaeology of prehistoric societies and by anthropology, rather than as illustrations of literary narratives, and the considerable complexity of both agency and outcome. However, these later twentieth-century studies of course generated readings very different from Haverfield's notion of progress toward the assumed virtues of "civilization" and "coherence."[16]

With hindsight, three works in English of the late 1970s and early 1980s, each offering new ways of thinking about "Roman government" of the Imperial period, posed the most significant challenges to the partitioning of scholarship between the Roman center – with its monopoly on power, initiative, and political agency – and the provinces, spheres of "culture" or, at most, reaction to Roman power. Fergus Millar's *The Emperor in the Roman World (31 BC–AD 337)*, first published in 1977, took to task the tradition of understanding the role of the emperor in terms of what he was "allowed" to do by virtue of the legal definition of his powers. Although Millar set out his study in polemically empirical terms ("the emperor is what the emperor did"), and sources on "what the emperor did" are inevitably doing more than just describing, it can be read most productively as a radically new response model of empire. Instead of the emperor (or, for that matter, "the Romans") having the monopoly on political agency, Millar's imperial subjects and inhabitants of empire substantially mold the practice of emperor and empire and alike by issuing requests and petitions to which the emperor responds. In Keith Hopkins' comparative, sociological essay, "Divine Emperors and the Symbolic Unity of the Roman Empire," published in his collection *Conquerors and Slaves* (1978a) the year after Millar's book, the Roman Empire is, by contrast, much less a matter of doing and much more a matter of believing. Empire is a belief system centered on emperors. Their cult functions as both legitimization and the means by which remote subjects "come to terms with his grandeur and power" (197). Hopkins makes a point of including stories and myths because "political power and legitimacy rest not only in taxes and armies, but also in the perceptions and beliefs of men" (198). Ironically, in the light of Hopkins' savage review of

---

[16] Particularly innovative examples include: Bénabou 1976; Webster and Cooper 1996; Mattingly 1997.

*The Emperor in the Roman World,* the differences between his own approach to the Roman Empire and Millar's seem rather smaller than they did in the late 1970s.[17]

My third example is Simon Price's *Rituals and Power: The Roman Imperial Cult in Asia Minor,* first published in 1984. Deeply informed by approaches to ritual, power, and kingship in anthropology, critical theory, and political science, Price's study locates the "power" of his title not only at the Roman center in two-way communication via the "imperial cult," but also in the multiple asymmetrical relationships (e.g., mass and elite, intercity rivalries, tensions between "Greek" and "indigenous" cultures) enacted through the practices and beliefs of the "imperial cult." As such, his study takes very seriously the local political structures and plural systems of religious authority in which the "imperial cult" is embedded and which it enhances.[18]

Two more recent, and justly influential accounts take forward the focus on empire as a belief system and continue to complicate the idea of a bipartite model that distributes power and agency neatly along the lines of "Romans" and "subjects" or "natives." Greg Woolf's *Becoming Roman: The Origins of Provincial Civilization in Gaul,* first published in 1998, might be viewed primarily as an offshoot that significantly transcends the "provincial cultures" tradition. The study centers on a shared imperial value-system encapsulated by the Latin term *humanitas* (which he translates as "civilization"), while the process of "becoming Roman" that Woolf signals in his title involves joining an "insiders' debate about what that package did or ought to consist of at that particular time" (11). The emergence and development of this value-system are tracked in the material culture of Gaul. Both the "debate" and the implicit gap between values and their material substantiation write in and account for substantial cultural variation. Baths and bathing, along with dining and writing, are Woolf's paradigmatic examples of articulations of and contributions to this value-system. Clifford Ando's *Imperial Ideology and Provincial Loyalty in the Roman Empire* (2000) significantly transcends the "government of the Roman Empire" tradition. Unlike Woolf's *humanitas,* Ando's belief system is not a particular value but consensus about the power and efficacy of the Roman imperial system itself, a system that connects the individual to the Roman state through participating in its rituals (that may be more or less

---

[17] For empire and specifically emperorship as response, cf. Millar 1984; Hopkins 1978b on Millar 1977.

[18] See, especially, Price 1984, chapter 9.

"religious" or more or less "political," e.g., the census, the granting of crowns, the communication of status and privilege, and the systematization of loops of correspondence through rescripts and archives).

In the last two decades, impressive initiatives to cross disciplinary, methodological, chronological, and regional lines in the sand have continued, while big questions about where we might go from here have continued to surface. Among these, I would single out exciting questions about the nature of Rome's Republican empire, following older traditions of enquiry about Greek perspectives on and engagement with the Roman empire to move beyond a narrower focus on "the Romans" as military and political actors. Michael Crawford's acute suggestion of the value of Millar's response model of imperial governance also for Rome's Republican empire is an invitation waiting to be taken up more fully, while the extension to "the west" of the sorts of deeply contextualized, culture- and politics-rich enquiries that have characterized the most successful studies of the Greek-speaking east, is very promising.[19]

Meanwhile, lively debate continues about how best to approach the study of change within the Roman empire and change attendant on empire, and how to disentangle the various strands. While there is an admirable desire to think through issues of identity and socialization beyond texts that represent the conscious and intellectualizing reflections of a small proportion of society, the hasty politicization and ethnicization of behavior such as bathing with the tag "Romanitas," or "being Roman" are not the answer. As we have begun to see, they risk confusing legal status, self-identification, and the less conscious but extremely complex processes of assimilation, and, not unlike Haverfield's account of the process, imply a state of completion or conversion that limits alternative interpretative possibilities, including those that work within local systems of authority.[20]

At the same time, systematic reassessments of particular types of material culture have begun to undermine some earlier certainties about the "spread of Roman culture." For example, the kind of third-century BCE black-gloss pottery identified as the production of the "Atelier des petites estampilles" had been understood as an indicator of both a Roman economic imperialism and aesthetic change. However, Roman Roth's recent reevaluations would emphasize the plurality of production sites in

---

[19] Crawford 1990, 102 with n. 50; promising new context-rich studies of 'the west': e.g., Prag 2007; Prag and Crawley Quinn 2013.
[20] E.g., Revell 2009, esp. 172; Woolf 2012; Revell 2016.

central Italy, the variation of types at the same time that we see increased standardization, and the different central Italian economic and social contexts within which the pottery was produced and used, suggesting different meanings. On a grander scale, turning to "globalization" as a model for the interplay between local distinction and broad common patterns of change has a number of advantages, not the least of which is that it encourages the discussion of connectivity and change without assuming that it is all about Rome. How far it will prove a useful model beyond conveniently tagging processes we were already beginning to recognize remains to be seen.[21]

The overall trajectory of change attendant on empire is likely to continue to be an area of keen debate. Should we think in terms of a progressive trade-off between "local" and Roman (or "global"/"international") political and cultural idioms, escalating between the later first and early second centuries CE, as scholarship on the northern and western provinces has tended to suggest? Or does the interplay between "local" and Roman or "global"/"international" have more subtle rhythms as local political bodies and individuals define themselves and assert their authority by instrumentalizing various idioms and *loci* of power?[22]

The question of trade-off becomes acute between the scholarly zones of "high empire" and late antiquity, when idioms associated with the Roman imperial state progressively dominate the articulation of power and efficacy. Examples of this progressive domination of idioms associated with the Roman imperial state include the phenomenon of portraying Egyptian and Near Eastern gods "in uniform," the distinctive military dress of the emperor or high officials (see Figure 1 for Horus), and the naturalization of Latin or Latinizing imperial formulas or legalese. It is tempting at first sight to interpret such tendencies in terms of a shrinking ability to think outside the all-encompassing Roman Empire and one's place within it. It might be tempting also to see them as anticipating or ultimately aligned with the loud, assertive statehood and central control of the late Roman Empire, arguably at the expense of the vibrant, city-based local political life that had been the mainstay of earlier Imperial energy, along with the exclusive

---

[21] Black-gloss pottery: Roth 2013, with some response to Morel 2009; cf. Roth 2007; Roth and Keller 2007; globalization: Witcher 2000; Hingley 2005; Hitchner 2008; Versluys 2014; Pitts and Versluys 2015; cf. the sophisticated approaches of Horden and Purcell 2000; Whitmarsh 2010; Woolf 2014.

[22] For different assessments, see e.g., Woolf 2011; Johnston 2017; compare different approaches to regions of the Greek-speaking east, e.g., Smith 1998; Andrade 2013.

Figure 1　Seated Egyptian god Horus dressed in the Roman military costume of an emperor or high-ranking officer, probably second to third century CE, British Museum. Photo by C. M. Dixon/Print Collector/Getty Images.

monotheism that seems to go hand-in-hand with it. But a closer look at the contexts of the use of idioms associated with the Roman imperial state reveals garbling, appropriations that do not feed the Roman imperial machine but myriad local and group purposes, juxtapositions with alternative *loci* of power, and occasionally outright rebellion. Recent assessments have also emphasized the less than streamlined unity of structures and belief in late antiquity, as the Roman state continued in active competition with other systems. The Roman citizenship was still (however surprisingly) invoked as a measure of status, alongside other measures. Plural legal systems remained available, while the alternative *loci* of power and authority that these plural systems imply remained active. The political activities that enacted organized grouphoods were transformed, rather than simply failed. Gaps remained between messages and their reception in thought and deed.[23]

## Empire and Political Cultures in the Roman World

This book is a thematic treatment of change attendant on the Roman empire that can be broadly classified as political, with its chronological focus between the early reception of Macedonian dialects of conquest and empire ca. 300 BCE and the "high" empire of the second to third centuries CE. This political dimension includes: the direct intervention or influence of representatives of the Roman imperial state; the emergence of imperial idioms associated specifically with Roman rule, and engagement in and appropriation of systems, rituals, and insignia associated with Roman sovereignty; the enactment and performance of Roman citizenship within local contexts; reconfigurations of civic community and other peoplehoods and grouphoods at the interface with the imperial center; and articulations of self-direction.

This book seeks to bridge the gaps between the Republican military/ political actions of "the Romans" and the "government of Empire" traditions, on the one hand, and between both of these traditions and the "provincial cultures" tradition, on the other. Qualifying "cultures" with "political" centers, I focus on articulations of statehood, peoplehood, and grouphood rather than on looser questions of cultural identity or mapping broader changes in material culture. I also take seriously the degree to which local communities, groups, and organizations of the Roman empire articulated political identity and self-direction within an imperial system that substantially depended on such self-direction, and actively fostered and even created groups and organizations (e.g., friendly kings, cities, militias, *koina, collegia*) rather than relegating such activity to "just" cultural expression. The plural "cultures" of my title signals the centrality of plural languages and idioms within the Roman imperial world, along with the presence of competing states and systems of authority and belief, something that is not immediately apparent in most "belief system" treatments of empire rooted in the "government of Empire" tradition. Insofar as there was sometimes everyday fuzziness about who was in control, about lines of command and subordination, this was not without

---

[23] Ando 2013 is a highly stimulating account of the strengthening of the late Roman state, and its narrowing of other possibilities; rather different conclusions are suggested by e.g., Garnsey 2004; Sandwell 2011; Humfress 2013.

risk to imperial security, but the opportunism and investment that this encouraged in general only lent dynamism to the imperial project. The book is necessarily an essay, with no pretensions to comprehensiveness.

Of the five chapters, the first, "Toward a Roman Dialect of Empire" is concerned with the ongoing processes of conceptualizing, enacting, and claiming modes of power and sovereignty associated with the Roman imperial state. It treats the ongoing process of the Roman imperial state coming to be at the interface with preexisting and competing systems and expectations of rule. In addition, it considers the increasing availability of modes of power and sovereignty of the Roman imperial state and its systems for the self-actualization and fulfillment of various ends of groups and individuals. Each of the four chapters that follow, "Territory," "Wealth and Society," "Force and Violence," and "Time," explores a theme that raises a fundamental set of primarily political questions about how and by what means the articulation of sovereignty, constitution, and self-direction (e.g., around the payment of taxes, minting coinage, setting boundaries, and articulating territory, keeping an army, or having a common calendar) on the part of states and other groups changed at the interface with the Roman imperial state. In the Epilogue, I briefly reassess the consequences of viewing the Roman empire through this lens, and what the "rise and fall" of empire looks like from this perspective.

# CHAPTER I

# Toward a Roman Dialect of Empire

## Anatomies of Roman Imperial Government

This, then, is the lay of the different parts of our inhabited world; but since the Romans occupy the best and the best-known portions of it, having surpassed all former rulers of whom we have record, it is worthwhile, even though briefly, to add the following account of them ... Of this whole country that is subject to the Romans, some is indeed ruled by kings, but the Romans retain the other part, calling it "provincial" (*eparchian*), and send governors (*hēgemonas*) and collectors of tribute (*phorologous*). But there are also some free cities, some of which came over to the Romans at the outset as friends, whereas others were set free by them as a mark of honour. There are also some potentates and phylarchs and priests subject to them. Now these live in accordance with certain ancestral laws. But the provinces have been divided in different ways at different times, though at the present time they are as Augustus Caesar (*Kaisar ho Sebastos*) arranged them; for when his native land committed to him the foremost place of authority and he became established as lord for life of war and peace, he divided the whole land into two parts, and assigned one portion to himself and one to the people.

Strabo, *Geography* 17, 3, 24–5, Loeb tr. H. L. Jones with minor adaptations

There are many ways of starting a conversation about empire and political cultures in the Roman world. Modern accounts of the Roman empire have traditionally begun where the early Imperial[1] geographer, Strabo, writing between the 30s BCE and the 20s CE with a perspective that zooms impressively between the global and the highly particular, ends his panoramic account of a Roman world newly centered on monarchy.

---

[1] Modern usage makes the fact that the Romans possessed an empire before they had emperors seem counter-intuitive. As a compromise, I capitalize Empire and Imperial when referring specifically to the period from January 27 BCE, when Augustus was granted this honorific name by the Roman senate. When referring either to the empire of the Republican period and its condition ("imperial"), or to empire spanning the Republican period and the world of emperors, I do not capitalize these terms.

Something along the lines of Strabo's anatomy of the Roman empire's parts, its personnel and basic institutions (provinces and governors, tax-collectors, the *princeps* himself, free cities, kings and other rulers paradoxically both subject to Rome and using their own ancestral laws), is generally reproduced as a straight description of Roman administration, how the Roman empire really was.[2]

Modern anatomies of Roman administration that lay out its constituent parts and the relationships between them are rooted in masterful nineteenth- and earlier twentieth-century analyses, a tradition dominated by Mommsen's account in his *Römisches Staatsrecht* (1871–1888) of the Roman state as a well-oiled machine that operated according to recoverable, legal rules. But there is, of course, no such thing as an unengaged and merely descriptive anatomy of the Roman empire. The telling of parts and powers is inevitably selective, aspirational, idealizing, or corrective, in various measures, whether it forms part of an official, Roman-state sponsored context, such as the later Republican *repetundae* ("extortion") law (Crawford 1996, 1, 1), or a literary text such as Strabo's *Geography*.

Strabo's panoramic vision of the distinctly Roman political geography of most of the inhabited world translates Roman imperial power into a centuries-old Greek vocabulary of sovereignty and rule with its own, substantial baggage and different semantic ranges. Along with this vocabulary go centuries-old expectations: highlighting free cities signals the ancient motif of "surrender-and-grant" that makes self-government the gift of imperial rulers, a prime illustration of the distinctive currencies of premodern empires, balancing precariously but productively on local structures and their bargaining power. As Strabo's *Geography* reaches its grand finale in this passage, Augustus' division of the provinces marks recognition of the *princeps'* supremacy over the best part of the inhabited world: Strabo's very project of universal geography is underpinned by the hereditary monarchy established by Augustus (cf. 6, 4, 2). There was no inevitable connection between ideas of universal history and monarchy: Strabo had to work hard to make this association seem natural and inevitable, just as the first *princeps* worked hard to place himself at the center of a vast, reordered world in his *Res Gestae*. At the same time, Strabo's connection of his project with that of Augustus alerts us to broader issues of agency and implication in the imperial project within

---

[2] Excellent introductions to Roman imperial administration include Millar 1981a; Braund 1988; Lintott 1993; Bowman 1996; Eck 2000; Galsterer 2000; "how the Roman empire really was": cf. Finley 1986a.

his *Geography*. The history of Strabo's own family, from Amaseia on the Black Sea, historically closely allied to the local kings, and with Mediterranean networks of its own, is enmeshed within, and gains and loses from, the dynamics of rival powers and individuals in the eastern Mediterranean and Asia Minor.[3]

Rather than presenting a "bird's-eye" view of the structures and operation of the Roman empire, this chapter focuses on the dynamic, ongoing processes of conceptualizing, enacting, and claiming modes of power and sovereignty associated with the Roman imperial state. I begin with a discussion of the Roman imperial state's self-fashioning at the interface with older and competing systems and expectations of rule, and move on to consider the ways in which various groups and individuals were able to use and claim the Roman state's modes of power and sovereignty for various ends including self-actualization.

## Among Empires

What we might think of as some of the classic, distinctive concepts and institutions of the Roman empire – including *imperium* in the sense of a single, territorial entity ("the Roman empire"),[4] provinces as administrative units of this territorial entity, Roman governors, the articulation of cities outside Rome as Roman or Latin in legal terms, the creation of community-level hotspots (theaters that juxtapose local elites with the Caesars, reproductions of the *Forum Augustum*, sanctuaries of the "imperial cult") that localize the power and centrality of Rome, instantly recognizable symbols of sovereignty and officialdom that invited appropriation (the emperor's head on the obverse of coins, consular dating, Latin or Latin-influenced legalese), and the Roman citizenship exercised as a privilege and honor within one's local town – are all products of processes that took many years to formulate in these particular ways. The early history of Rome's Republican empire is one of negotiation between ideas and institutions of imperial power specific to Rome and preexisting or competing

[3] Greek translations of Roman imperial power and institutions: Mason 1974; Crawford 1977; Richardson 1979; Derow 1979; Dubuisson 1985; "surrender-and-grant": Ma 2002, 111–13, with bibliography; Strabo and his contexts: Bowersock 1965; Prontera 1984; Clarke 1997; 1999a; Dueck 2000; Dueck, Lindsay and Pothecary 2005; universal history: Clarke 1999b; Alonso-Núñez 2002; Liddel and Fear 2010; Augustus' own geographical projects: e.g., Nicolet 1991; Cooley 2009.

[4] "Among empires" alludes to Maier 2006, but my interest is in the ways in which ancient understanding and actions were affected by experience of different imperial systems (cf. Dandelet 2014 for an early modern case-study) rather than in how we might compare historical empires from our early twenty-first-century perspective.

ideas and institutions of empire in the Mediterranean world, often involving the literal or figurative processes of translation. While long memories of empire are most readily apparent in the eastern Mediterranean, mediated to us primarily in the Greek language and via Greek cultural motifs, comparable processes also played out in the western Mediterranean as well as in northern Europe.

Polybius' later second-century BCE account of "by what means and under what kind of government the Romans in fewer than fifty-three years succeeded in subjecting almost the whole inhabited world to their sole rule (*archē*)" (1, 1, 5) beautifully illustrates these processes. It begins with the Romans crossing the sea to Sicily in 264 BCE and ends in 146 BCE with the sacks of Carthage and Corinth. In writing of Rome's rise, Polybius engaged in an early kind of "comparative empires" exercise. This is explicit in his "succession of empires" scheme that starts with the Persians and continues with Sparta and Macedonia, culminating in Rome as the most recent and greatest (1, 2). It is implicit throughout his narrative in the continuum of imperial vocabulary and institutions he applies to Rome and to other competing, expansionist states in the Mediterranean, both Greek and "barbarian," including Carthaginians, Syracusans, and the Oscan-speaking Mamertini (former mercenaries of Agathocles, ruler of Syracuse). The "succession of empires" motif first appears in historical writing of the classical period, but it is a key feature of Hellenistic and Roman historical geography. It is more than just a literary trope: it indicates the process of modeling and abstracting a concept of empire, and it suggests both the typical morphology and behavior of empires and past precedents for dealing with them.[5]

These processes are apparent at least as early as the fifth century BCE both in the more reflective contexts of historical writing and within the ideology of the Athenian empire. Athens engaged extensively with ideologies and practices of the Achaemenid (Persian) empire, which arguably provided *the* quintessential model of what empire was. The most significant feature is the regularization of tribute, but we should add to this garrisons, colonies, and dedicated, supervisory personnel, all of which would come to add up to a recognizable and long-lasting "package" of empire in the Mediterranean world. Persian models informed the language of imperial ceremonial and imperial centers. The procession depicted on

---

[5] Modern "comparative empire" approaches that include the Roman empire include Doyle 1986; Alcock et al. 2001; Burbank and Cooper 2010; Mutschler and Mittag 2008; Scheidel 2009; Vasunia 2011; for "succession of empires," e.g., Momigliano 1982, 542–9.

the Parthenon frieze recalls that of the reliefs of the Apadana, the audience
hall of the palace of Persepolis, even if the public ideologies are dramatically different.[6]

The preexistence of models of empire and behaviors associated with it
especially encourage both the self-conscious following of patterns and the
explicit rejection of major elements, often simultaneously. Athens' self-
conscious reception of Persia as an imperial model anticipates the importance of the Achaemenid and Pharaonic past, as well as that of other Near
Eastern kingdoms, for the successor kingdoms of Alexander the Great.
These processes of self-fashioning with reference to predecessors are nicely
illustrated in later foundation stories of Macedonian rule that involve the
deeds of Alexander the Great, involving the "wedding" of Macedonian and
Achaemenid practices in dress and ceremonial as well as the literal marriage
of Alexander's Companions and ordinary soldiers to Asian women (Plut.
*Alex.* 45, 1–2; 47, 3–5; 70, 2; *De Alex. fort.* 1, 7–8; 2, 6; Arr. *Anab.* 4, 7, 4;
4, 9, 9–11, 9; 7, 4, 4–8; 6, 1–5).[7]

Herodotus' later fifth-century BCE account of the rise of the Persian
empire and its defeat by the Greeks, written with Athens on the cusp of
imperial ascendancy, and Thucydides' early fourth-century account of the
rise and fall of the Athenian empire, written with consciousness of its
defeat by Sparta in 404 BCE, work through more reflectively the behavior
and trajectories of empire. Both accounts are prime examples of a classical
trope and strategy of representing empire as a type of tyranny, the
antithesis of the idealized self-direction of the polis and its citizens. As
Herodotus traces the origins of Greek-barbarian conflict, he looks to the
beginnings of Greek subjugation to barbarian power: while it was painfully
clear to some fifth-century observers that you did not have to be a
barbarian to be a tyrant, there was nevertheless something barbarous about
tyranny. Herodotus' telling of events on which he presumes to pronounce
truth or falsity begins with the *archē* of Croesus of Lydia over the Greeks of
western Asia Minor in the mid-sixth century, an ongoing subjugation
exacted by tribute that runs in parallel with a relationship of "friendship"
extended to the Spartans. Croesus' *archē* is explicitly distinguished from
smash and grab raids and is the antithesis of freedom (1, 5, 3–1, 6).
Tribute and "enslavement" likewise signal the beginnings of Athenian
*archē* in Thucydides' account of the period between the Persian and the

---

[6] Root 1985; Boedeker and Raaflaub 1998; Raaflaub 2009.
[7] Kuhrt and Sherwin-White 1991; Sherwin-White and Kuhrt 1993, 40–52; Hatzopoulos 1996;
Ma 2002; 2003, 183–6; 2009; Briant 2010; Manning 2010.

Peloponnesian Wars (1, 89–118), accelerating to the point at which Athens could be portrayed by her own leaders as a "tyrant city" (2, 63, 2; 3, 37, 2), despite her professed aim of leading an alliance to continue hostilities against the Persian king.[8]

Croesus' option of subjugation through "friendship" and Athens' professed aim alert us to the degree to which ancient imperial relationships relied on "soft" mechanisms that were regularly articulated as being mutually beneficial.[9] Imperial relationships were brokered in part through traditional, ostensibly voluntary networks that maintained connection and ordered power and proximity in the Mediterranean world, including friendship, gift-exchange and "kinship diplomacy." Rome's expedition to Sicily in 264 BCE was made in response to the appeal of the Oscan-speaking Mamertini, former mercenaries of Agathocles of Syracuse who had gone rogue and taken over the Greek city of Messana. Finding themselves in trouble with Syracuse, they appealed to Carthage, who installed a garrison, and to Rome, appealing to ties of kinship, *homophylia*, perhaps based on a notion of common Italian-ness, a notion with its own peculiar history of power relationships (Polyb. 1, 8–12). This episode illustrates beautifully broad awareness across international communities in the third-century BCE Mediterranean of how to play the imperial game in its variations, with the stakes or counters that made most sense in any particular social and cultural environment.[10]

Rome's experience of international languages and practices of empire did not begin only when it crossed the sea to Sicily in 264 BCE but was apparent already in modes of self-representation, victory, and continuous subjugation of multi-ethnic peoples (including Greeks and "Hellenized" communities) exercised in Italy decades earlier. Rome's management and domination of vast tracts of space by road-building, the annexation of territories, and the movement of whole populations, militaristic colonial foundations, and concessions of status such as limited grants of citizenship-without-the-vote suggest engagement with international models of domination, including those of the Deinomenids of Sicily and, most recently, the Hellenistic successor kingdoms to Alexander the Great. Coin-motifs of third-century Rome, eclectic in comparison with the coinages of other

---

[8] For empire as tyranny, see Tuplin 1985; cf. Lavan 2016.
[9] Cf. the pioneering initiative of Badian 1984 (1st edn. 1958) to portray a Roman empire fueled by interpersonal relationships rather than by the impersonal structures of "annexation," even if the role of patronage is over-emphasized (cf. Eilers 2002).
[10] Kinship diplomacy and friendship: cf. Sahlins 1972; Jones 1999; Morris 1986; Erskine 2001; Burton 2011, 63–75; Mamertini: Russo 2012.

southern Italian cities, fasten for their inspiration particularly on the martial and imperial iconography of Athena, goddess of Athens, and Alexander.[11]

Livy, writing in Latin in the Augustan age, but almost certainly drawing on the near-contemporary Greek account of Polybius, depicts the Roman proconsul L. Aemilius Paullus delivering his pronouncement on the settlement of Macedonia in 167, after the Roman defeat of King Perseus, and the dissolution of the Macedonian kingdom as follows:

> Aemilius gave notice for the councils of ten from all the cities to assemble at Amphipolis and to bring with them all archives and documents wherever they were deposited, and all the money due to the royal treasury. When the day arrived he advanced to the tribunal, where he took his seat with the ten commissioners, surrounded by a vast concourse of Macedonians. Though they were accustomed to royal power (*regio imperio*), this novel assertion of authority filled them with fear; the tribunal, the clearing of the approach to it through the mass of people, the herald, the aide, all these were strange to their eyes and ears and might even have appalled allies of Rome, to say nothing of a vanquished enemy. After the herald had called for silence Paullus, speaking in Latin, explained the arrangements decided upon by the senate and by himself in concert with the ten commissioners; Cn. Octavius the praetor, who was also present, translated the address into Greek. First of all it was laid down that the Macedonians were to be a free people, possessing their cities and fields as before, enjoying their own laws and customs and electing their annual magistrates. They were to pay to Rome half the tribute which they had been paying to the king. Secondly, Macedonia was to be broken up into four separate cantons. (Livy 45, 29, Loeb tr.)

This evocative representation of the spectacle of Roman imperial power zooms in on the issues of translation (literal and metaphorical) that are an intrinsic aspect of operating "among empires," acute at the initial point of succession but always there at the interface between the dominant power and older or alternative sources of power. Aemilius Paullus' judgment has much in common with other highly charged type-scenes of the arrival of Roman power: it is somewhere on a spectrum between Polybius' account of Scipio Africanus capturing New Carthage with highly calibrated terror (10, 15, 4–6), and the handshake that confirmed *amicitia*, familiar from both literary and artistic representations.[12]

---

[11] Roman imperial practices in Italy: Frederiksen 1984, 193–8; Purcell 1990b; 1994; Dench 2003; coin-motifs: Burnett 1986.

[12] Terror: Chapter 4; friendship: Burton 2011, 1–2.

It was hard to decouple empire from monarchy in the ancient world, however loud protests might be from and on behalf of the Athenian democracy or the Roman Republic. Although the world into which the Romans expanded was not exclusively monarchical, it was one dominated by the model of monarchy, specifically the model of Alexander cultivated by and much beyond the Hellenistic successor kingdoms (the Antigonids, the Seleucids, and the Ptolemies). In the passage from Livy, the spectacle is on one level all about the new power's self-distancing from the Macedonian monarchy. Its emphasis on "freedom" and on halving the tribute plays on both immediate and historical knowledge of what empire was, while the alien trappings and ceremonial of Roman power and the use of a foreign language drive home the cultural difference.[13]

The idea of Rome as the antithesis of kingship surfaces strongly in ancient traditions on the Seleucid king Antiochus IV Epiphanes. The king's madness (for which he earned the alternative epithet "Epimanes") is manifested in his topsy-turvy behavior, dressing up as a Roman Republican magistrate, canvassing for election, and sitting on an ivory chair to dispense justice. The idea of Romans as not-kings was not just an intellectual game. We can see this from the passage of *1 Maccabees,* a Jewish text written in Greek around 100 BCE, and treating the dramatic date of 161 BCE, with Judas Maccabaeus seeking alliance with the Romans. Among the attractions of the Romans is that, despite the fact that they are both king-makers and destroyers of kingdoms, there is no king, no-one who wears the trappings of kingship, diadems and purple, even if there is, tantalizingly, only one man chosen to rule them each year (8, 11–16).[14]

The "natural" opposition between regal Macedon and Republican Rome quickly breaks down in the passage from Livy, just as the real-life boundary could be usefully fuzzy: monarchy and the Roman Republic sometimes operate as polarities and sometimes as analogies. Having the Roman propraetor, Cn. Octavius, translate the proconsul's proclamation into Greek underlines the power of appropriation, just as bilingual and  even trilingual inscriptions articulate ancient imperial powers' mastery of multiple systems and cultural groups. When the ceremonial associated with a Roman Republican proconsul is compared with "regal power," the use of the Latin word *imperium* here collapses the difference between

[13] A more benign version of grappling with alien models at the "coming of Rome" is apparent in importation of the loan-word *patrōn* in inscriptions of Greek cities from the late second century BCE to express a new relationship that no Greek term quite encapsulated: Eilers 2002.
[14] Antiochus IV Epiphanes: Polybius 26, 1, 5–7 = Athen. 5, 193d; Diodorus 29, 32; cf. Livy 41, 20, who is significantly less interested in Antiochus' cultural and constitutional inversions.

king and magistrate. *Imperium* signified the power vested in certain of the highest officers of the Roman state (praetors, propraetors, consuls, proconsuls, dictators, and masters of the horse), specifically the power to exact obedience to their orders, symbolized by the *fasces* that functioned as a portable punishment and execution kit. By the mid-second century BCE, *imperium* was beginning to acquire the more abstract meaning of the "sway" of the Roman people, their imperial rule. The terror inspired by the spectacle of Roman power even among those used to regal ceremonial might remind us of Polybius' tripartite, post-Aristotelian analysis of the Roman state, which identifies consuls as the "monarchical" element (and the senate and Roman people respectively as the "aristocratic" and "democratic" elements) (6, 11, 11–18).[15]

Roman *imperatores* were slotted into regal roles with some regularity, with more or less emphasis on the awkwardness of fit. One famous example involves L. Aemilius Paullus again, upcycling an inscribed pillar base at Delphi that was intended for a golden statue for Perseus, king of Macedon, literally slotting himself in to the place reserved for Perseus, and inscribing it in Latin thus: "L. Aimilius L. F. inperator de rege Perse Macedonibusque cepet" ("Lucius Aemilius, son of Lucius, imperator, took this from King Perseus and the Macedonians") (*CIL* I [2] 622 = *ILLRP* 323). Aemilius' action acknowledges the symbolic place of Delphi as a center of the Greek world in the tradition of other aspiring superpowers who had made dedications there, including Croesus of Lydia. The phrasing of the inscription marks the parallel between Aemilius Paullus and Perseus but highlights the differences embodied also in the use of Latin: "inperator" vs. "rex." At the same time, Aemilius Paullus explicitly trumps Perseus: his inscription makes the gift to Apollo that the Macedonian king had intended into war booty as well.[16]

There are many other instances of Roman authorities slotting themselves into, or being slotted into, the spaces newly vacated by Hellenistic monarchy, including palaces and public buildings of the old regimes. Cicero's depiction of Verres, the rogue Roman governor of Sicily, living in and operating out of Hieron II's palace in Syracuse (*Verr.* II, 4, 54; II, 5, 80), hints at the complex lived experience of Roman rule's continuities and

---

[15] Polarity and analogy: Lloyd 1966; empires and linguistic mastery: Adams 2003, 637–41 on the Gallus inscription; Kuhrt 2007, 135–58 on the Bisitun (Behistun) inscription of Darius; *imperium:* Richardson 1991; 2008, 43–4; 54; *fasces:* Schäfer 1989, chs. 5, 7.

[16] The pillar base at Delphi: Plut. *Aem. Paull.* 28; Pollitt 1986, 155–8; Ferrary 1988, 560–5; cf. Edmondson 1999 for the cultural gymnastics of Aemilius Paullus and Antiochus IV more generally; "upcycling": cf. Rous 2016.

disruptions of preexisting institutions and their associated structures. The transition from kingdoms to Roman rule was played out also in cult. Subjects and allies sought to extend to the new Roman power established religious ways of thinking about monarchical power, and harnessed that power to the local community. The cult's complex struggle with monarchy is visible on many levels. The cult-figure of Roma is first attested in Smyrna in 195 BCE, and attestations rapidly increase after the fall of Macedon in 168. While the cult of Roma might remind us most immediately of the personified community of Athens or the *demos*, the cult, ideology, and trappings of the goddess Roma compare most closely with those of the Hellenistic kings. At the same time, cult was regularly addressed directly to individual Roman generals: "good" generals refused such honors, but "bad" ones did not, and there was clearly a hazy area in between.[17]

The idea of kingship continues to function as a Roman imperial resource well beyond its intervention in the eastern Mediterranean in the third to second centuries BCE. The Romans became king-makers, endorsing and even appointing the "friendly" kings who feature in Strabo's depiction of empire, although there was sometimes in practice greater ambiguity about who needed whom more than his account would suggest. These interactions with Rome further blurred the boundary between the Roman Republic and "foreign" kingship as kings increasingly adopted the ceremonial and behavior of Republican *imperatores* and were honored by gifts that the Romans imagined were appropriate to kings, a combination of recreated memories of their own regal past, experience of actual Hellenistic kings, and the more king-like costumes and attributes of high Roman officers and triumphant generals, including the curule chair, gold crown, and ivory scepter. Meanwhile, within the Roman state, consciousness of empire's traditional entanglement with monarchy encouraged attempts to regulate the conduct and careers of officeholders by norms and laws, even while competing Roman dynasts narrowed into a hereditary Roman monarchy. This consciousness would ultimately help to naturalize Strabo's equation between world rule and sole rule, as well as to formulate the peculiar institution of Roman monarchy.[18]

[17] Roman governors moving in to preexisting spaces: Haensch 1997; Meyer-Zwiffelhoffer 2002; Roman imperial cult: Mellor 1975; Beard, North and Price 1998, vol. 1, 158–60.
[18] "Friendly kings": Braund 1984; Millar 1996; cf. Cornwell 2015; distinctive Roman ideologies and practices of monarchy: Rawson 1975; Wallace-Hadrill 1982.

While much of the complex dance around monarchy takes place in the eastern Mediterranean, Iron Age Britain, at the northern edge of the Roman world, makes a fascinating case-study of how models of kingship gelled between local and international ideas. Julius Caesar's *Gallic War*, his account of his campaigns in Gaul and the first conquest of Britain, proceeds by polarity and analogy to write the political geography of Britain into recognizably international terminology, leaving space for the different and strange. Notably, his account identifies "kings," suggesting a complex process of interpretation in the translation of the term (e.g., *BG* 5, 20; 22). We tend to forget how crucially such intellectual processes underpin the practical workings of an empire that depended so substantially on local structures. On the British side, Iron Age coins suggest that local rulers drew eclectically on Hellenistic, Roman republican, and early imperial iconography, but could also find expression for the significance of older, local traditions. The coinage of Tincomarus in the south of England drew on the older, local significance of horses and ancestor cult in portraits that evoked the internationally recognizable equestrian pose and Octavian's self-representation as Divi F., "son of the deified Caesar" in its legend C. F., "son of Commius."[19]

The rich and dynamic interactions between Roman and local concepts of imperial figureheads do not end with the Republic. Portraits of emperors can be made to project a distinctive local vernacular, even in cases where communities were demonstrably well aware of the different kinds of images favored in Rome and Italy. Thus, the local people of Samos made at home both a portrait of Augustus as a very Roman exemplar of *pietas* with veiled head *and* a portrait of Augustus according to the conventions of a Hellenistic king, rather different from the distinctive "between citizen and king" model of the emperor in Rome and Italy.[20]

Roman rule's interface with kingship might be seen as a synecdoche for Roman imperial interfaces with local structures and expectations more generally. L. Aemilius Paullus' decidedly ambivalent Macedonian audience in 167 were informed that they would for the future pay to Rome half of the taxes formerly due to the Macedonian kingdom, and enjoy self-rule but rearranged in a new geography determined by Roman authority. It is hard to think of a better example of the subtlety of grafting new onto old, or of the sophisticated appeal to hard-wired ideas about the incompatibility of freedom and empire.

---

[19] *VA* 375: S7 with Creighton 2000, 101–5; 188–97; 2006, 35–45; Williams 2005, 73–7.
[20] Boschung 1993, 157 (plates 76, 2;3; 173, 2); 156 (plates 176–7); Mayer 2010.

## Making a Roman Imperial Dialect

The traditional account of Roman imperial government is a bird's-eye view of the development of systems (provinces and taxation, the making and deployment of a standing army, the role and duties of the Roman governor) and of distinctive imperial ideologies. Such frameworks risk tracing institutions and ideologies as if they were substantially separable from their diverse fields and relationships of imperial engagement and are encouraged particularly by the legalizing approaches that we considered briefly in the first section of this chapter, and to some extent also by a semantic and literary focus. Interestingly, however, any narrow view of Roman imperial government that tries to nail its trajectory to what the Romans did or thought begins to collapse even and especially at the most empirical level. For example, the study of Roman imperial taxation necessitates thinking about the interface with earlier and competing systems, as well as the embeddedness of tax collection in local structures. This is an inspiring challenge as long as one does not retreat to a model of the Roman empire as "laissez-faire," one traditional means of maintaining the clean detachability of Roman systems from the mess of imperial contexts. The messiness of the contexts within which Roman imperial institutions developed will be a recurrent theme in the later chapters of this book.[21]

The Roman state was certainly capable of both interventionist behavior and not intervening in spheres where we might expect them to intervene, as we will see shortly. But recent, sophisticated work has emphasized the degree to which Roman imperial government was responsive rather than proactive, presupposing, reinforcing, and actively creating local structures, groups able to function as bargaining units, and even quite ordinary individuals (including women) attuned to the vagaries of the system. To study Roman government is therefore necessarily to think deeply about sites and modes of interaction and communication.[22]

An embedded study of Roman imperial government of this kind is one of the increasing visibility, and indeed domination, of motifs (linguistic, iconographic, architectural) and practices that suggest Roman sovereignty

---

[21] Superior accounts of Roman imperial institutions and ideologies include: Brunt 1978; Bowman 1996; Eck 2000; Ando 2006; Richardson 2008; Roman imperial government as laissez-faire (sometimes qualified by economic or religious spheres, or in comparison with the later or late empire) e.g., Rostovtzeff 1926, 159; Salmon 1944, 255.

[22] Roman emperors as responsive: Millar 1977; 1984; cf. Crawford 1990, 102 with n. 50 for its application to the Roman Republican empire; interaction and communication: especially Ando 2000.

- Imperial cult
- Decrees
- Military presence

or channel systems and institutions of the Roman state, or localize imperial power in hotspots, even if these substantially co-exist with alternative loci of power. Examples include local appropriations of Roman magisterial titles and insignia, or of Latin or Latinizing vocabulary, formulas, legalese or material forms such as the "double document" occupying a register of power and efficacy. Another familiar manifestation of this phenomenon is acknowledging Roman coinage as the "top" coinage, and taking its forms, language, and iconography as the epitome of statehood. Elsewhere, architectural or iconographic motifs of the city of Rome were cited within discrete local contexts, or consensus was reached around distinctive, non-metropolitan imperial modes of localizing power (e.g., the cult of Roma or temples of Capitoline Jupiter). We could also think of the readily recognizable and diffused iconography of the divinized imperial family, and its interference in the representation of both local divinities and prominent local individuals. We shall consider specific examples of this increasing visibility and its contexts in later chapters.[23]

The Roman state and its officers were acutely conscious of the power of spectacle, an important aspect of discussions of metropolitan political culture in recent years, particularly that of the politically dynamic middle and later Republic with its ceremonial, memory theaters and plain theatricality structuring, socializing, and reinforcing the social and political order. In the broader imperial sphere, the significance of spectacle is deeply dependent on context. Rome's earlier practices, notably the reconfiguration of the Italian landscape through centuriation and road-building, were informed by the ideologies and practices of competing powers as she emerged as a serious contender, first in Italy and then in the Mediterranean. Polybius' engagement with Roman use of spectacle is inevitably comparative, sometimes overtly so. Whether depicting atrocities visited on towns unfriendly to Rome (10, 15), or the ceremonial of a Roman magistrate (assuming that the treatment of L. Aemilius Paullus' settlement of Macedonia in Livy Book 45 is indeed rooted in a Polybian account), Polybius offers a sophisticated, discursive take on the implication of observers in interpreting and calibrating spectacle.[24]

If these are all examples of the grander, one-off spectacle of the Roman state and its officers, it is important not to minimize the impact and

---

[23] Interplay between imperial and metropolitan forms: Purcell 2000.
[24] Spectacle and metropolitan political culture: Hölscher 1984; Linke and Stemmler 2000; Morstein-Marx 2004; Hölkeskamp 2005; 2006; 2011; Beard 2007; early Roman spatial ideology and practices in context: Catalano 1978; Purcell 1990a; 1990b.

engagement of observers in the sorts of spectacle that will become more or less routine, ranging from the assize-circuit of a Roman governor to the much rarer journeys of emperors themselves. Above all, we should factor in the everyday performance of the privilege and power associated with the Roman state and imperial family on the part of minor Roman officials (soldiers, customs officers, imperial procurators), and indeed private Roman citizens and Italians (Roman by association in this context), sufficiently recognizable to be the focus of an orchestrated massacre in the "Asian Vespers" of the First Mithridatic War of 88 BCE (Val. Max. 9, 2, 3; Plut. *Sull.* 24, 4; App. *Mith.* 22–3), a massive *anti*-Roman spectacle.

Ancient empires of the Near East and the Mediterranean world traditionally staged participatory rituals in which rulers and subjects played distinctive parts. If the Apadana reliefs of Achaemenid Persepolis represent an idealized version of an imperial tributary system as the willing presentation of ethnically suitable gifts, the Athenian allies were required to bring their tribute to the festival of Dionysus and to participate in its procession. They also contributed a cow and panoply in the Great Panathenaea and were treated as if they were "honorary" Athenians. In the Seleucid Empire, exchanges of royal letters and local civic decrees sought to frame imperial power relations as the sort of reciprocal exchange of benefactions and honors that managed social relations within the *polis*. Roman imperial rituals, with origins at some point on a spectrum between institutions of the Roman state, Roman institutions formed "for export," and local practices, required their own, distinctive patterns of subject participation. These included the census, a Roman state institution that encountered parallel but not quite the same institutions in its imperial contexts, notably Egypt, extended first to Italy and from the Augustan age to the Roman Empire as a whole, the most obvious occasion for subjects to encounter Roman bureaucratic peculiarities. Orchestrated oath-swearing extended to provincial inhabitants (nominally, at least) older practices of soldiers swearing loyalty oaths to their commander, or subjects to their king. The practice of petitioning Roman dynasts and subsequently Roman emperors (or members of the imperial family) developed as the Romans progressively became *the* brokers of privilege and *the* arbitrators of the Mediterranean as well as much of the Near East and Europe. Besides encouraging the development of embassies as a new, translocal form of politics, it created ancient versions of "paper trails" that might cohere into applicable legal findings, instrumentalize local "memory theaters," or encourage the curation of cherished, valuable personal documentation, as well as habituating individuals and communities to a particular language of *politesse,* praise, and honors most likely to get things done.[25]

By writing of "spectacle," "performance," and "ritual," I would not want to minimize the sometimes catastrophic effects of physical and economic harm done to subjects within imperial contexts, but rather to emphasize the habituation of subjects to the particular expectations and opportunities of empire, from which some will indeed gain at the expense of others. But the language of "spectacle," "performance," and "ritual" also introduces a story within which the direct and deliberate intervention of the Roman state of its officers plays only a small part in comparison with some other premodern imperial systems. Examples from early (Qin and Han) China illustrate vividly paths not taken by Rome in the imposition of practices and customs: the universal application of a common script; the circulation of an authoritative state calendar; and imperial officials encouraged by rewards and punishments to impose the normative customs characterized as *li.*[26]

These counter-examples from China point out major structural differences in the Roman case that are played out across sets of issues. These include the referral of authority over a community's religious practices to local officials without imperial oversight in both the charter of the Roman citizen colony of Urso of 44 BCE and the mid-third century CE decree of Decius on universal sacrifice. This is of course not "toleration," as the ejection or annihilation of practices associated with security threats to the Roman state and its holdings makes clear. In the correspondence between Trajan and Pliny the Younger, the emperor beautifully 'corrects' Pliny's knee-jerk reaction of thinking in terms of Roman law or material expertise within a provincial contexts, reminding him of the appropriateness of local custom and local resources (*Letters* 10, 17–18; 37; 39–40; 49–50; 61–2; 68). The sporadic emergence of Roman officials specifically tasked with economic supervision within cities (*curatores rei publicae*) between the later years of the first century and early years of the second century CE, some of whom were requested by cities, and some of whom were appointed to cities that did not pay tribute, might suggest the importance above all of

---

[25] Apadana reliefs: Root 1985; Boedeker and Raaflaub 1998; Raaflaub 2009; requirements of Athenian allies: succinctly Osborne 2000, 98–9; Seleucid imperial exchanges: Ma 2002, chapter 4; on Roman imperial rituals, see especially Price 1984; Ando 2000; cf. Revell 2009 for interesting attempts to use structuration theory to argue for the socialization of provincial inhabitants through specific spatial configurations, even if the theory promises more than the case-studies deliver.

[26] On intervention in Qin and Han China, see e.g., Bodde 1986, 56–8; Loewe 1986, 655–7; 686–8.

the financial well-being that suggested the broader health of empire, delicately balanced between individual centers and the imperial whole.[27]

These illustrations of Roman structural difference might be considered alongside the notorious passage of Tacitus' *Agricola*, chapter 21, in which Tacitus' eponymous protagonist, his father-in-law, steers the Britons toward a lifestyle that should neutralize security threats to Rome, an indirect form of disarmament. "Agricola" is present and offers encouragement and incentives in building (temples, fora, and houses) and lifestyle changes (hanging out in porticos, baths, and at feasts), until the Britons unknowingly and inadvertently enslave themselves in seeking to acquire highly desirable *humanitas* ("civilization"). The passage engages in much longer traditions of thinking about the luxury engendered by empire, but also tells a sophisticated (and not morally unproblematic), psychologizing, and surely over-coherent story about the extremely complicated and generally indirect relationship between Roman imperial presence and material change in provincial contexts. Although the passage has been read directly onto the fabric of provincial towns from Haverfield onwards, it is, importantly, a highly discursive passage that works on the level of esteem and self-worth with a mix of sociopolitical norms rather than operating as an architectural pattern book for a provincial town. We close the gap within imperial contexts between feelings, ideas, influence, preference, and norms at the interface of Roman state and local peoples, on the one hand, and precise material forms, on the other, at our peril.[28]

## Reproducing Roman Power

Our discussion in the previous section of spectacle, performance, and ritual outlined some of the major imperial interactions that would habituate the inhabitants of empire to imperial systems as well as creating significance and even form. The analysis of the processes by which these imperial systems were created, communicated, understood, and applied has changed radically in recent decades. For much of the twentieth century,

---

[27] Local religious authorities: Rives 1999; Rüpke 2006a; 2006b; Ando 2007b; 2008, chapter 5.; for a critique of "toleration," see North 1979; on *curatores rei publicae*, see Burton 1979; 2004; cf. the essays in Eck 1999 for the delicate calibration of local autonomy.

[28] For Tacitus *Agricola* 21, see e.g., Clarke 2001; Dench 2005, chapter 1; for the role played by a Roman legate charged with "care of the temple" to be built by Smyrna to Tiberius, Livia, and the senate after the city was granted permission to build such a temple (Tac. *Ann.* 4, 55–6), see e.g., Burrell 2003, 29; Rubin 2008, 11–12; cf. more generally Jones 1997 for important problematization of reading ethnic self-identification from material culture.

it was hard not to think of the chilling use of mass media by the Nazi and Fascist regimes of Europe in the 1930s and 1940s, including radio, film, and television as well as print, especially given these regimes' appropriation of classical imagery and reframing of Roman sites and artifacts. A centripetal model of magnetic attraction to a "Roman culture" that implies loyalty to Rome, somewhat along the lines envisaged by Haverfield (and for him very much a constant and inevitable aspect of empire), persisted within discussions of "Romanization" within the provinces that are concerned primarily with baths, pottery, and urbanization. Meanwhile, within the largely separable conversation about political culture of empire centered squarely on the city of Rome, the ghost of "propaganda" loomed large but encouraged big questions about the relative roles of message, medium, maker, and consumer.[29]

The nature of these questions can be illustrated by two different visions of the relationship between power and "culture" (in the sense here of the "high" culture of literature and fine art) in the Augustan principate across the twentieth century: Ronald Syme's treatment of ideology, poetry and historiography in two chapters (29: "The National Programme," and 30: "The Organization of Opinion") of his *The Roman Revolution* (first published, significantly, in 1939) and Paul Zanker's *The Power of Images in the Age of Augustus* (1988: the English version of the 1987 German book, *Augustus und die Macht der Bilder*). Syme's account of the Augustan principate is the story of the establishment of a "party," its members and adherents, including literary figures, rewarded by the goods and honors of patronage. Nevertheless, the literary talents of Virgil, Horace, and Livy elevate their works beyond propaganda, functioning as layers of interference in the promulgation of any singular imperial message, even if their loyalty is beyond question. In Zanker's vision, there is a more or less free flow between message, producer, and user in the normalization of a particular new fusion of imperial imagery and ideology (of new beginnings, moral rectitude, and the central importance of princeps and dynasty to this new world order) that enables its empire-wide reproduction and consequent saturation.

Zanker's Augustan world is to some extent the artistic expression of the growing tendency in the 1970s and 1980s to figure empire as a belief system in which subjects and inhabitants are significant actors and agents. This is the case even if the structures and processes and particularly the

[29] For Europe of the 1930s and 1940s, see e.g., Visser 1992; Ades et al. 1995; Marchand 1996, chs. 7–9; Nelis 2007.

relative roles played by officers of the Roman state, producers and con-
sumers in Zanker's world are more shadowy than they are in, say, Simon
Price's more obviously social scientific account in *Rituals and Power*
(1984), or Clifford Ando's comprehensive explication of empire as consensus in *Imperial Ideology and Provincial Loyalty in the Roman Empire*
(2000). I have no desire to return either to the model of a "natural" pull
toward the supposedly superior and more coherent culture of empire, or to
that of the deliberate and total domination of minds implied by "propaganda." At the most basic level, neither model factors in the reliance on
local structures that was fundamental to the workings of the Roman
empire. But the model of empire as a belief system risks underplaying
the significance of these local structures and agencies too, of equating
reproduction too quickly with loyalty, and minimizing the friction, interference, mishearing, and redirection of energy that needs to be reintro-
duced lest the machine becomes too close to the dystopian, science-fiction
vision of *The Matrix* (1999), in which what people experience as reality
turns out to be simulated by machines fed by people's own body heat and
electrical activity.

Andrew Wallace-Hadrill's incisive criticisms of Zanker's *The Power of
Images* are applicable to the belief/consensus model of empire more generally. Wallace-Hadrill points to the existence of demonstrably variant
"readers" of the architecture of Augustan Rome, most obviously Ovid,
and to ongoing tensions in the adoption and juxtaposition of registers and
systems of meaning (in this case, notably "Greek" and "Roman" systems)
within and beyond the Augustan age. Wallace-Hadrill also suggests how a
spelled-out version of Zanker's model of the process of reproduction of
imperial imagery might complicate things, through an example from his
own work on the numismatic iconography of victory and virtue. The coin
user has a stake in the prestige and winning quality of the imperial imagery
that is distinct from that of the maker (let alone that of the emperor, a
notoriously difficult role to pin down in the early Empire): the prestige and
winning quality associated with the imagery is transferred to the coin itself,
with implications for the success and faithfulness of the transaction. In the
context of the empire of belief/consensus more generally, to focus more
squarely on users and contexts of use is to raise questions about the
singularity of the belief system, its relationship with other systems, and
who or what benefits in the process.[30]

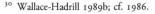
[30] Wallace-Hadrill 1989b; cf. 1986.

To develop this argument, I begin with the phenomenon of reproducing in non-Roman contexts the rituals, performance, or iconography associated with the power of the Roman state when this demonstrably has nothing to do with loyalty to Rome. Earlier in this chapter, we considered the story of the Seleucid king Antiochus IV dressing up as if he were canvassing for a Roman magistracy and performing the duties of a Roman magistrate as an illustration of imagining a powerful kind of sovereignty that was the "opposite" of kingship, in the form of the Roman Republic. Availability of this alternative recurs in ancient traditions on Salvius the leader of the second Sicilian slave war. Traditions on both Eunus, leader of the first Sicilian slave war (135–32 BCE), and Salvius of the second (104–100 BCE), are densely interwoven with motifs of contemporary kingship in the eastern Mediterranean, notably references to the Seleucid kings: Eunus' alter ego, "Antiochus," in whose name he minted coins, ("basi(leos) Antio(chou)"), is a dead giveaway. But traditions on Salvius (whose alter ego, "Tryphon," was not at all coincidentally the name of a Cilician pretender to the Seleucid throne in Syria) are even more interesting: he is made to assume a hybrid costume that pairs Roman toga with *chiton*, the generically "Greek" costume of the increasingly polarizing world of the second-century Mediterranean, and to have lictors bearing axes go in front of him. Diodorus Siculus, the Sicilian Greek narrative historian of the late first century BCE, interestingly sums up his performance as "and in general he affected all the trappings that go to make up and embellish the dignity of a king" (36, 7, 4), perhaps implicitly acknowledging the blur between Roman *imperator* and king in signaling sovereignty at this time.[31]

As we move into the first century BCE, the iconography and might of the Roman state are increasingly visible in the claims of rebels and pretenders. Notoriously, in the Social War of 91–89 BCE, the rebellious Italian allies minted coins that closely mirrored the coinage of the Roman state in weight, denomination, and iconography, and even described the Samnite general C. Papius Mutilus as *embratur* (the Oscan version of *imperator)* even as the bilingual Oscan-Latin legends and the coins' message – at their starkest, the Italian bull goring or raping the Roman wolf – insisted on separatism and domination. The literary tradition on the rebel allies' political organization and aspirations at their capital, Corfinium (significantly renamed Italica), explicitly mirrors the Roman

[31] Shaw 2001, 107–29.

state, with a senate of 500, two annual consuls, and 12 praetors (Diod. Sic. 37, 2, 4–7).[32]

The trajectory of the third-century CE self-representations of Zenobia and her son Vhaballath makes for a suggestive case-study from the "high" empire. This noble family of Syrian Palmyra elevated their realm to a "kingdom" and until the spring of 272, in the time-honored fashion of locals co-opted into the service of the Roman empire, they guaranteed the military security of the Roman empire against the Parthian empire to the east, initially under Zenobia's husband Odaenath and then, after his death, under Zenobia herself and their son Vhaballath, whose Aramaic name means "gift of Allath." Vhaballath was a Roman citizen, whose full name, Lucius Iulius Aurelius Septimius Vhaballathus, records close connections with the dynasty of Roman emperors and hyphenates his Palmyrene origins, retaining his Aramaic name as a Latinized cognomen. Their self-representation was at first culturally eclectic, but careful to acknowledge the supremacy of the Roman empire. Their coinages utilize the three languages of Palmyra (Latin, Greek, and Aramaic), and draw selectively on three different cultural traditions with some points of intersection: young gods of Palmyra, "friendly kings" of the Roman empire, and the "king of kings," the formula used by rulers of the Parthians and Sasanians who set themselves in the tradition of Achaemenid Persia. On coins minted at Antioch and Alexandria, Vhaballath's portrait on the reverse is twinned with the Roman emperor Aurelian on the obverse. Aurelian, as Imperator Caesar Aurelianus Augustus, appears with his radiate crown, while Vhaballath appears with his diadem and laurel wreath, looking two ways, to Greek and Roman pasts. On other coins, he is portrayed with long hair, perhaps an allusion to the local "young gods" of Palmyra.

From the spring of 272 CE, Vhaballath and Zenobia broke away from the Roman center and started ruling in their own right. The more independent and dangerous they became, the more they portrayed themselves exclusively as Roman emperor and empress respectively. On coins, Vhaballath was completely slotted in to the iconography of third-century emperors, with his crown, short hair and titles ("Imperator Caesar Vhaballathus Augustus") (Figure 2). By the third century CE, when it came to asserting imperial power in the traditional territory of the Roman empire, it was hard to envisage being anything other than a Roman emperor.[33]

Appropriating dominant forms of sovereignty is not the only way of framing a rebellion. The destruction of statues, representations, or shrines

[32] Wallace-Hadrill 2008, 88–9.    [33] cf. Long 1996; Schwentzel 2010; Butcher 2003, 328.

Figure 2    Obverse of silver Antonianus of Vhaballath of Palmyra with radiate
crown as Im(perator) C(aesar) Vhabalathus Aug(ustus), uncertain mint,
272 CE, ANS 1944.100.30790.
Courtesy of the American Numismatic Society.

that distill the ruling power in the most concentrated way is familiar from
the Roman world and revolutions the world over, while refusing to be
taxed is similarly incendiary. Language and particular facets of religion and
culture can become highly charged and used in self-identification with
groups and states distinct from and at odds with Roman rule. Certain cases
of this phenomenon can be identified relatively easily, notably the exclusive use during the Great Revolt of 66–70 and the Bar Kokhba Revolt of
Hebrew and paleo-Hebrew slogans on the coinage of the insurgents. In the
case of the Social War bull and wolf coins, the aggressive nature of this
image encourages us to see the gap between these and coins of the Roman

state, as well as aspirations to statehood implied by the appropriation of formal aspects of Roman coinage.[34]

In the last part of this chapter, I will consider the quieter reception of tropes of Roman power that do not always look to the Roman center or necessarily entail loyalty to central Roman authority. Roman rule profoundly changed the structures of local societies, and the fact of Roman sovereignty was marked in every sphere of life. But we find numerous examples of individuals and groups who seek to harness the efficacy of Roman power to all sorts of personal and local ends, that, however benign, have nothing to do with loyalty to the Roman center.

My first set of examples concerns the representation and self-representation of local magistrates. From the second century BCE, long before there was anything particularly desirable about adopting Roman culture outside the city of Rome, and long before the city of Rome functioned as a model for civic communities, we see the proliferation of Latin loan-words for Roman magistrates in the Latin and Oscan inscriptions of Italian towns that were still at that time subject to Rome. Loan-words, such as *pretores* and *kvaisstures*, appear alongside more traditional *meddices* and other local designations. These Latin loan-words helped to express the new diversification of office in Italian communities, but they also represented the appropriation of elements of the imperial power to which the Italians were subject into strictly local situations. There is no doubt here that the Italians believed that Roman power was efficacious, and even the epitome of a dominant power, but there are no particular implications of loyalty to that Roman power: many Italian communities notoriously fought against Rome in the Social War of 91–89 BCE.[35]

By the end of the Republic, the status of cities in relation to Rome in Italy and the west was formally defined in legal charters, a process that paralleled the incorporation of individuals into Roman citizenship. The responsibilities of local magistrates of Roman colonies and other privileged communities were set out in these legal charters, with explicit references to city of Rome practices. In theory, communities and individual magistrates knew their place, which was inevitably subordinate to the city of Rome and its magistrates. Town charters contained clauses that specified the number and type of attendants wielding *bacilla* (axe-less fasces) a local magistrate could have, significantly fewer than a high magistrate of Rome.

---

[34] Jewish coins: Schwartz 1995, 27; the visibility of the gap in mimesis: Bhabha 1994a; Fuchs 2001; problems of reading resistance from material culture: Jiménez 2008.

[35] Campanile and Letta 1979.

The "rule book" mentality plays a significant role in the making of a juridically Roman or Latin town in the early Empire. Holders of the duumvirate, the top magistrates in Latin and Roman towns, were allocated one pair of *bacilla*-wielding lictors, compared with the six pairs attending a Roman consul. Jurisdiction was circumscribed, and military command under local officials' own auspices and independent foreign policy were obviously out of the question.[36] Augustan legislation and actions of the *princeps* reinforced notions of order that emphasized the distinct place of groups and individuals within a hierarchy: theater-seating legislation models this beautifully, as we will see in Chapter 3. The very emergence of a *princeps* focused attention keenly on gradations of power, such as questions about the appropriate recipients of a triumph and suitable spaces for the self-display of senators and other individuals outside the imperial family. Ironically, this encouraged a more clearly articulated "Republican-ism" than ever before.

So what are we to make of the (probably) early Augustan monument honoring C. Cartilius Poplicola (Figure 3), dedicated in a lengthy inscription "at public expense . . . by decree of the decurions and consensus of the colonists," to the eight-times holder of the office of duumvirate in the Roman colony of Ostia and three-times censor, as well as to his children, descendants and wife? The imposing marble monument is decorated with a triumphal-type frieze depicting a sea battle, as well as infantry and possibly cavalry, no fewer than 16 bundles of *bacilla* flanking what may originally have been a representation of a curule chair, and was almost certainly topped off with a *rostrum* (ship's beak), the paraphernalia of naval victory.[37]

On an obvious level, the monument looked to the Roman center, taking its inspiration from the highest Roman officials of the Roman Republic, and perhaps even from the archaizing exceptionalism of Augus-tus himself. Scholars have suggested an exact parallel for the rare adjective used to describe Poplicola, *preimarius,* "first and foremost": the famous elogium of the mid-third-century BCE consul and censor A. Atilius Cala-tinus. This elogium had enjoyed something of a revival in the late Repub-lic, perhaps encouraged by wishful thinking about the emergence of a positive kind of first man. The Ostians' choice of Poplicola as duumvir "both in absentia and while present" is also signaled, and this association of

---

[36] *Lex Coloniae Genetivae* 62 (Crawford 1996, 25 with note at p. 433); cf. Schäfer 1989, 217–21.

[37] Inscription: Bloch 1958 with Panciera 1966; monument and its decoration and date: Squarciapino 1958; Gismondi 1958; Schäfer 1989, C7, 385–6 with plate 93, 1; Pensabene 2004.

Figure 3    Heavily restored monument to C. Cartilius Poplicola of Ostia, eight-times duumvir and three-times censor, showing one half of eight pairs of bacilla (axe-less fasces), frieze with sea battle and infantry soldiers, and beginning of long inscribed dedication "at public expense." Probably early Augustan, outside the Porta Marina, Ostia.
Photo by Art Media/Print Collector/Getty Images.

*in absentia* elections with exceptionalism has a particularly Augustan ring to it. This emphasis on *in absentia* election will find a famous historicizing parallel in the elogium of Marius, traditionally attributed to the Forum Augustum, finally dedicated in 2 BCE (*CIL* 6, 41024; *Inscr. It.* 13, 3, 17): "three times he was made consul in absentia." The very cognomen Poplicola, "the People's Friend," which C. Cartilius apparently acquired at some point during his second duumvirate, almost certainly recalls that of the suffect consul of the foundational year of the Roman Republic, the colleague of Brutus, and iconic expeller of kings, named Poplicola by the grateful (and arguably rather fickle) people, finally reassured that he was not aiming at tyranny. Livy's account of the Poplicola story, with its complex negotiation of kingship, suggests how this episode resonated in the early years of the principate (2, 7, 3–8, 4).[38]

Poplicola's memorial has generally been interpreted as an endearing example of the kind of "over-expression" associated most readily with freedmen Augustales or *vicomagistri,* perfectly aware of their humble position in the Roman imperial eco-system but a little starstruck by the Roman imperial center with its associated ceremonial. In the case of a Roman colony like Ostia around the turn of the eras, we would probably talk rather about an equally endearing and anodyne "local pride," based on Ostia's ancient and special relationship with Rome, newly manifest in a developed sense of what it was to be a Roman city. I would of course not want to deny the Ostians' pride in their celebration of Poplicola, or to see anything non-benign in their "over-expression" of his achievements and virtues: Ostia was, after all, an "extreme" Roman colony, believed to have been founded almost at the beginnings of Rome itself. But I do want to think of the monument within a much broader context of empire-wide engagement in or reproduction or appropriation of rituals, insignia, or hotspots that suggest Roman sovereignty or reproduce Roman centrality at home, and at one end of a long spectrum of that runs all the way via gaming the system or siphoning a bit off for yourself or your community to outright usurpation of the executive power of the Roman state.[39]

Viewed within this context, the Ostian monument is a striking statement of statehood expressed in the symbolism of a world power. We might single out the astonishing display of multiple axe-less fasces, a celebration of the power to enforce that stops short of execution, and a reminder of the centrality of coercion in the reception of imperial power and violence as an expression of self-determination. Also striking is the *princeps*-like exceptionalism of their leader, played out as a distillation of grand statesmanship, culminating in an Actium-like sea battle (and perhaps the grandest imaginable battle, by all conceivable means). Last but not least, we should note the Ostians' showcasing of their sovereign political institutions ("colonists" and "decurions," as well as officers such as Poplicola) in action

---

[38] Inscription's language of exceptionalism: Bloch 1958.
[39] Freedman paramagistrates and "over-expression": Whitehead 1993 (cf. Petersen 2006 for critique); cf. Prag 2006; Laird 2015.

(electing and honoring, their political community perhaps mirrored in the "brothers-in-arms" iconography of land soldiers in the frieze).[40]

The Poplicola monument is an excellent illustration of the impact and internalization of Roman imperial symbolism. This arguably extends even to the internalization, at least on one level, of rules that reinforced hierarchical relationships. It is hard to believe that the 16 *bacilla* represented on the monument are "only" a multiplication of the two axe-less fasces to which Poplicola, as *duumvir*, was entitled, by the eight times that he held this office (let alone "only" artistic license). But the mathematical precision, as well as the absence of axes, remains suggestive of an applied legalism and awareness of how far to push the boundaries of possibility and respectability. At the same time, there is a magnificent boldness in this boundary-pushing, which reminds us of other, less benign and more self-interested acts of appropriating the paraphernalia of the Roman imperial state and diverting its power and efficacy to ends that have nothing to do with enacting loyalty to the center.

The so-called "Babatha archive" takes us well beyond receptions of the authority and power of the Roman empire on the part of Roman citizens or those who were close to Roman citizenship in status.[41] Babatha was not a Roman citizen, but a wealthy Jewish woman, who lived in the "friendly" Nabataean kingdom, which became during her life time part of the Roman province of Arabia (established in 106 CE). Her "archive" is a collection of legal documents dating from between 96 and 132 CE, detailing her affairs and those of some of her family members. They were found in a leather bag in a cave near the Dead Sea. It has been conjectured that Babatha fled to the cave during the Bar Kokhba Jewish revolt (132–135 CE) and never returned home. The documents are written in Nabataean Aramaic (the major language of the Nabataean kingdom), Aramaic (a legacy of Persian rule and influence), Hebrew (the language of Jewish scriptures and hence a cultural, religious, and ethnic marker of Jewish diaspora communities in the Roman empire), and Greek (the major language of official business in the eastern Roman empire, as we have seen). Some individual documents are written in a combination of several of these languages. Babatha's complicated personal life, including her two marriages and disputes with

---

[40] Actian imagery of late first century BCE: Avilia and Jacobelli 1989; Kellum 2010.
[41] For what follows, see fundamentally Lewis, Yadin and Greenfield 1989; Bowersock 1991; Goodman 1991; Isaac 1992; Cotton 1993; Millar 1993, s.n. "Babatha"; Yadin, Greenfield, Yardeni and Levine 2002; Katzoff and Schaps 2005; the Babatha "archive" illustrates beautifully the "ground-up" workings of Roman legal culture discussed by Humfress 2011; 2013.

a number of people over the guardianship of her "orphan son," Jesus, her son by her first husband, and over property, can be reconstructed from contracts, summonses, and other documents. While the persistence of such documents as land leases, sales, and marriage contracts in "Semitic" languages suggests the plurality of authorities after the establishment of the Roman province of Arabia in 106 CE, the degree to which Babatha sought the authority of Roman rule to resolve her various problems is striking.

The presence of Roman authority is most overt and direct in a copy of a census document dating to 127 (*P. Yadin* 16) and in a number of summonses and counter-summonses before the Roman governor, issued by and against Babatha (*P. Yadin* 14; cf. 15; 23; 25; 26). The census return is a fact of Roman rule, not a matter of choice, but the summonses suggest a willingness to turn to Roman authority, and specifically the highest Roman authority available at the local level, the governor, to resolve disputes. This was a facility that was learned very quickly during the first generation of direct Roman rule. A number of the summonses relate to the guardianship of Jesus, and the "archive" includes three copies of a Greek version of the Roman praetor's pronouncement on guardianship that we know about from Gaius' *Institutes* (*P. Yadin* 28–30; cf. *Inst.* 4, 47). Although Jesus' guardian had been appointed by the local city council of Petra, Babatha pursued this important personal issue extensively through *Roman* rather than local legal avenues.

Elsewhere, Roman authority is targeted much more loosely, rather than appealing directly to the Roman governor as judge or invoking Roman law. One excellent example is the marriage agreement of 128 CE between Babatha's stepdaughter Shelamzion and "Judah, surnamed Cimber" from En-gedi on the Dead Sea in Judaea (*P. Yadin* 18). While Babatha's own second marriage document was written just a few years earlier in Aramaic, the contract between Shelamzion's father and her husband is written in Greek, and refers explicitly to "Greek" custom, although the parties and witnesses sign off on it in Aramaic. The extent to which the arrangements reflect Jewish practice has been much debated. The document begins by identifying the year both by consular dating and by reference to the new province of Arabia, striking echoes of Roman official practice. The scribe indicates his "job-title" by a Latin word transliterated into Greek, probably *libellarius*. These various features reflect the reception of new models of what an "official" document looked like, whatever the realistic nature of its target audience. It should be Greek, an "official" language of the eastern empire used by both the city councils and institutions of Roman administration in a way that local, "Semitic" languages were not. It should have distinctively "Roman" features, especially in dating formulas that seem almost to define official discourse, and the odd loan word from Latin will only increase the authority of a document.

As if these features were not enough, the document was clearly intended to look "official" at very first glance, and without anyone needing to read it: like other documents in the "archive," including even some written in Aramaic, the papyrus was folded in an obvious reference to the wooden tablets that were associated specifically with official Roman contexts, such as census returns or military *diplomata*. This phenomenon has been illuminated in Elizabeth Meyer's eloquent study of *tabulae*, often called "double documents," because there are distinct inner and outer sides, with the outer side typically summarizing the inner one. These local approximations are far from homogeneous, as the languages and materials of the documents in Babatha's "archive" illustrate. Most importantly, this phenomenon gives us a beautifully complicated sense of "consensus." Local peoples might certainly use the double document form (and the legalese that went with it) to target the Roman authorities specifically, for example when sending a petition to the governor. But these forms are also employed in contexts which Roman authorities can never have been intended to see, such as marriage contracts written in an unfamiliar language.[42] This approximation of a specifically "Roman" official form appears to be expected to work far beyond the reach of Roman authority: to some degree it has taken on a life of its own.

By the late first and early second centuries CE, the degree to which specifically Roman trappings of power and authority are "targeted" by local groups and individuals is striking. It was not the case, however, that Rome was the only source of power and authority so targeted. On both the human, political plane and the divine plane, there were attractive alternatives, as the Palmyrenes' choice of the Parthian/Sassanian "king of kings" and the phenomenon of hyphenating gods in the western and northern provinces, such as Minerva Sulis and Apollo Granius, illustrate. These plural sources of power are not evidence of passive "survival" but of the continuing, dynamic processes of translation, equivalence, and distinction that were features of the beginnings of Roman overseas expansion.

---

[42] Meyer 2004, especially 178–206; cf. 54–5; 103–7 for the *tabula* form and legal language of Roman curse tablets, and the legalese of British curse-tablets, following Tomlin 1988, 70–1.

## Roman Middle Grounds

Richard White's *The Middle Ground* (1991), a case-study of the early history of encounters between Europeans and Native Americans in the Great Lakes region, offers a suggestive model for thinking about the dynamic interface between Roman rule and competing systems and local structures. White characterizes a situation in which "badly frayed or even cut" cables run out from the centers of French imperial power, as they lose the power to control and coerce and have to compete with other loci of power, the Iroquois, Algonquians, and smaller entities, such as Huron, the Illinois, the Miami, and the Ottawa as well as more distantly, the British. His "middle ground" erodes only gradually, initially in fits and starts, as European approaches switch from mediation to coercive alliance, from upholding the authority of chiefs to dictating terms to them, and, from the 1750s, with the arrival of competing imperial armies of occupation, the French and the British.

In the case of the Roman empire, the power to control and coerce was of course the aspiration of Roman *imperium,* and threat and terror very real: we shall explore the role of force and violence in the rhetoric and practice of imperial relationships in Chapter 4. But the thinly stretched nature of that Roman power, or at least its coexistence with competing systems of power and authority is clearly visible in the making of empire, at its edges and at times of crisis. Parallels with White's "badly frayed or even cut" cables are most obvious here. What I have argued in the last section of this chapter is that there are suggestive parallels to some extent also in everyday, business-as-usual Roman imperial relationships, encouraged by the substantial reliance of the Roman empire on local authorities and structures for even basic functions of state. This phenomenon becomes hard to see if we join the dots between periodic articulations of rules that more clearly nest local authority within and subordinate to central imperial power, and because it can be hard to look beyond the comparative domination of Roman imperial motifs, and more closely at structural contexts, interests, and ends.[43]

---

[43] I fully take on board Andrade's criticisms (2013, 11–14) of the use of White's "middle ground" theory to characterize the articulation of cultural identity as if there were bordered entities of "Greek" versus "Syrian" etc. I am concerned rather to read "middle ground" theory in terms of the stretched and gappy quality of imperial *power.*

# *Territory*

## One World?

Aelius Aristides' second-century CE panegyric *To Rome* notoriously portrays the city of Rome as a single, vastly inflated *polis*, receiving and showcasing goods and arts from all over the world-empire, possessing an immense territory protected at the edges by walls and soldiers standing shoulder to shoulder. The empire is pacified and civilized, its rivers, mountains, and deserts mastered. The firm, god-like authority of one man rules the city's vast domain. He rules by letters that are dispatched as if flown by birds, arriving instantaneously. These truths of spatial control, unity, and centralization are asserted so loudly that we need to work hard to hear other arguments. We can start by observing the cracks in the panegyric itself, its obvious conceits: the absurd trope of the world city, the admission that the emperor cannot actually be in all places at one time behind the fiction of airmail faster than Fedex, the tensions between Rome as central place and Rome as physically encompassing the world, and between the systematized mastery of Roman monarchy and the freedom and self-government of cities. These cracks and conceits alert us to the perspective and agenda of Aelius Aristides, a provincial subject writing Rome as imperial center in very particular ways rather than merely observing it.[1]

When thinking about the Roman empire in terms of its physical, material, and territorial presence, modern scholarship has also tended toward big, "one world" visions, although through most of the twentieth century, these competed with Manichean universes of oppressors versus the oppressed, or "Romans" versus "natives." At the beginning of the twentieth century, Haverfield, as we saw in the Introduction, regarded the Roman message of civilization as a self-evident end-point that was

---

[1] Esp.13; 31–3; 36; 58–65; 79–84; 92–102; Starr 1952; Harris and Holmes 2008.

readily observable in the roads, towns, Latin inscriptions, and changing tastes of Roman Britain. While he might regret the loss of local color and spirit, civilization seemed so obviously to be preferable to what had prevailed before that he dwelled little on the processes of delivering and acquiring it. At the end of the twentieth century, Woolf and Ando both write the Roman empire as a more or less singular belief system. For Woolf, that belief system is again civilization, but unlike Haverfield he offers a comprehensive exploration of both the value and the practical and psychological processes of reception, internalization, and application, whether in the physical appearance of the gods or the order and amenities of towns. Also in contrast to Haverfield, Woolf does not restrict his explanation of change to the western or northern provinces, but he addresses the more complex relationship between the material culture of cities of the Greek-speaking east and the processes that he describes as "becoming Roman." In Ando's version of empire as a belief system, the Roman authorities have strong ideas about political community, and are not hesitant to impose them, but the significance of material culture is much reduced except insofar as it is a proxy for the loyalty rituals that bind individuals and communities to the Roman center.[2]

Late twentieth-century models of the Roman empire as a belief system liberate the study of towns, and especially colonies, in the Roman empire from the more literal notion of reproducing or copying the city of Rome. They also liberate the study of Roman frontiers from the expectation that we will be able to correlate the position of markers on the ground more or less exactly with centralized policy. In this chapter, I will emphasize the significance and reach of ideas, including territorial domination, a defining aspect of imperial power in the ancient world, alongside civilization and loyalty, and noting intervention on the part of Roman officials as well as the more spontaneous targeting of the Roman imperial state or metropolitan center on the part of local communities and individuals. We should also emphasize process and the multiple perspectives that suggest plural, and potentially conflicting, ideas and ideals. This complexity looms large at foundational moments: when Roman road networks are established not so much by constructing the roads themselves but by changing the road signs, as seems to be the case in the earliest years of the province of Asia, or when colonies are "sent out" to areas in which preexisting towns or cities offer established ideas of community within their structures, as is the case at Paestum. It also looms large at the frontier, where peoples and towns on

[2] Haverfield 1915; Woolf 1994; 1998; 2003; 2012; Ando 1999; 2000; 2011.

the other side may appropriate the symbolism of Roman power to benefit from its perceived efficacy without implying political loyalty to Rome. This is an exaggerated form of the everyday plurality of loyalty and interest focuses within the provinces of the Roman empire. It suggests itself, as we will explore more fully in Chapter 3, "Brave New World," not least when "euergetism" (the reciprocal and unequal exchange of public gifts and individual honors), the sociopolitical power-force of the Hellenistic-Roman city, goes viral, giving shape, meaning, and impetus to organizations both within and beyond the city.[3]

## Making Imperial Territory

Whether they were seen as betterments of the world or as ugly structures of domination, the mechanisms of Roman territorial mastery used to seem comparatively simple: networks of roads facilitated movement or carved up older territories and connections; colonies were mini-Romes, whether they brought civilization to their neighbors or the shock of alien culture, lifestyle, and mindset, while centuriation scarred landscapes into patterns of Roman order and ownership, humiliating or reeducating local populations; frontiers were barriers that kept out barbarians. The establishment of provinces was an event that swiftly followed conquest. One burning question was why Rome did not "annex" more territory into subject provinces before the late Republic, and the other was what the consequences of this reluctance to annex were for her ratings as an imperial power.[4]

In recent years, much of this picture has started to seem less certain: third- to second-century BCE Roman rule was predicated not on provinces and structures of provincial government but on the ability to exact obedience to Roman orders; the making of provinces as units of an imperial system was a process (or rather a series of processes), that was only beginning to cohere into repeat patterns as the second century BCE progressed. Early Latin colonies were not mini-Romes; they had no original, ritual foundation moment and were perhaps not even nucleated, and probably not centuriated. Furthermore, centuriation was not a practice peculiar to Rome and is probably not to be understood as a punitive early step in the colonization process, but as a secondary development that enacts particular ideologies of community. The erosion of confidence

---

[3] For a "deep history" of euergetism, see Gygax 2016.
[4] Annexation debates: e.g., Badian 1968; criticism: e.g., Badian 1958; Derow 1979; Kallet-Marx 1995.

about certain formative actions of the Roman imperial state raises fundamental questions about how far we should pinpoint any one historical
moment as decisive for the development of territorial systems. While there
are good reasons to see the Augustan principate as particularly dynamic in
terms of the interconnection between innovative systems and the ideology
of a world newly centered on a single individual, it is equally important to
recognize the much longer trajectories of both systems and ideology.[5]

In this section, I focus on road-building, which has escaped relatively
unscathed from these new questions. We will consider frontiers in the next
section and colonies along with cities more generally in the last; modern
assessments of both frontiers and the making of cities have changed
profoundly in recent decades. The Roman road-building system greatly
impressed Polybius with its careful and frequent calibration of distance,
such that it could be used to measure the extent of Carthaginian mastery of
the west before their defeat, and stages of Hannibal's expedition, with the
implication that the Carthaginians had no such integrating system (Polybius 3, 39, 8). The degree to which the Romans engaged directly or
indirectly with other imperial systems (e.g., Seleucid and Macedonian
road-building and ultimately the Persian Royal Road) in the earlier stages
of construction is an open question, while those legendary straight lines
through uneven territories might have been facilitated by broader intellectual developments, notably Pythagorean mathematics. Large-scale road-
building, ensuring and threatening swift passage for the Roman army and
ultimately direct connection between colonies and the city of Rome, began
with the building of the Via Appia as far as Capua in 312 BCE, cutting its
way assertively through Roman and non-Roman territory in a statement of
long-distance control. Within the course of the second century BCE, roads
not only radiated outwards from Rome in all directions of peninsular Italy,
but cut right across the Apennine mountain chain and connected the
Tyrrhenian to the Adriatic Sea, marked by milestones and monuments
that proclaimed mastery by the Roman state. Intense road-building in
Cisalpine Gaul between the late third and late second centuries BCE mark
out this zone as one of initially intense military presence, and subsequently
as one of more general Roman visibility, significantly marking out the
Roman imperial presence beyond Italy and beyond the spider's web of
roads centered on Rome. Road-building (or flagged appropriation of
earlier systems, as seems to be the case in the province of Asia) beyond
Italy will become from at least the later second century BCE one of the

---

[5] The Augustan moment: Nicolet 1991 with Purcell 1990a; cf. Clarke 1999a.

expected ways to designate a province as a unit as well as signaling intense, onward activity at the edges of "hard" Roman power in frontier zones.[6]

For all of this intensity, with hindsight Roman road management can look to us like one of a number of imperial incompletes, precisely because it leaves room for pretensions of local sovereignty in the provision of infrastructure. For all the intensity of technological and territorial ambition in the earlier stages of Roman road-building, or major innovations for a pre-modern state, local authorities retained responsibility for the regular maintenance of roads. The rhetoric of benefaction in road-building and maintenance beautifully illustrates the tension between layers of sovereignty and authority that typifies the early Roman Empire. The emperor largely monopolizes road-building and restoration in Italy in the first two centuries CE, in his role as "highest building supervisor," but in the provinces the emperor's personal role in funding building and restoration projects, especially major infrastructure work such as bridges, is the exception rather than the norm. Other work was done in the name of provincial governors, but it is the role of local elites that is the most interesting, alternatively "invited" by governors to play their part in maintenance and repairs, or more spontaneously "reproducing" the grand Roman imperial/ Roman state official language of benefaction in advertizing their own big man versus the natural order actions. This slightly awkward compromise between local and central roles may be the major reason why emperors do not in fact make more of roads in their central ideology. If this is the normal state of play in the first three centuries of the Empire, Richard Talbert makes the interesting argument that the origins of the Peutinger Table, with its representation of a whole networked world of roads and cities, belong to the Tetrarchy's ideology of unusually assertive and direct territorial control.[7]

## Frontiers

Much of the discussion of Roman frontiers in recent decades has focused productively on what they were *not*. Insofar as they were ever defensive

---

[6] Persian Royal Road: Briant 2002, 172–83; 357–77; 505–7; Pythagorean mathematics: Humm 1996; Roman road-building in Italy and Cisalpine Gaul: Wiseman 1970; Frederiksen 1984, 213–14; Coarelli 1988; Purcell 1990b; Asia: Thonemann 2004; cf. Prag 2013 for the significantly earlier episode of Roman road-building in Sicily as an extension of Italy.

[7] Innovations e.g., the courier system: Kolb 2001; 2002; local versus imperial road-building: Pekáry 1968; "highest building supervisor": Kissel 2002, 146–7, cf. Alföldy 1991; Tetrarchy versus early empire: Talbert 2012; cf. Salway 2005.

barriers in the early Empire, that does not preclude the possibility, or indeed the strong likelihood that they were imagined also, and perhaps even primarily, as advance posts toward further territorial gain. To the extent that we can talk about centralized strategic policies of the Roman state, we will be hard put to find on the ground anything that approximates the particular kind of twentieth-century ideal of rational, "scientific" defensive boundary envisaged by Edward Luttwak as the *telos* of Roman imperial strategy in his provocative and influential *The Grand Strategy of the Roman Empire* (1976). If Luttwak's lines of approach and the sorts of questions he asked were informed by Cold War military strategy, the different sets of questions raised by the early twenty-first century experience of migration of peoples and goods across state borders in all its forms and with its vast range of effects on and challenges to institutions, economies, identities, law, and statehood itself, resonate across both ancient and modern historical studies of space and frontiers.[8]

Once we have acknowledged that the frontiers of the Roman empire are unlikely to have functioned in a way that mirrors closely a particular vision of the modern nation-state, securely fenced in with rationally set borders, it gives us license to explore the kinds of engagement that the Roman state and its officers *do* display with issues of territory and sovereignty. As we have seen, third- and second-century BCE Roman notions of imperial power are focused on the ability to exact obedience to commands rather than on "annexation" of territory or controlling it by particular institutional means. Hence, the scope of imperial power is fuzzily and exuberantly vague: even as the rhetoric of world mastery begins to take, the edges are not in focus. At the same time, physical domination of the territory by increasingly networking roads asserts point-to-point and coast-to-coast connections, surmounting natural geography, but always the possibility of a jumping off point to more: as Benjamin Isaac eloquently argued, *limites* are routes, not stopping points, in later Republican and early Imperial Latin.[9]

These grand ambitions of Rome's earlier overseas empire co-exist with equally important but much more narrowly focused territorial concerns, neatly illustrated by L. Aemilius Paullus' settlement of Macedonia in 167 BCE, which is tightly focused on the reconfiguration of the kingdom into

---

[8] Reevaluations of the Roman frontier: Isaac 1990; Whittaker 1994; 2004; new wave ancient and comparative modern approaches: e.g., Hekster and Kaizer 2011; St. John 2011; Alcock, Bodel and Talbert 2012; Kosmin 2014; Herzog 2015.
[9] Third- to second-century notions of imperial power: Derow 1979; *limites*: Isaac 1990; cf. Purcell 1990b.

districts (*regiones*), each with its *caput*, a central city to which the barebones functions of the new administrative unit are assigned: council, the collection of [tax] money, and the election of magistrates. The territory of each *regio* is designated by reference to geographical features (the "natural" boundaries of rivers and mountain ranges), with emphasis also on the hotly contested Paeonians (and their land, "Paeonia"). The particularity of the external border with "barbarians" is marked by permission to retain militias, suggesting acute fear of insurrection. Intermarriage and land ownership across *regiones* is forbidden. The settlement represents an exaggerated concern to enforce the reconfigured units by policing some of the most obvious forms of human (and particularly elite) interests that complicate the neatness of ancient state territories, as befits the aggressive dissolution of the Macedonian monarchy. Livy's account retains the shocking simile of dismembering an animal (45, 29–30), a resonant image of Roman violence, as we will see in Chapter 4. But the terms of the settlement are almost entirely directed to the establishment and policing of internal boundaries, and even there not to everyday mobility of goods and peoples but to high-end investment in kinship ties or property over these boundaries.

Interestingly, however, the most notorious early example of overseas Roman territorial insistence, the "day of Eleusis," when C. Popilius Laenas drew a line in the sand around Antiochus IV Epiphanes in 168 BCE, concerns arbitration in the territorial claims of others: the Seleucid king's encroachment on the Ptolemaic kingdom of Egypt. Occasional, dramatic interventions such as this will help to establish Rome's status as a "go to" authority in more everyday situations of territorial dispute between neighboring communities or individuals, one of the major day to day tasks of a Roman governor, and an important example of the reactive management of much of Rome's Republican as well as its Imperial empire.[10]

In terms of territorial boundaries to be *observed* by Roman officials, rather than those imposed by them, legislation from the later second century BCE forbids magistrates from leaving their provinces without the permission of the senate and Roman people. This measure suggests increasing concern about the possibility of treading on the toes of either a fellow Roman official, or a different state recognized by Rome or, indeed, of overstepping the authority delegated by the Roman people. Let out clauses in this legislation, excusing overstepping boundaries in both

---

[10] Day of Eleusis: Kosmin 2014, 129–30; governors and territories: Burton 2000; Ando 2006; reactive government as phenomenon of Republic as well as Empire: Crawford 1990, 102; cf. Millar 1977.

routine (e.g., travel to and from the province) and exceptional conditions (e.g., pursuing a perceived threat), suggest how closely tied the original sense of *provincia* as task has become fused to the more recently acquired, additional sense of *provincia* as bounded territory.[11] Thinking in provinces will never wholly replace other ways of imagining and enacting human geography, whether on the grand level of the Roman state (e.g., Augustan or Hadrianic displays of *ethnē*, peoples of the world of Roman experience, that include some provinces but are not restricted to them), or on the more intimate level (e.g., individual commemorations that normally identify people by their original, immediate birth community). Nevertheless, we can see as early as the first layer of the Monumentum Ephesenum, dating back to soon after the creation of the province of Asia in the early 120s BCE, the extraordinary care to delineate the fiscal boundaries of a province in establishing customs points. The notion of province as fiscal unit will only be enhanced by the Augustan generalization of censuses to provinces. This focus on usable units perhaps helps to explain (to us) the curious myopia of early Roman mapping practices, insofar as we understand them to date, and at least before the third century CE, with anything remotely resembling a map recognizable to modern eyes showing a comparatively small scale. Large-scale representations (of "the world," or rather the parts of immediate interest to the Roman state) quickly slide into abstraction, no longer requiring the map-like detail that we recognize in order to function.[12]

From the last decades of the Republic, we begin to see a qualitatively different concern with edges and with imagining a contiguous whole within those edges, coloring in between and beyond the lines of *limites*. The careers of Pompey and Caesar as well as their own cultural contributions make more expressly territorial Polybius' notion of Rome bringing about the subjection of "almost the whole world." We might think of the vote of *imperium* to Pompey against the pirates in 67 BCE, defined by miles from the Mediterranean as well as with reference to the *provinciae* of regular magistrates, or his identification with Alexander the Great pushing the connection between individuals and the unrivaled territorial expansion of empire, or Julius Caesar's configuration of geography in his *Gallic War*, with a Germany that is for better and for worse an anti-Gaul (*BG* 6, 11–28). The civil war between Pompey and Caesar, and the later

---

[11] Succinctly Lintott 1993, 22–5.
[12] Thinking outside (or in much smaller units than) the province: Talbert 2004; Monumentum Ephesenum: Mitchell 2008; small-scale maps: Brodersen 1995; Hänger 2001, 29–36.

large-scale carving up of responsibilities and war between Antony and Octavian would make the sovereign reach of Rome felt more painfully than ever before. This carving up of the world would culminate in a ceremony that Ovid commemorates on January 13, 27 BCE, as the occasion on which "every province was returned to our people" (*Fasti* 1, 589). Later accounts would put rather more emphasis on what happened next, that Augustus took back the more troublesome, military provinces, leaving the others to the people and to the traditional manner of appointing senatorial governors, by lot. Ovid's account, with its emphasis on Octavian's giving back to the people, harmonizes well with the famous *aureus* of 28 BCE that celebrates Octavian's restoration of "laws and rights to/of(?) the Roman people." This ritualized giving back between 28 and 27 BCE is reminiscent of the "surrender-and-grant" ritualized behavior that John Ma has identified for Near Eastern and Hellenistic kings, and in adapted form for the Athenian democracy, whereby the king – or Athenian people – first takes cities into his control, demonstrating that their future is wholly in his hands, and then grants them their autonomy. The self-government that was essential to the traditional ideal of the *polis* (even if this ideal was, in practice, regularly compromised) becomes, with beautiful irony, the king's gift. The Augustan ceremony takes this regal ritual of potential territorial mastery but actual magnanimity and protection of local custom and autonomy, and runs with it in an internal context, the governance of the Roman state. This ceremony might take its place in the company of Augustus' subsequent makings of geography, unprecedented in scale and ambition, from the intellectual and ideological scope of his *Res Gestae* to the physical rearrangement of the city of Rome and Italy and the extension of the Roman citizen ritual and institution of the census, with its archived documentation of people and property, to the provinces, the themes of Claude Nicolet's path-breaking *Space, Geography and Politics in the Roman Empire* (1991).[13]

One of the most striking features of Augustus' *Res Gestae* is the author's concern to represent himself as pushing the geographical limits of Roman knowledge and influence (26; 30), and of power itself in his mastery of kings (27; 31–3). Major recent threats at some of the edges, the Germans and the Parthians, are neutralized in the account, more or less dubiously (26, 31, 33). This attention to edges is important for claims that Augustus has surpassed all possible competition, whether in the past or in the

---

[13] Ma 2002, 111–13; Ma 2009; Octavian's restitutions: Rich and Williams 1999.

present. After the exceptional escalation of conquests and acquisitions in the last two centuries of the Republic, Augustus' contemporaries could not agree on whether he had finished the conquest of at least every part of the world that was worth it, or whether there was more to be done, perhaps in subduing the Indians and Britons. The realization of Roman dynastic monarchy will considerably stabilize expansion driven by intensely competitive desire for glory and honor: that stabilization is dramatized in the tradition of Augustus, in a document left behind on his death, instructing Tiberius not to expand the empire (Tac. *Ann.* 1, 11). Nevertheless, expansion will long remain what an emperor ideally does, leading to more isolated spikes of acquisition memorialized as spectacular achievements of the near impossible (e.g., Claudius in Britain, Trajan in Dacia), alongside an emerging rationalizing rhetoric of cost versus benefit, with Britain as Exhibit A (e.g., Strabo 4, 5, 3; Appian, Pref. 5 cf. 7).[14]

This increasing attention to the edges is immediately apparent in the emergence of frontier zones, where military, economic, and policing considerations will create concentrated hotspots of Roman state presence, often in the form of army units. These hotspots of Roman state presence will encourage the diversion of resources from the Mediterranean center, and new and extended networks of supply and trade that typically work in both directions of the frontier. At the same time, communities will be reconfigured, founded, or become established, ranging from "friendly kingdoms" with their distinctively "middle ground" enactments of sovereignty (e.g., Commagene, or Bosporus), through to ad hoc civilian settlements in the vicinity of army camps (e.g., Noviomagus/Nijmegen), preexisting local towns changed by the presence of army units and veterans (e.g., Dura Europus), and colonies (e.g., Colonia Agrippinensis/Cologne/Köln). Across the frontier zones, we will expect to see intense communication (including the development of long-distance trade routes, e.g., across the Sahara, or via India all the way to east Asia), fusions, juxtapositions, and creations of religious ideas and cultural practices, and, in some cases, significant economic and political knock-on effects on local peoples.[15]

However, this intense communication of goods and ideas should not be understood as implying consensus about the meaning of goods and ideas

[14] Rhythms of Roman expansion: Harris 1979; Cornell 1993; Woolf 1993.
[15] "Friendly kingdoms": Braund 1984; Millar 1996; Schörner 2011; civilian settlements near army camps: Hanel 2007; Dura Europus: Pollard 2000; Kaizer 2016; Sahara: Schörle 2012; India/east Asia: Liu 1988; Casson 1989; de Romanis and Tchernia 1997; Ying 2004; economic and political knock-on effects on peoples beyond the frontier: Halsall 2007; 2009.

within different political contexts. For example, Roman iconography of power is targeted by a number of groups outside of the Roman empire, but the contexts of appropriation and translation differ considerably, as does the degree to which Roman iconography is the single locus of power. At the most basic level, appropriations of Roman iconography of power cannot be equated with aspirations to *be* Roman. Roman symbolism of power, particularly in the form of military officials' belt-sets (with their elaborate buckles, fastenings and other attachments), was received more or less exclusively as *the* locus of power among peoples of late antique "free" Germany, even as trousers, arguably worn for their associations with "barbarian" soldiers, were banned by the Theodosian Code (14, 10, 1–2). On the other hand, the citizens of the caravan city of Hatra, just across the Roman-Parthian frontier, whose relationship with both the Roman and Parthian Empires was, to say the least, complicated until it surrendered to the Sasanians between 240 and 241 CE, kept their focus tightly on chosen local deities of Hatra and took a keen interest in the Arsacid fire cult, but at the same time thoroughly naturalized as a god the Roman legionary standard, gave it an Aramaic name, Samya, and placed it in the company of Mesopotamian gods.[16]

Amidst this intense activity, the power and efficacy of the Roman empire and its finite nature were felt and enacted to different degrees and in different ways across place and time. Fiscal control was strongly asserted in some frontier zones, such as the care to delineate customs procedures in the *Monumentum Ephesenum*, the customs law from the province of Asia that preserves layers from the beginnings of the province to the age of Nero, and that differentiates taxes on imports into the Roman empire from taxes on imports from other areas of the empire. We can compare first-century CE concern at Berenice, on the coast of southeastern Egypt, to monitor and provide a final check on taxes paid earlier on goods bound for long-distance trade routes to India, the primary reason for a conspicuous military presence that operated almost like its own little state, imposing its own tax, the *quintana*, on traders entering the military zone. As more of the extraordinarily well-documented existence of military units is illuminated by papyri, ostraka, and wooden tablets, such as the *ostraka* pass permits of Mons Claudianus from the beginning of the second century CE, we can see ever more clearly the Roman preoccupation with surveillance and information-gathering, monitoring to-ing and fro-ing in

---

[16] "Free Germany": Halsall 2009; Hatra: Dirven 2011; Dirven 2013; Andrade 2013, 1–2.

frontier zones and other areas that were sensitive from an economic or security point of view.[17]

Monitoring and surveillance seem to have been the primary reasons for the construction of a system of ditches, walls, and forts across a frontier zone of North Africa in the early second century CE. Even the southwards extension of the system between the later second and the early third century seems to have been focused primarily on surveillance and monitoring the major access routes to water sources, rather than on keeping nomadic peoples out, as we can deduce from the positioning of the network. It also makes sense to think in these terms when we  consider Hadrian's Wall, built in northern Britain in the 120s CE, punctuated with mile castles, watchtowers, and gates that manage the through traffic. The Vindolanda Tablets vividly illuminate the movement of supplies and people that constitutes this through traffic. At this point, we should emphasize that surveillance is not an activity directed exclusively toward outsiders, and also that it was not necessarily an inoffensive pursuit: Benjamin Isaac has brilliantly identified the pattern of concentrating troops in the towns of Judaea, in small desert guardposts and along roads not so much as a means to keep intruders out but rather as symptomatic of occupied territory. As we will see in Chapter 4, the Romans were certainly alert – some would say that they were hyperalert to the point of making things a lot worse – to the possibility of internal disorder spilling over into internal threat. Certain situations and territories, notably Britain and Alexandria, as well as Judaea, made them particularly nervous. The context of Hadrian's Wall differs from the North African system of ditches, walls, and forts insofar as the area to the north of it had been an active zone of Roman warfare within living memory. Even if the construction of the Antonine Wall several decades later from the Firth of Forth to the Firth of Clyde in what is now Scotland undermines any notion of Hadrian's Wall as a permanent, defensive barrier, Hadrian's Wall is more immediately a physical symbol of the distinctively Roman variety of peace that comes when war is actively extinguished than is the North African system.[18]

The Rhine-Danube frontier zone and what we might refer to in shorthand as "the Euphrates frontier zone" were the areas of the Roman empire most intensely contested by external peoples and states. The history of Roman intervention in Germany begins in a manner reminiscent of

[17] Berenice: Nappo and Zerbini 2011; Mons Claudianus: Fuhrmann 2012, 208–9.
[18] Isaac 1990, chapter 3.

intervention in northern and western areas like Gaul and the Spains, whose pacification was not always easy, but which was ultimately regarded as complete. It will come to look rather more like Britain in the sense that completion was obviously questionable. As we observed in the previous section, Julius Caesar made of Germany and Germans an anti-Gaul across the Rhine, the people calibrated as more primitive, further from the center and civilization, and their land encapsulated by the Hercynian Forest, vast, unknowable, and the home of strange animals (*BG* 6, 21–8). His account draws a line that conveys a sense of completeness about his conquest of Gaul, but it also leaves open possibilities, particularly in signaling that the Rhine is crossable in both directions. Caesar himself relies happily on his German cavalry, probably the direct ancestors of the Imperial Batavian cavalry, and notes the presence of "colonies" from Gaul to the east of the Rhine, assimilated to the Germans in their customs and moral uprightness (6, 24). Augustan ambitions for a huge province that would stretch from the Rhine to the Elbe, encompassing "free Germany," are suggested by the archaeological discovery of a monumental and rapidly built civilian site at Waldgirmes, with an orthogonal street plan, *forum*, basilica, and monuments of the imperial cult, including parts of a life-sized equestrian statue in gilded bronze, a shockingly incongruous new central place that suggested distinctive community ideals.[19]

These particular ambitions were to be quietly abandoned in the aftermath of Varus' disastrous losses in 9 CE, and Germanicus' return to Rome in 15 (*Ann.* 2, 26, 3), but attention remained very much focused on the Rhine-Danube region. The legacies of this attention include the west bank settlement of Colonia Agrippinensis (Köln/Cologne) at oppidum Ubiorum, and the assertive declaration in the reign of Domitian of Upper and Lower Germany as no longer just military zones but provinces, although most of their territory was to the west of the Rhine, reassigned from Gaul. To the east of the province of Upper Germany as well as that of Raetia, also expanded in the Flavian age, where they stretched assertively beyond the Rhine and the Danube respectively, were linear structures, probably begun in the immediate aftermath of the creation of the provinces, although parts were at least improved or strengthened if not actually built for the first time in the age of Trajan. Improvements continue in the course of the second century CE, in the form of sturdier and more continuous wooden palisades, wooden towers exchanged for stone ones,

---

[19] Waldgirmes: Weiler 2007; Strobel 2007.

the construction of earth banks and ultimately stone walls in some parts, along with shifts forward until Upper Germany reached its greatest extent in 161 CE.[20]

While these structures are undoubtedly important in enacting a distinction between two sides at the frontier, arguably this distinction is achieved at least as much by negotiation. Marcus Aurelius and Commodus' regulation of the movements of tribal chieftains across the frontier into the Roman empire by a series of treaties granting land and requiring military service and the payment of tax are a notable example. We might contrast these actions with traditional Roman thinking about rivers or other "natural" geographical boundaries, as positively inviting an ambitious commander to cross them, confounding their very nature. Repeatedly reversing this trajectory, as Marcus Aurelius and Commodus did, presumably under some pressure, both enacts the frontier as boundary and places a question mark over the expectation that the Romans will always push forward.[21]

The Romans shared the "Euphrates frontier zone" with the successor states of the Achaemenid Empire, the Parthians, and later the Sasanians, the only external power that was even occasionally acknowledged by Imperial period Roman sources to be roughly comparable with their own empire. The Parthian presence, in addition to that of other, smaller but sometimes assertive kingdoms made fluent in the language of imperial bargaining between the fallout of the Seleucid kingdom and the coming of Rome, made the Near East a volatile region. While the Roman military presence in the province of Syria, a "province of Caesar," was doubled in the reign of Tiberius, Roman hold over the region before the Flavian period rested extensively on the hope that "friendly kings" were doing it primarily for Rome, rather than the frightening possibility that they might be doing it primarily for themselves or even for another power. The results were mixed: Commagene and (occasionally after 4 BCE) Judaea had their problems, while Armenia, ruled in some episodes by members of the Arsacid (Parthian) dynasty endorsed by Rome, suggests how tenuous Roman power was in this region. While the presence of these "friendly kings" made this frontier zone broader and fuzzier even than usual in the early Roman Empire, face offs and diplomatic exchanges between Rome

---

[20] Rhine/Danube frontier: Creighton and Wilson 1999; Wilson 2006; Oppidum Ubiorum/Colonia Agrippinensis: Eck 2004; Matijević 2010.
[21] Treaties: Potter 2013, 328–30; rivers: Braund 1996; Campbell 2012; Purcell 2013.

and Parthia significantly took place at the Euphrates, on bridges or by symbolic crossings, demarcating the river as boundary.[22]

After Antiochus IV of Commagene, under suspicion of being too close to Parthia, was deprived of his kingdom in 72 CE and the territory incorporated within the Roman province of Syria, we see a flurry of road and fort-building in the immediate vicinity of the Upper Euphrates. Direct Roman intervention in the region, challenging the uneasy balance of power between Rome and Parthia, will reach its peak in Trajan's Parthian Wars, with the provocative establishment of the short-lived provinces of Mesopotamia and Armenia, intensified road-building, and the physical presence of Trajan himself in the Near East for three years. This focus of attention and resources anticipates and arguably helps to provoke the emergence of the formidable Sasanian dynasty in the third century CE, and ultimately Shapur I's claims of mastery over three Roman emperors.[23]

It seems quite clear from our brief survey of frontier zones, structures, and natural features enacted as borders that their configuration was not directed by any centralized plan, let alone by a single author. Although it is naïve to suppose that the Romans had nothing approximating a modern understanding of policy (in general terms of sustaining broad intentions) with regard to the various frontiers, both textual sources and the nature of manufactured structures suggest that decisions about where to set stopping points were generally made in an ad hoc way, by commanders who were actually there. While manufactured structures or natural features could be used defensively and were regularly used to police traffic moving across the frontier zone, a number of factors suggest that the message of manufactured structures was directed at least as much toward those within them as toward those outside of them. Recent studies of Hadrian's Wall suggest that it is configured back to front if its primary purpose is to keep people out: the *vallum*, the impressive ditch and mound earthwork, is on the south side of the wall rather than the north, while the Wall is to all intents and purposes in the middle of nowhere rather than obviously protecting strategic sites. Roman agents and forces regularly intervened in the business of peoples and land on the far side of manufactured structures such as Hadrian's Wall. David Potter's formulation of the boundaries of empire as marking divisions between spheres where Rome exercised "hard" power

---

[22] Roman recognition: e.g., Strabo 11, 9, 2; Tac. *Ann.* 2, 56; Jos. *AJ* 18, 46; Just. *Epit.* 41, 1, 1; imperial bargaining: Andrade 2013, 67; Euphrates as boundary: Millar 1993, 33; 58.

[23] Millar 1993, 99–105; Potter 2004, chapter 6; Wheeler 2007.

through imposing and enforcing the provincial system, and those where it might exercise "soft," hegemonic power, is a helpful one.[24]

The image of Rome as "fortress empire," surrounded by walls, fences, and barrier-like natural features, like a single, enormous army camp, was increasingly resonant from the second century CE (e.g., Appian Pref. 28; Aelius Aristides *To Rome* 81–4), and a marked ideological feature from the third century, sometimes retrojected to the Augustan foundations of the Empire. There are real problems with understanding such evocations as a simple, accurate description of the aims of manufactured structures in frontier zones. In many cases, neither their appearance nor their primary function conforms to such an image of a "fortress empire." We should, however, take seriously the symbolic and performative character of Roman building in frontier zones, which does not mean that such building was *only* symbolic and performative. Early examples include assertive building in the Rhine frontier zone, especially the dramatic construction we have observed of the short-lived town at Waldgirmes, which anticipates by roughly a century the monumental forum complex of Lopodunum in Upper Germany across the Rhine, on the pocket of land between that river and the Danube (the area referred to as the *agri decumates:* Tac. *Germ.* 29), in the age of Trajan. Although we cannot know for certain in either case, the speed, scale, and construction methods all suggest directed Roman involvement, probably on the part of army units. In terms of boundary structures, Hadrian's Wall is the obvious example of monumentality, making a statement not unlike that of earlier roads in its coast-to-coast reach, but considerably surpassing even them in visibility and physical Roman presence, dominating both the landscape and human interactions. There are signs on other frontiers of more modest gestures toward monumentality from the second century CE, including more robust structures on the Rhine-Danube frontier and, in the third century CE, the imposing fort at Bu Njem in North Africa. It is tempting to think of these signs of increased monumentality as being connected both with the "fortress empire" ideology and with a semantic shift observable in the third century CE from *limites* as routes to "limits," as empire's edges were more deliberately configured to signal what it meant to live within or pass through Roman territory.[25]

---

[24] *vallum:* Wilmott 2009; Potter 2013.
[25] Lopodunum: Wilson 2006; Hadrian's Wall: Breeze and Dobson 2000; Hanson 2002; Thorne 2007; Breeze 2008; Hingley and Hartis 2011; Bu Njem: Mattingly and Hitchner 1995; *limites:* Isaac 1990; Graham 2006.

## Rome and the City

Within early twentieth-century receptions of the Roman Empire, Roman urbanization, especially of the northern and western provinces, was a central part of its *mission civilisatrice*. Here as elsewhere, it has been hard to escape Tacitus' evocative image of Agricola's plot to settle down the Britons and get them used to pleasure, notably by giving them psychological and material incentives to build "temples, *fora* and houses" (*Agricola* 21), fostering competitive pride and luxury, a passage still frequently cited as major evidence to be taken literally for the mechanisms of city-building in the Roman west and north. While the association between cities and civilization is a significant aspect of the Roman discourse of urbanism and urbanity from the late Republic, it is far from clear that we should retroject such an ideal to the earlier Roman empire, or that we should ever imagine the Roman state to have been primarily concerned with the fabric of city-building, or that civilization was the only or even the primary ideal that inhabitants of the Roman empire associated with towns.

For much of the twentieth century, the first generation of Latin colonies in the third century BCE seemed to exemplify perfectly the foundational moment for establishing a "Rome away from Rome," with all that that entailed in terms of planting an external value system in the urban fabric of the colony. E. T. Salmon's Latin colonies are distinct from juridically Roman and politically and materially dependent colonies by being political entities in their own right, *polis*-like, "blue-print" reproductions of Rome itself. As such, they are key elements in the "Romanization" of Italy. Salmon's *polis*-like reproductions of Rome were inspired not least by Frank Brown's interpretation of his excavations (1948–1972) of the Latin colony of Cosa, established on the coast of south Etruria in 273. The site of Cosa seemed to Brown to fit perfectly Aulus Gellius' mid-second century CE characterization of colonies as "of the greatness and majesty of the Roman people ... miniatures, as it were, and in a way copies" (16, 13, 9, tr. J. C. Rolfe, LCL), but interpreted less abstractly and more literally as a material reproduction. Cosa's rituals of Roman city foundation (substantially modeled on Plutarch's version of Romulus' foundation of Rome, *Rom.* 11), and its "master plan" layout, centered on a forum integrated with public buildings including spaces for the central organs of the Roman state and a temple to Capitoline Jupiter on the *arx*, modeled a readily recognizable, new miniature version of Rome. In the process, it slightly improved on the original, insofar as it had a regular street plan.[26]

The more recent excavation of Cosa directed by Elizabeth Fentress in the 1990s has begun to cast doubt on many of Brown's fundamental interpretations. These begin with a circular argument: Brown's assumption that Cosa was a mini-Rome encouraged him to identify elements at Cosa that he associated with the fundamental DNA of early Rome, and then to use the colony to reconstruct unknown elements of early Rome. As a result of more recent excavations, the earliest, third-century BCE phase of Cosa is now looking much starker, stripped down to city walls, a "*curia*" ("senate-house": the persistent identification of buildings by Latin names that suggest typologies is a minefield), with a small enclosure next to it, an "*aerarium-carcer*" ("treasury-prison"), and a puzzling lack of houses.[27]

The reexamination of the nature of the first settlement of Cosa has encouraged fundamental reevaluation of earlier models of late fourth- to early third-century colonies as substantial material outposts of a specifically Roman value system and a nucleated presence, and a wholesale decon-struction of both ancient and modern assumptions about early colonies. Extensive fieldwork on the broader geographical environment of early Latin colonies by Jeremiah Pelgrom has suggested that we should think less in terms of a nucleated, city-like settlement with its territory and more in terms of predominantly hamlet-like settlements, clustering close to the farmland in still hostile territory. The first phase of Cosa might be better understood as a fortified gathering place rather than a town. While Roman and Latin colonies are undoubtedly "statist" projects in a way that earlier Greek colonies are not, Pelgrom would further suggest that the energy of the Roman state was not invested in establishing colonies as self-governing centers but in direct control of confiscated land, the Roman *ager publicus*, which was not ceded to Latin colonies.[28]

Clearly, much more work needs to be done to further our understand-ing of early colonies. Considerable disagreement is likely to continue for quite some time about fundamental aspects, such as the dating of the earliest street plans, or distinctively elongated *fora* flanked by long blocks

---

[26] Cosa's foundation: Brown 1951; Brown, Richardson, and Richardson 1960; 1993; Salmon 1969, 29–39; Brown 1980.

[27] Reevaluation of ancient and modern assumptions: Crawford 1995; Bispham 2006; Stek and Pelgrom 2014; third-century Cosa: Fentress 2000a, 14; lack of houses, and hypothesis of third century forum and street plan: Sewell 2010, chapter 6.

[28] Pelgrom 2008; Wilson 2004 for the recent identification of Etruscan settlement in the vicinity of Cosa, long thought to be a "greenfield" site.

of houses, or types of civic building. Nevertheless, the recent reevaluation of the construction of the *forum* at Paestum, a preexisting Greek-Lucanian city to which a Latin colony was "sent out" in 273 BCE ("twinning" it with Cosa), begins to suggest that a colonial settlement can exist without particular spaces or community ordering. Furthermore, a colony's enactment of ideals of space and community that marked its close relationship with the Roman state and the Roman metropolis was a complex process rather than a single, foundational moment. The *forum* of Paestum was constructed ca. 200 BCE, so several generations after the "sending out" of the colony, and co-existed with continued use of the earlier *agora*, suggesting less of a rupture and more of a juxtaposition of different models of central place and political community.[29]

As the third century BCE continues, we begin to see clear signs of enacting Latin colonies as discrete political entities: an early generation of magistrates at Beneventum and its "twin" Ariminum (both destinations of colonists in 268 BCE) named *cosoles* like their Roman counterparts; toponyms of Cales and elsewhere that adapt names of topographical features from the city of Rome, such as "vicus Esquilinus"; colonies minting coins with various standards and iconographies. Taken together, these look like different experiments in constituting a group along state lines, with more or less engagement in the major model of a state for many of the settlers, Rome. The degree to which the new community is an offshoot of Rome and the degree to which it is a distinct entity with executive powers is beautifully undecided at this point and, as far as we can see, up to the settlers themselves to figure out. These examples certainly suggest a burgeoning sense of community and grouphood, but it is a sense of community and grouphood closer to that of an early kibbutz than to top-down new builds such as Milton Keynes, Belmopan, or Brasilia.[30]

However, perhaps as early as the late third century BCE, and thus overlapping with some of these examples, we begin to see reliably attested interest on the part of Roman commanders and other officials in gesturing toward acts of foundation and constitution outside of Rome. The most explicit commemoration of an early act of constitution is that of the triumvir T. Annius Luscus, leader of a *supplementum* ("additional settlement") at Aquileia in 169 BCE, and remembered for establishing the

---

[29] Fundamental treatments of early colonies include Coarelli 1988; 1992; Gargola 1995; Torelli 1999, chapter 2; cf. more recently Sewell 2014; Paestum: Crawford 2006.

[30] *Cosoles* and adapted Roman topographical names: Bispham 2006; coins: Bradley 2014; kibbutz analogy (for early Greek colonies): Malkin 2011, chapter 4.

colony's laws, co-opting its senate "three times," and having a temple built. Contributing both to the fundamental constitutional elements and to the fabric of the town gestures toward a foundational moment (or at least brief foundational period), an episode of intense intervention signed off in a commemoration that initiates self-governance, a set of laws to call her own. T. Annius Luscus' contribution of a temple might be understood in relation to a new phenomenon in the second century BCE: the Roman censors' commitment in 174 BCE to fund (with public funds and occasionally private ones) infrastructure and amenities in Roman colonies, other Roman citizen communities, and occasionally Latin colonies (Livy 41, 27).[31]

The example of T. Annius Luscus might help to illuminate more obscure acts of Roman officials that gesture toward foundation and/or constitution. Acts that were later remembered as "foundations" in Spain, such as Scipio Africanus' "foundation" of Italica in 205 (App. *Hisp.* 38), seem likely to have been much humbler, no more and perhaps considerably less than the commemorated actions of T. Annius Luscus. We can only speculate about the reasons why the later third to early second centuries BCE brought new Roman interest in the phenomena of foundation and constitution. Certainly, however, Rome's increasingly international scope of imperial interaction and intervention brought it into ever closer contact with the successor kingdoms of Alexander the Great and their emulators, within which the foundation of cities was a measure of imperial success. Notable in this respect is Philip V's famous letter to the people of Larisa, trying to persuade them to loosen restrictions to their citizenship using the example of Rome founding "seventy colonies" (perhaps not coincidentally the number of cities believed to have been founded by Alexander), buoyed up by her practice of enfranchizing ex-slaves (*SIG* 543). Philip V's historical accuracy may leave something to be desired, but the fact that he draws Rome into a very Macedonian conversation that associates foundation with imperial prosperity is highly significant.[32]

The "upgrades" funded by the Roman censors of 174 BCE might be best understood within a much broader second century BCE context of enacting colonies as towns from their foundation, a burgeoning sense of colonies as discrete communities, and increased economic prosperity and

[31] Gabba 1958 for possible identification of a third-century "constitution" of Brundisium; T. Annius Luscus: Galsterer 2006; Bispham 2007; 174
[32] Cf. Sewell 2014, who dates Macedonian influence on Roman urban planning to the fourth century BCE.

security together with inspiration from international models of city foundation. As a variation on this theme, the additional settlement (*supplementum*) sent out to Cosa after the Hannibalic War in 197 was marked by
intense building: temples, the extension of a *"curia-comitium"* complex, a
*basilica*, and two sizes of standardized houses constructed along grid-plan
streets flanking an elongated *forum* give the town an emphatically planned
(even if notably austere) appearance. The scale and outlay of the project, as
well as the standardized houses, are probably best interpreted as pointing
toward a Rome-sponsored "refoundation," but insofar as assumptions or
ideals are written into the fabric of the town, they seem to be rudimentary
socio-political ones about a hierarchical community centered on a *forum*
rather than fleshed out cultural or religious ideals. Colonies enact notions
of religious community that <u>may</u> target cults associated with the Roman
state (e.g., in some cases the Capitoline triad, with its associations with
Roman victory), or cults inflected as Latin, but there is no one pattern or
correspondence of cults with a town's juridical status.[33]

The Oscan law written, remarkably in Latin script, on one side of the
two-sided Tabula Bantina, from the Oscan-speaking town of Bantia in
Lucania, can be interpreted as a striking example of appropriation not of
the cultural values of a colony, but of the phenomenon of foundation-
constitution with a very Roman twist that we have been discussing. Of
uncertain date (even whether to date it before or after the Social War, and
therefore whether to associate it with a non-Roman, non-Latin allied
community or a *municipium*, a Roman citizen town, remains a matter of
dispute), the Oscan law may be inspired by the constitution of the nearby
Latin colony of Venosa. Bantia's law ordains a census, names for officials,
and procedures for trials. It is in obvious ways inspired by Roman institutions, but the point is surely not to "become Roman" – inscribing the
law in the Oscan language makes such an aspiration particularly unlikely –
but to become a more prestigious community, to have a set of laws to call
its own, albeit a set of laws perceived to be particularly efficacious precisely
because of their Roman model.[34]

The first century BCE sees the escalation of phenomena we began to
observe in the late third to second centuries. In the aftermath of the Social
War of 91–89 BCE, constituting through legal charters former allied

---

[33] Second-century "new build" colonies, e.g., Luni: Laurence, Esmonde Cleary, and Sears 2011,
55–7; second-century Cosa: Fentress 2000a; Sewell 2010; religious identities: Torelli 1999,
chapter 2; Bispham 2006; sociopolitical community: Ando 2011b; cf. Pelgrom 2008 on evidence
for measured land allotment as a Gracchan/post-Gracchan phenomenon.
[34] E.g. Crawford 1996, 271–92; Bispham 2007, 142–52; cf. Wallace-Hadrill 2008, chapter 3.

(non-Roman and non-Latin) and Latin towns of Italy as Roman citizen towns (*municipia*) highlights the enormous problems of delineating sovereign responsibilities for such communities on the one hand and for the city of Rome on the other. These problems and the responses to them mirror the enormous difficulty in figuring out both in theory and in practice what it means to be a Roman citizen resident hundreds or even thousands of miles from Rome. Cicero's notorious formulation in his *Laws* (2, 3–5) of the "dual citizenship" experienced by Cato the Elder and himself, with one citizenship "by nature" and one "by law," locates their obligations toward and intense love for their homelands in the tombs of their ancestors. These sentiments are trumped by the higher obligations toward and affection for Rome, for whom they should lay down their lives if necessary. This is only one, idealized way of resolving the tension. Nevertheless, one important after-effect of the "municipalization" of Italian towns, mirroring the enfranchisement of Italians in the Roman citizenship, will be the progressive interpretation of Roman citizen and Latin status as examples of prestigious, hierarchical social statuses brokered by Rome.[35]

If the late third and early second centuries BCE introduce a tentative connection between individuals and city foundation/constitution/benefaction, the issue intensifies from the dictatorship of Sulla. Sulla and subsequently Julius Caesar claim by virtue of their territorial expansion of empire the right to extend the *pomerium*, the ritual boundary of the city of Rome, a right supposedly rooted in the regal period of Rome: individual exceptionalism finds expression outside the constraints of the Republic, in naturalized paradigms of *Roman* kings as founders. The personalized late Republic foundations of Pompey and Caesar are altogether grander and closer to the acts of Hellenistic kings. In settling the east in the 60s BCE, Pompey trod evocatively in the footsteps of Alexander and the Seleucids at their height, allegedly founding thirty-nine colonies (Plut. *Pomp.* 45), a spectacular number from a Roman perspective, including Pompeiopolis and Magnopolis, and honored as a divine founder. Of the Caesarian colonies in the west, we know most, at least in terms of ideals and aspirations, about Urso in Spain, founded by the dictator shortly before his death in 44 BCE. Fragments of the town's charter dating from its monumental, bronze version, probably inscribed in the early principate, survive: the wording of the charter itself seems to belong to the period of

---

[35] Frederiksen 1965; Crawford 1998; Bispham 2007, chs. 4–5; prestige: cf. Mouritsen 1998 on Roman citizenship.

foundation. The name of Colonia Iulia Genetiva (Urso) and the fact that her charter ordains an annual commemoration of Venus in a festival appended to the celebration of the Capitoline triad (Crawford 1996, 25, 71) are constant reminders of the divine associations of the founder.[36]

As we will see in Chapter 3, "Brave New World," Urso's charter articulates specifically metropolitan benefaction models for the new colony, and also explicitly hands over a significant decision to the city's magistrates, the determination of festival dates, durations, and sacrifices to be made (Crawford 1996, 25, 64), in addition to the prescribed shows, games and spectacles funded by the local magistrates for Venus and the Capitoline triad (70–1). These are two important articulations of self-government for a city of Roman status. At the same time, the charter almost reflexively assumes the institutional model of metropolitan Rome even as it delineates obligations and responsibilities of self-government. Thus, for example, it refers back to the powers of "a military tribune of the Roman people" when characterizing the military powers granted to a local magistrate or his appointee to deal with a security problem (103). The late Republic and early decades of the principate see much greater self-consciousness about what makes a specifically Roman city, played out in different experiments in "new build" colonies, delineated in the writings and drawings of the *agrimensores* ("land-surveyors"), and theorized in Vitruvius' notions of distinctively Roman architecture.[37]

As suggested by Sulla's and Caesar's extension of the *pomerium*, this is the age of antiquarian "revival" of quintessentially Roman rituals of city foundation and demarcation of space: Varro details the "Romulean" rituals of city foundation in his *De Lingua Latina* (5, 143). This self-consciousness is extended to foundations and re-foundations outside Rome. Urso's charter demarcates the colony by its sacred boundary, "drawn around by the plough" (14; 73), and "traditional" Roman foundation rituals were commemorated in coins, a relief or inscription for a number of towns, including Capua, Aquileia (Figure 4), Mérida, Berytus, and later Aelia Capitolina (on the site of Jerusalem), suggesting the local

---

[36] *Pomerium:* Richmond, North and Lintott 2012; late Republican colonies: Broadhead 2007,160–2; Pompey's foundations: Magie 1950, vol. 2, 1232–4; Mitchell 1993, vol. 1, 31–2; Jones 2001, 16; fragments of Urso's charter: Crawford 1996, 25; Caballos Rufino 2006; 2010.

[37] Decisions on sacred calendar and euergetism in Urso's charter: Rüpke 2006a; 2006b; "new build" cities: Laurence, Esmonde Cleary, and Sears 2011, 48–51; 55–7; agrimensores: Campbell 2000; Vitruvius: Wallace-Hadrill, 2008, chapter 4.

Figure 4   Early imperial relief from Aquileia depicting a plowing ceremony probably
meant to represent the demarcation of the sacred boundary associated with "traditional"
Roman city foundation. Museo Archeologico Nazionale di Aquileia, 1171.
Photo by DEA/A. DAGLI ORTI/De Agostini/Getty Images.

importance of these rituals in conferring the religious, cultural and social
capital now associated with juridically Roman city status.[38]

In this context, one surprising but persuasive recent argument is that,
although centuriation, the measurement out of equal allotments of land,
has been conventionally interpreted as a punitive act immediately
following Roman conquest and part of the act of founding colonies, it is
hard to find clear evidence for such allotments before the Gracchan age
with its very distinctive populist ideology. More remarkably, there are very
late examples that seem to follow an elevation to Roman colonial status:
the measuring out of land has become a ritual of foundation that reenacts
the supposed beginnings of the city of Rome itself. Tarraco, Barcino
(Barcelona), Emerita Augusta (Mérida), and Arausio (Orange), elevated

[38] Capua: *CIL* X 3825; Aquileia cippus: Museo Archaeologico Nazionale di Aquileia, inv. 1171; coins:
Sisani 2014, 382–3n117.

to or founded as Roman colonies between the Caesarian and Augustan periods all seem to fit this pattern. Possible receptions of an association of centuriation and the prestige of (re)foundation have been tentatively identified also in the territories of non-Roman cities of North Africa, with the grids measured by the Punic cubit, a studiedly local enactment of the phenomenon.[39]

While the phenomenon of targeting Roman constitutionalism in laws of governance or titles for magistrates is attested by the later third century BCE, and Latin colonies were inspired to adapt Roman toponyms for their own purposes, the fabric of the city of Rome was not an inspiring model before the Augustan age. As has been long observed, towns and other monumental centers in Italy looked directly or indirectly to the eastern Mediterranean for international models before the Social War. Although Roman imperial activity was of course closely implicated in both access to these models and the economic boom that escalated Italian (and e.g., North African) building projects from the second to the first century BCE, the city of Rome notoriously lagged behind Italian communities in, for example, the building of monumental stone theater complexes. The developing city ideals enacted by "new build" colonies are expressions of abstract Roman community rather than directly inspired by the fabric of the city of Rome.[40]

The direct quotation of city of Rome buildings in Italian and provincial cities belongs to the post-Augustan age. The most remarkable examples are mid-first-century CE quotations from the Forum Augustum complex such as those at Arretium, Corduba, and Mérida, each version different enough from the original through its selections or framing to be simultaneously a homage and a commentary. Other naturalizations of city of Rome models include Capitoline temples, rarer and more regionalized than they were once thought to be. While direct quotation or tributes *may* articulate a particular closeness to Rome, such as Roman citizen status, it does not seem to follow any particular rules, spoken or unspoken. We should rather see this phenomenon on a continuum with localized "hotspots" targeting the Roman center of the kind we identified in Chapter 1, such as "imperial cult" centers, which typically bear no visible relation to city of Rome models, but which nevertheless signal their localization of Roman power by architectural choices,

---

[39] Classic treatments of centuriation: Settis et al. 1983; "new wave" centuriation: Pelgrom 2008; Palet and Orengo 2011; north Africa: Stone 2013, 516–17.
[40] International architectural inspiration/Roman access and economic boom: Zanker 1976; Wallace-Hadrill 2008, chapter 3; Stone 2013; abstract Roman community: Ando 2011b.

imperial statues, language and/or monumentalized imperial correspondence. The increasing concern to designate these heterogeneous "hotspots" targeting the Roman center serves also to throw into relief local gods, histories, styles, and practices, which may be juxtaposed (or, in the case of the Greek cities, as we will see in Chapter 3, "The Economic Role of the Roman State," literally placed on the other side of the coin), or positioned in a past that still more or less actively communicates with the present. Occasionally, as we have tended to forget in recent decades, these "hotspots" can be the focus of rebellion, and the "local" that was so comprehensively a by-product of empire can be evoked in defiance.[41]

In all this, it is far from clear that Rome had any policy of urbanization along the lines envisaged by Haverfield, through his reading of Tacitus' *Agricola* 21. With very few exceptions (the short-lived city at Waldgirmes is perhaps one), it is notoriously difficult to identify direct Roman agency in the building of towns and cities as such. The more familiar glimpses we do get of involvement of Roman authorities would suggest that Agricola's constant hovering over his charges' building of "temples, fora and houses" is a compressed and exaggerated version of imperial preferences typically conveyed in reaction to local request or action: Vespasian granting permission to the magistrates of Sabora in Baetica to move their town down to the plain (*CIL* II, 1423); the people of Oxyrhynchus in Egypt granted permission to use money collected to adorn their *nome* capital, which did not enjoy the particular sovereign privileges of a 'Greek city,' with baths, and praised for doing so (*P.Oxy.* 43, 3088); Trajan referring Pliny's requests for advice about the over-ambitious building plans of Nicomedia, Nicaea and Claudiopolis in Bithynia-Pontus back to him (Pliny *Letters* 10, 37–40). These imperial preferences might also be expressed more quietly (at least to us) in the form of gifts, hints of the dynamic interface between Roman officials and the local community. These interchanges undoubtedly reiterate a power relationship in which representatives of the Roman state are the arbiters of good urban management, just as they are brokers of differential city statuses across the Roman empire. However, while this suggests consensus around the terms of the constant competition that fostered the extraordinary vibrancy of city life, the competition itself was played out within or between the cities themselves.[42]

---

[41] Forum Augustum quotations: Jiménez 2010; Capitoline temples: Quinn and Wilson 2013; focus of rebellion: Temple of Claudius at Camulodunum, Tac. *Ann.* 14, 31; going "native" in Civilis revolt: Tac. *Hist.* 4, 12.

[42] Oxyrhynchus' upgrade: Bowman and Rathbone 1992, 123; differential city statuses: succinctly Reynolds 1988; civic competition: Jones 1978, chs. 10–12; Burrell 2003; Heller 2009.

The call by Louise Revell and others to focus less on the immediate foundation and building processes of towns in the ancient world, and more on the ways in which they were experienced, especially behavior that is scripted by the specific configuration of a town in the Roman empire and its amenities, is timely, although the execution of this idea is in its early stages. One problem lies in assuming a monologue or singular chorus of voices rather than dialogue, and too restricted a script. It is easy enough to identify subscription to broadly held imperial ideals of a town, even when local versions may be strong on gesture and weak on execution, but harder to tune in to significant absence, avoidance, and appeal to alternative models. *We* might home in on the close association of towns with civilization (and sometimes hyper-civilization) that is a leitmotif of classical literature and that aligns neatly with modern civilizing traditions. We might also identify new kinds of bodily grooming as the prime ways in which northern Europeans experienced directly a lifestyle changed by new amenities such as bath-buildings. There is probably some truth in this, but it risks being reductive, along the lines of saying that shopping malls the world over introduce the quasi-religious (American?) capitalist experience of shopping as destination and achievement, missing the significant differences in behavior at, and ultimately meaning of, a mall in Japan, Nairobi, or New England.[43]

In the rush to identify urban rituals and behaviors as communing with an imagined Roman center, or with embodying particular imperial ideals, such as civilization, it is easy to overlook perhaps the most obviously abstracted urban behaviors. If the model of the Greek *polis* arguably to some extent stunted Hellenistic political thought, the Hellenistic-Roman city, with its vibrant enactment of hierarchical reciprocity through euergetism, proved not only good to think with, but reproducible, especially in the sub-urban or extra-urban format of associations based on common worship and/or occupation and/or place of origin. We will explore the impetus to form and maintain these viral grouphoods in the last section of the next chapter, "Knowing Your Place?".

---

[43] Experience and behavior: Revell 2009; Woolf 2012, 222–5; global malls: Jewell 2015; Dávila 2016; Lepik and Bader 2016; local avoidance of particular kinds of buildings or ingredients: Laurence 2012, 68–9.

# CHAPTER 3

# Wealth and Society

## Between the Devil and the Deep Blue Sea

The normally impeccable politeness of recorded honors in the cities of the Roman world does not always fully conceal the tensions, struggles, and anxieties of the Roman imperial experience.[1] A first-century BCE inscription from the Achaean *polis* of Messene contains three documents relating to an extraordinary Roman demand for 100,000 denarii to fund a military expedition (*IG* 5, 1, 1432–3). The dossier includes two decrees honoring an Aristocles. In the first, the Council of Messene honors him as their secretary, focusing specifically on his scrupulous conduct in making the assessment, collecting the funds, and above all in managing the announcement of a shortfall in front of the Roman praetorian legate Vibius at a public meeting in the theater, avoiding the possibility of the councilors having to carry the burden or the community having to resort to loans. The second decree, in the name of the Council and people, focuses more generally on Aristocles' fiscal propriety and exemplarity, including the benefits he secured from Roman officials. Both decrees emphasize the honors awarded to Aristocles by the legate Vibius (the second decree also names a Memmius, the proconsul) in this public audience: the right to wear a gold ring and for a statue to be erected for him. Importantly, these honors are endorsed and matched by the councilors themselves, while the costs of the statue and its pedestal are to be met by the public funds of Messene. The third document details figures for the assessment, initial collection, and shortfall, revealing the intricacy of late Hellenistic/early Roman fiscal categories that include a wealthy Roman citizen diaspora community.

---

[1] Cf. Zuiderhoek 2009, chapter 6 for benefaction as a symptom of internal political tensions, especially inequality; see also Gygax 2016 for developments in the ideology and practice of benefaction between the classical Athenian and Hellenistic *polis*.

The circumstances commemorated by the inscription were unusual both in terms of the exceptional nature of the Roman demand and the exemplary behavior of the council's secretary. We see a community under considerable pressure, with Aristocles' management of the situation not just averting potential disaster but ending with emphatic happiness. There are also clues of broader norms. The emphasis on Aristocles' management of this delicate situation and the assertion of the community's own political infrastructure and processes, even and especially under the gaze of Roman officials, hint at fears of what unshielded and unmediated Roman power might feel like, and the hearty praise of Aristocles' exemplary fiscal behavior inadvertently reminds us of how traditional opportunities for personal enrichment on the part of the elite could be exaggerated and obfuscated by their role as intermediaries in the context of Roman rule. The specific praise in the second decree for Aristocles using his own funds to entertain Romans further hints at opportunities for invoking Roman authority to enjoy a public slush fund, a literal, financial version of the phenomenon we noted in Chapter 1 in the example of the Poplicola monument of Ostia (Figure 3): siphoning off a little extra (displayed power in that case) for oneself.[2]

The inscription from Messene (often referred to as the "*oktobolos eisphora* decree" after the amount levied) neatly introduces the major themes and questions of this chapter. These include the nature and limitations of direct economic interventions of the Roman imperial state, which is the subject of the next section, "The Economic Role of the Roman Imperial State". They also include the often subtle and complex processes of economic change accompanying empire within local communities. These processes are illustrated firstly by a discussion of Pausanias' allegation that the Romans destroyed democracy ("Putting Down Democracies?"), and secondly by a discussion of imperial ideologies and practices of theater seating and benefaction ("Brave New World"). In the final section ("Knowing Your Place?"), I discuss a famous inscription from the Latin town of Lanuvium concerning the foundation or refoundation of a *collegium* (voluntary association) in honor of Diana and Antinous. Despite the unusualness of oversight of the *collegium* by the town's patron and the Roman senate, its bylaws articulate elegantly the potential of voluntary associations more generally to feed ambitions, status, honor, and a sense of belonging on a relatively small scale, both responding to and exacerbating

---

[2] Wilhelm 1914; Migeotte 2008; for arguments about the date (which would help to determine which military expedition is behind the demand for money), see succinctly Rizakis 2001, 93n100.

the scrabble for place and space within the profoundly unequal Roman imperial world.

## The Economic Role of the Roman Imperial State

Two very different but similarly influential works from the early years of the twentieth century and both written in America, the Kansas-born Tenney Frank's *Roman Imperialism* (1914) and the Russian-born Michael Ivanovich Rostovtzeff's *The Social and Economic History of the Roman Empire* (1926), offer valuable insight into the particular debates about the relationship between economics and empire in the Roman world that continued for much of the twentieth century. They also offer a provocative starting-point for considering the economic role of the Roman state within an imperial landscape from an early twenty-first century perspective. Frank and Rostovtzeff offer quite different responses to a question that would become particularly urgent as the notion of imperialism as economic exploitation, deliberately going after foreign markets, increasingly took shape through the works of the British economist J. A. Hobson (*Imperialism*, 1902) and Lenin (*Imperialism: The Highest State of Capitalism*, 1939; originally published in 1917). These questions include the extent to which Roman expansion was directly motivated by "mercantilist" or "capitalist" desires or, rather, followed such activities: in Ernst Badian's evocative language, whether "trade . . . preceded the flag."[3]

Tenney Frank's Roman Republic is a gentlemanly state that continues as such into the first century BCE, run by a careful and conservative senate indifferent to expansion as an end, but propelled to military action in order to defend itself from attack by foreign powers: Frank coined the term "defensive imperialism" that would remain a dominant means of characterizing the Republican empire until the late 1970s. According to Frank's thesis, the Republic's socioeconomic tone was long set by such a senate of landowners who had no real use for trade: Roman citizens embarked on trade late in comparison with their neighbors, and even then it was an occupation for those of foreign descent rather than the home grown. The unorthodox rise of Pompey, the first figure associated with deliberate imperial expansion, promoted by "capitalists" in the form of *equites*, who

---

[3] Badian 1968, 70. These debates were, of course, not entirely new to the twentieth century: see e.g., Mommsen 1854–1856, vol. 3 for Roman conquest and expansion as primarily reacting to external threats and pressures (e.g., 3, 10) and "mercantile" interests pursued in the destruction of Corinth in 146 and prospering on the defeat of Rome's major rivals in this activity, the Carthaginians (3, 1; 3, 12; 4, 1).

had been sponsored politically and economically by C. Gracchus' system-atization of public contracts in the newly acquired province of Asia in 123, and were now hell-bent on the business opportunities of Asia Minor, are shocks to a Republican system that will soon be killed off by the far more calculating imperialism of Caesar.

In comparison with Frank, Rostovtzeff traces enthusiastically the rise of "capitalist" ventures and the urban "bourgeoisie" (of Roman Italy, initially) who, along with the traditional Roman aristocracy, enthusiastically embrace them with increasing alacrity from the late Republican period onwards. If even Rostovtzeff characterizes Roman motivation for conquest and expansion in the Republic primarily in terms of preventing threats from outside, he is in no doubt at all about the economic opportunities taken by both the Roman elite and Italian traders and businessmen on the back of this reluctant expansion on the part of the Roman state. Rostovt-zeff's is a comprehensive (and imaginative) vision of the arc of Roman history and of the connection between politics and socioeconomics at its heart. Roman history is a continuous class struggle, and the particular sequence that runs from the late Republic to late antiquity concerns the conflict between this urban bourgeoisie, aligned with the aristocracy, and the peasants, dispossessed by the rise of capitalism but eventually turning against them as the military instrument of later Roman emperors. With hindsight, and with, especially, a little distance gained from the particular distorting effects of an unguarded superimposition of the Russian Revolu-tion onto Roman history, Rostovtzeff's account has the real merit of loosening the over-tight connections that were generally imagined between particular political events, agents, and economic opportunism in argu-ments about Roman imperial economic interests in the earlier twentieth century, as well as bringing industry and trade squarely into the discussion of the Roman economy.[4]

The terms of the earlier twentieth-century debate about "mercantile" and "capitalist" interests and their relationship to imperial expansion can seem both narrow and obviously anachronistic to early twenty-first century eyes. However, it is worth emphasizing the immensity of issues raised by this debate, and their ongoing relevance within contemporary scholarship. Behind the sorts of specific questions that were the preoccupation of scholars for decades, such as whether the *equites* could be characterized as a class in socioeconomic terms or in terms of mode of production, lie fundamental questions about the distribution of power, decision-making,

---

[4] Bowersock 1986; 2003; Shaw 1992.

and economic opportunity, not only in the empire of the Roman Republic, but throughout the history of the Roman world.[5]

Among the modern arguments that would most profoundly change the parts of the debate that related most closely to the connection between "mercantilism"/"capitalism" and Roman imperial expansion in the later twentieth century, the importance of William Harris' *War and Imperialism in Republican Rome, 327–70 BC* (1979) is obvious.[6] After Harris' systematic sociology of the Roman state and its constituent parts, fueled by the intense, aggressive expansion of the middle and later Republic, along with detailed analysis of how each war started and the disentanglement of notions of just warfare from reluctance to go to war, it becomes difficult to sustain the belief in "defensive imperialism" that underpinned Frank's and Rostovtzeff's very different accounts. Harris' impact in shifting the terms of the debate is clear also in his earlier article, "On War and Greed in the Second Century BC" (1971), in which he separated evidence for awareness of the likely economic consequences of conquest and imperialism on the part of agents of the Roman state, and for reaping the benefits of conquest and imperial rule, from the specificity of "mercantilist" motivation for imperial expansion.[7]

Moses Finley's *The Ancient Economy* (1973) was similarly a timely argument against thinking about the ancient economy in terms of "capitalist common-sense assumptions," as Peter Bang has incisively put it (2007, 7). Finley's argument about the complete lack of "economic principle ... economic analysis ... efficiency of production, 'rational' choice, marketing" in Xenophon's *Oeconomicus* (1973, 19) holds true for his more general portrayal of both the individual and the state in classical antiquity. At the same time, the absence of such principles and modes of operation from the state cannot be understood as providing for a "free market economy," which would precisely presuppose such principles and modes of operation. Finley, like Harris, never denies the appreciation of economic benefits on the part of the state and individuals: his quarrel is with assuming that the ancient state or individual actors were capable of exploiting or maximizing profits in the manner of early modern or modern capitalist thinking and action.

While Finley's argument about the modesty of growth in the economy of the Roman empire has sometimes been misrepresented in critiques of

---

[5] Important reappraisals of the socioeconomic positions of the *equites* include Badian 1972, esp. chapter 3; Brunt 1988b; Andreau 1999; Wesch-Klein 1999.
[6] See also the new Preface to the 1985 paperback edition.     [7] On Harris 1979, see North 1981.

the work, and "primitivism" has become something of a term of abuse, the fundamental substance of Finley's thesis has been substantially upheld in recent decades. Hydraulically powered industry seems at the moment to have made only modest advances before 200 CE, in what remained largely a world of cottage enterprises capable of joining the dots at boom times. The proliferation and growth of towns adorned with buildings and amenities is a noticeable feature of the "western" empire in particular, but the vast majority of the population of the Roman empire did not live in towns. The progressive enrichment of an imperial elite, along with a small but noticeable sub-elite is rendered striking to us by the textual, monumental, and art-historical materials that we have traditionally most favored, but Scheidel and Friesen's recent calculations would estimate that these groups would exclude approximately 90 percent of the population of the empire, with the elite making up only about 1.5 percent of the total. However, while recent accounts would emphasize along these lines that any "trickle down" effect was very limited, the boom times enjoyed by a small, lucky percentage are suggested by long-view measures, particularly the numbers of ship-wrecks (peaking between the second century BCE and the second century CE), and lead- and copper-levels in Greenland ice cores. Levels of lead, a by-product of silver-mining, especially important in coinage, peaked in the mid-first century BCE coinciding with intensive mining in Spain, and reaching levels unmatched before the thirteenth century CE. Levels of copper (also used in producing coins) peaked twice, slightly before 100 BCE and toward 200 CE, levels not matched until the eighteenth century CE.[8]

The Roman imperial state was not, it would seem, a significant beneficiary of economic growth, particularly over the long term: official levels of taxation were comparatively low. This is not, of course, to deny the immediate enriching effects of control of new peoples and new territories, both through the diversion of direct (land and poll) and indirect (customs, monopolies, etc.) taxes and other demands made, as well as booty. As it has often been noted, keen awareness of these possibilities is suggested by reflections from the early principate on whether the annexation of Britain and other "barbarian" territories is worthwhile in terms of balancing expenditure with income from tribute (Strabo 4, 5, 3; cf. Appian, Preface 5; 7). Similarly, spheres of state expenditure were limited beyond the army,

---

[8] Recent broad discussions of scale and growth include: Jongman 2002; Bang 2007; Saller 2002; Scheidel and Friesen 2009; hydraulic engineering: Wilson 2002; Bang 2007, 17n36; lead, copper and shipwrecks: Callataÿ 2005.

which accounted for a massive 50–75 percent of annual expenditure
(compared with annual defense and international security assistance
expenditure in the US, currently reckoned at approximately 16–20 percent
of the federal budget, and very considerably out of line with that of other
states, including China).[9]

But the actions of the Roman state do, it seems, play a significant, if
unintended role in the economic growth of certain sectors within the
empire. Keith Hopkins' model in "Rome, Taxes, Rents and Trade"
(2002), revisiting and considerably refining an argument first made in
1980, reasoned that tax demands on the part of the Roman state, together
with rents and less official demands had a generally stimulating effect on
provincial economies, encouraging the production of agricultural surpluses
and other economic activities in order to make these payments. The recent
reevaluations of wealth distribution in the Roman world would suggest
that Hopkins' model of general enrichment within the empire through this
economic stimulus is over-optimistic: we might therefore emphasize
instead his short evocation of the particular opportunities for the enrichment of individuals on the back of imperial rule and their enhancement of
an already regressive tax system (2002, 204–8).

It is worth spelling out some of the main avenues for enrichment that
are most closely tied to Roman imperial expansion and rule. In the
Republic, these include short bursts of enrichment on the part of Roman
generals and governors, able to exploit opportunities that were more or less
above board during their term of office. Such opportunities included
acquiring large tracts of land to farm and to rent, money-lending, receiving
gifts, and embezzlement. This was a phenomenon that survived the end of
the Republic and that arguably thrived despite and because of the structural changes of the principate. Another avenue for enrichment that went
hand in hand with imperial expansion was the well-explored phenomenon
of tax-farming contracts that involved bidding a fixed sum at auction. Even
if collecting the once-lucrative direct taxes of Asia was redirected to the
*poleis* in 48 BCE, privatized tax-farming remained the norm for the collection of indirect taxes throughout the Empire. The growth of empire also
brought the radical adjustment of hierarchies and networks of privilege and
power at a local level that facilitated enrichment, complex phenomena that

---

[9] The economic health of the Roman state: e.g., Tan 2015; 2017; Scheidel 2015; competing
estimates of expenditure on army: Duncan-Jones 1994, 45; Hopkins 2002, 208n40; US defense
spending: https://en.wikipedia.org/wiki/Military_budget_of_the_United_States; for debates over
the role of taxes in kind versus private enterprise in the grain-supply of Rome, see e.g., Erdkamp
2005, chapter 5; Bang 2007, 5–6n5 for bibliography.

we will explore in the next section of this chapter. It sponsored individuals dubbed by Peter Bang "portfolio capitalists," who supplied goods to those who had most immediately reaped the benefits of empire, and who were themselves enriched in the process.[10]

The unevenness of opportunities for acquiring wealth on the back of empire was intensified by the establishment of a dynastic monarchy that progressively accumulated wealth through the very fact of its power and primacy. When emperors were named beneficiaries of wills and default beneficiaries of the intestate, the result was the escalating privatization of considerable swathes of land in estates with a staff acting on and leveraging the authority of the emperor. Emperors were the recipients of increasingly regularized "gifts" that marked particular occasions, especially the *aurum coronarium* ("gold for a crown," effectively a tax on the communities of empire levied to mark special events in an emperor's reign, but one that maintained a fiction of voluntariness on the part of emperor and community alike). This accumulation of wealth underwrites the discretionary spending that plays a key role in the ideology of Roman monarchy: the emperor can afford to be generous in funding local infrastructure projects, but does so always as a major favor, not as an expected or regular obligation. The emperor and his family served as particularly prominent and powerful models of euergetism for Italian and provincial elites, who were able increasingly to leverage their power and privilege to reap considerable financial benefits, not least through tax-collecting liturgies and rent-collecting opportunities. Such individuals are the virtual descendants of Aristocles of Messene, able to play their relationship with Rome in such a way as to enhance their standing in their local community and even to suggest themselves as quasi-imperial benefactors at home. The stabilization of a standing army was also connected with the beginnings of monarchy, and private contractors played an important role in supplying this standing army (supplying the army remained substantially a matter of private enterprise into late antiquity). Meanwhile, officers and soldiers used their authority as imperial representatives to requisition billets, transport, and other supplies from local populations, a system wide open to abuse.[11]

The Roman imperial state was, then an epicenter of opportunism rather than the maker of policy or instigator of mechanisms that were directly

---

[10] Enrichment of Roman officeholders and elite: Kiser and Kane 2007; Tan 2015; 2017; Brunt 1990a; "portfolio capitalists": Bang 2007; cf. Subrahmanyam and Bayly 1988 for early modern India.

[11] Emperors and privatization: cf. Millar 1963; Brunt 1966; Burgers 1993; Lo Cascio 2000; *aurum coronarium*: Ando 2000, 175–90; requisitioning: Mitchell 1976; Roth 1999, chapter 3.

responsible for systematic economic exploitation. This has a profound effect on patterns of wealth distribution within the Roman empire. Occasionally, the economic benefits of empire were made available long-term to a large group without further discrimination: the indefinite suspension of direct taxation (*tributum*) of Roman citizens in Italy in 167 BCE would be the most obvious example. In general, however, the distribution of opportunity does not fall at all neatly along the lines of Romans/subjects: privilege and proximity to the central power of the Roman state matter a great deal in determining the pattern of those who were able to siphon off significant shares of wealth and those who lost out.

To conclude this discussion of the economic role of the state, we will briefly consider three institutions of the Roman state at the interface with its members and subjects: taxation, the census, and coinage. In the case of each of these institutions, we will look particularly at patterns of behavior and more discursive reflections to explore consciousness, manipulation and, more neutrally, uses of the Roman state's distinctive but generally indirect economic role, and, finally, we will illuminate uneven patterns of opportunity accompanying empire.

Rome's expansion of power overseas both capitalized on and suffered from long memories of empire as an evil that endangered the freedom and autonomy that our mainstream classical narratives idealize as the property of the *polis*. The "evil empire" compromises this freedom and autonomy particularly by military force and fiscal oppression: horror stories proliferate of physical atrocity and limitless imperial greed, coupled with the gratuitous glitter of the tyrants or tyrant-like figures who embodied the "evil empire."[12]

Such memories rendered the particularity of Rome's imperial systems highly visible, especially in sensitized contexts. We can see the Romans' powerful manipulation of the heavy ideological baggage of taxation in the early years of their interference in the affairs of the Greek-speaking world, and specifically in their play-off with the kingdom of Macedon: Flamininus' declaration of the freedom of the Greeks, in the extraordinarily calculated context of the Isthmian games of 196 BCE, and L. Aemilius Paullus' halving of the tax formerly due to the Macedonian kingdom in his settlement of 167 BCE are the most obvious examples. But the highly deliberate use of both taxation and other financial demands and remissions is more generally one of the major ways in which the Roman state

---

[12] Greed and glitter: Harris 1971; Kurke 1992; 1999, 131–7; cf. Lavan 2013 for a reappraisal of the ideology of slavery within a Roman imperial context.

articulates its system of privilege on a scale that goes way beyond the brokerage of its Hellenistic predecessors in the eastern Mediterranean. Among Rome's more powerful statements, one might include the "payment plan" demanded of Carthage after the Second Punic War, to be paid in installments for fifty years. Rome's refusal in 191 to accept the balance as a lump sum enforced repetition of this act of subjection. One would also surely include the diversion, after the destruction of the Temple of Jerusalem, of the Temple tax previously paid by Jews to a fund for the new temple of Capitoline Jupiter, at whose altar Roman triumphs were celebrated, and the extension of liability to include women and children. A less obvious but still very significant statement is the rarity and preciousness of grants of "free and immune" status to communities, the only way of designating freedom from Roman taxation to provincial communities. Occasional, highly advertised remissions of tax or forgiveness of debts, such as Hadrian's alleged remission of a spectacular 900 million sesterces of tax (Dio 69, 8, 1) also stand out. While it is important not to minimize the material consequences of such extraordinary demands and remissions, it is equally important to acknowledge their significance for the standing and honor of a community. From the perspective of the Roman state, they also suggest that it was not only, or even primarily, about the money, a conclusion suggested also by the limited scope of public spending and the absence of reserves.[13]

On the other hand, the considerable "freelance" opportunities open to officers and representatives of the Roman state and *publicani* (private holders of state contracts for tax collection and other state enterprises) and their staff result in frequent complaints and even more frequent murmurings and render issues of answerability very murky. This murkiness is compounded by a general inability to recognize what to our eyes seems an obvious structural flaw, and to engage with the problem instead almost entirely at the level of individual "bad eggs," preferably low status ones at that. Roman monarchy arguably both enhanced the problem (with its intensive privatization of land and the public prominence of a large, private staff) and extensively capitalized on it. Above all, the emperor becomes the prime corrector of abuses, and the spokesperson for the system's fairness, as we can see in many well-known examples, including

---

[13] Carthaginian installment plan: Gruen 1984, 291–3; Jewish tax: Schürer, 1973–1987, vol. 1, 528; de Lange 1978; Goodman 1989; extraordinary remissions and forgiveness of debts: Duncan-Jones 1994, 60; Scheidel 2015, 248–9; standing and honor: e.g., App. *Mithr.* 9, 62 with Chapter 5, "Past, Present, and Future."

the most recent, Neronian stratum of the *Monumentum Ephesenum*, a palimpsest of customs tax legislation from the earliest years of the province of Asia, or Tiberius' special concern reported in the *Senatusconsultum de Cn. Pisone patre* to end the abuses of Piso's former neighbors by Piso himself, his freedmen, and slaves, avoiding just complaints of allies of the Roman people (Potter and Damon 1999, 84–90). One unexpected consequence of this articulation of the emperor's role is that his rhetoric can be voiced back to him when taxpayers, implicated in this web of exchange, occasionally try to exercise their bargaining power. We will consider in Chapter 4 the famous case of the Thracian villagers of Skaptopara who petitioned Gordian III in 238 CE.[14]

Among the more noticeable and notorious of Rome's imperial systems was the census, in its original form the periodic "reckoning" of Roman citizens that included moral judgment along with (mainly) agricultural worth, fitness for the stations that determined one's place within Roman society, and concluded with a religious ceremony of cleansing and renewal. The census was extended to the newly enfranchised Roman citizens of the Italian peninsula in the first century BCE, a period characterized by coming to terms institutionally and ideologically with a citizen body inflated massively beyond the experience of classical antiquity. During the principate of Augustus, the census in a considerably adapted form was instituted province by province, a significant intervention on the part of the Roman state. One of its less immediate legacies is the adoption of local approximations of the "double document" as *the* format that came to signal officialdom through much of the Roman world. The form of the "double document" had its origins in the wooden tablets used by census officials to record details in one of the most widespread direct encounters between individuals and the Roman state, an excellent example of both impact and appropriation.[15]

The census' intrusiveness and general impact are signaled casually in the emperor Claudius' remark in the Lyon tablet of 48 CE, in the context of extending privileges to the "Long-Haired Gauls," that the Gauls remained peaceful when his father Drusus introduced the census, despite the fact that Drusus was called away to war with the Germans (*ILS* 212, II, 36–41). It is signaled dramatically in the story of Jesus' birth in a

---

[14] Individual bad eggs: Steel 2001 (but as a peculiarity of Cicero); cf. van Nijf 2008 for shifting the blame for tax-collecting abuses onto lowlier agents; Neronian stratum of the *Monumentum Ephesenum*: Rathbone 2008.

[15] Roman census and its extensions: Neesen 1980, 39 ff.; Nicolet 1991, 133–8; 2000; double document: Meyer 2004.

well-known passage from the Gospel of Luke, "And it came to pass in those days, that there went out a decree from Caesar Augustus, that all the world should be taxed" (2:1, King James Version; the Greek term translated as "taxed" is *apographē*, registration for the census), requiring Joseph to travel to Bethlehem, his "own city," together with Mary, his heavily pregnant wife. The passage raises notorious questions about the date of Jesus' birth, but also about the notion of a decree of Augustus ordering a universal, coordinated census. Other evidence strongly suggests that individual provincial census were held in different years, and according to different rhythms, often conducted close to the time of provincial settlement, and linked with the institution of taxation. It seems simplest to  conclude that the author of the Gospel has compressed different provincial censuses into a global and universal decree of Augustus, making a highly effective, rhetorical statement about the might of the Roman emperor, and his power to interfere with ordinary lives, an ironic, earthly portent of the spiritual power of Jesus.[16]

The Roman imperial state, unlike the Athenian empire, never insisted on the use of its coinage within its sphere of rule, by legal or other means. A broad outline history of the emergence of Roman state coinage(s) begins with the appropriation of a plurality of different local coin-types and standards, in the last decades of the fourth century BCE. It was not until the 270s BCE at the earliest that the Roman state developed a monetary system of its own, introducing the silver denarius as the nominal whole of which smaller bronze coins made up parts only in the later 200s, an impulse probably stimulated above all by the escalation of overseas conquest and the increasing need to regularize outgoing and incoming expenses (above all, the payment of soldiers and collection of tribute). The sharp uptick in circulation of coinage between the mid-second and early first century BCE contributed to the pollution levels in the Greenland ice core that we observed earlier. In broad terms, we can see a pattern whereby locally produced coinage of the western provinces (Britain, Spain, Gaul, and Africa) first tends to converge toward the weight standards, shapes, colors, and even designs of Roman state coinage, before beginning to use only Roman state coinage from around the mid-first century CE. Meanwhile, examples of locally struck coinage of Greek cities, together with Roman colonies of the (predominantly) Greek-speaking world, range from exclusively "local" iconographies on both obverse and reverse of a coin through combinations of "local" and "imperial" iconographies (with

[16] Gospel of Luke: succinctly Schürer 1973–1987, vol. 1, 399–427.

the emperor's image typically as the "head" and an image of a local myth, building, or topographical feature as the "tail") to "imperial" imagery that represents Roman sovereignty exclusively.[17]

The geographically variable processes by which Roman coinage became the "top" coinage are clearly complex. They reflect growing consensus about the efficacy of the Roman state and its status as a "gold standard" power, but that consensus does not necessarily imply loyalty or the negation or subordination of alternative *loci* of power: this is most obvious when rebel powers seeking to identify themselves as a rival or replacement state target the iconography of Roman coinage, as we saw in "Reproducing Roman Power" in Chapter 1. The famous trick question allegedly posed to Jesus in Jerusalem on the lawfulness of paying the *kēnsos* (the poll-tax, payable according to the *census*) in the early first century CE illustrates both the impact of the Roman state on local consciousness and the ability to question its dominance and relationship with other *loci* of power. Jesus is made to refer to an actual *dēnarion* with its distinctive portrait and inscription, asking his audience, "Whose is this likeness and inscription?" When they reply, "Caesar's," his response is, "Render to Caesar the things that are Caesar's, and to God the things that are God's" (Mark 12:13–17; cf. Matthew 22:15–22; Luke 20:19–26). The regular delineation of tax-amounts in Roman monetary units undoubtedly encouraged the association of Roman coinage with Roman power and officialdom. It is not a coincidence that this episode uses two loan-words from Latin to denote tax due to Rome and the monetary unit closely associated with paying tax (*kēnsos* and *dēnarion*). Code-switching to Latin suggests the particular register of institutions of imperial power, comparable with Roman state dating formulas.[18]

The geographical variation in the use of locally versus centrally minted coinage, along with the greater diversity in the iconography of coins of Greek cities, including the possibility of "local" iconography, have often been interpreted as an indication of the distribution of cultural capital (the prestige of ancient civilization could generally be claimed more effectively by the communities of mainland Greece and the Near East, rather than by e.g., Gauls or Spaniards), or of political integration, split along "eastern" (or "Greek-speaking") versus "western" (or "Latin-speaking") lines. But

---

[17] The theoretical possibility of demanding that cities use "our" coins, weights, and measures is raised by "Maecenas" in Dio 52, 30, 9; history and circulation patterns of Roman state coinage and coinage that targets imperial imagery: Crawford 1969; 1985; Burnett 2005; 2011; Howgego 2005; von Reden 2010, 47–63; 86–91.

[18] Latin loan-words: Adams 2003, 390–3.

there are subtler ways of reading patterns of "retention" and "adoption" of coinage systems, while Carlos Noreña has made the persuasive argument that the power and standing of the elites of Latin-speaking communities were by no means effaced by or subsumed within the power of the emperor in the adoption of Roman state coinage from the mid-first century BCE, but rather played off it. He points to their replication in inscriptions of the particular vocabulary of imperial morals and virtues that was constantly reproduced and illustrated on Roman state coinage from the Flavian period, and suggests that this effectively superimposes their identities on those of the emperor, just as characteristic juxtapositions of gods, emperors, and local elites in public spaces encouraged viewers to make upwards connections. It is hard to deny a pattern of cultural capital that tends to cluster more in the old world of the eastern Mediterranean and Near East, while the adoption of Roman state coinage in the Latin-speaking west means that there is no opportunity to advertise on coins the *loci* of alternative power systems that we sometimes see in the Greek *poleis*. Nevertheless, the use of coinage to assert local power that regularly harnesses the might and efficacy of the Roman imperial state is not wholly dissimilar.[19]

## Putting Down Democracies?

We have begun to consider the nature and limitations of Roman state intervention in the economic lives of imperial inhabitants, and have emphasized the economic opportunism of privileged individuals and groups, as well as the broader impact of state systems and their sometimes unexpected afterlives. In this section, we zoom in on the starkest ancient testimony on the Roman imperial will to bring about political, social, and economic change. This is Pausanias' second-century CE account of the Roman commander L. Mummius' actions in Achaea in 146 BCE after the storming and destruction of Corinth. Hitting out at the autonomy of communities that had fought against Rome, Mummius is said to have immediately destroyed city walls and disarmed inhabitants, and then, together with his co-commissioners, to have "put down democracies and established magistracies from property-ratings (*timēmata*)," imposed tribute, forbidden property holdings in another community, and put down ethnic leagues (Paus. 7, 16, 9).

---

[19] Noreña 2011, chs. 5–6; cf. Burnett 2005; cf. more generally Johnston 2017.

Pausanias' account clearly distills voices hostile to Rome. The notion of the Romans being anti-democracy or engaged in a kind of reverse class warfare against Greeks[20] is an interesting variation on the construction of "Greek" and "Roman" ideal types that is an important aspect of imperial discourse between the later Republic and early empire. As such, it at the very least exaggerates differences to make full-scale polarities, as we can begin to see if we look at internal changes within both the *poleis* and the Roman Republic in the third and second centuries BCE. Democracy was a prevalent political and social ideal in the Hellenistic world, but it could take different forms in the decidedly plural environment of "Greek" *poleis*, and rarely bore much close resemblance to the "radical" democracy of later fifth-century and again fourth-century BCE Athens that was one iconic model. Some changes in the sociopolitical landscape of Hellenistic *poleis* were slow-moving, such as the multiplying statues of individuals in the public space of the agora, an increasingly tight connection between bene-faction and office, the growing visibility of women and families, and religious and even civic honors for women. Others were correlated more closely with single events, such as nervous suspicion of radicalism, espe-cially the cancellation of debts and redistribution of land, much intensified after the shock of the Spartan revolutions of Agis IV and Cleomenes III in the mid- to later third century BCE, giving rise to renewed interest in the character and place of democracy in the post-classical age, not least in Stoic explorations of justice, equality, and private property. These developments began independently of the "coming of Rome," but later in this section we will explore the ways in which the Roman imperial presence might have accelerated such processes.[21]

On the other hand, the intense exploration of the theory and practice of democracy in later second-century Rome, through engagement with Hel-lenistic political philosophy, especially Stoicism, *is* directly related to Roman imperial expansion. Polybius' identification of "democratic" elem-ents within the Roman state suggests the dynamism of political theory in the rapidly changing world of the later second century BCE. He admits that the senate (his "aristocratic" element) controls the purse-strings and that the consuls (his "monarchic" element, despite the fact that there were two of them) have absolute power when it comes to preparing for war

---

[20] For some complication of this view, see Briscoe 1967.

[21] Recent assessments of such changes within the Hellenistic *poleis* include van Bremen 1993; 1996; Cartledge and Spawforth 2002, 48–52; Hoepfner 2006; Erskine 2011; Dickenson and van Nijf 2013; Ma 2013, chapter 6.

and when in the field itself. However, he finds the sovereignty of the
Roman *dēmos* in the functions of the major voting assemblies of Rome: in
electing candidates to office, in punishing crimes, including those committed while in highest office, in passing laws, in deciding war and peace,
in ratifying alliances and treaties (6, 14). In his continuing discussion of
the "plēthos" ("the crowd"), he asserts that "almost everyone" is engaged in
public contracts in Rome (6, 17). In very obvious ways, Polybius elides
distinctions and omits details that would undermine the analysis. He does
not distinguish between the roles of the different citizen-assemblies or,
crucially, their different arrangements, such as the importance of census-
rating for the weight and order of votes in the centuriate assembly. He
omits the facts of group-voting in the assemblies, and their lack of
deliberative function (Roman *contiones* were rallies convened and orchestrated by magistrates, not substantive discussions). When he talks about
public contracts, he must be thinking primarily of *equites*, non-office
holding members of the highest census class in his day, and thus a highly
exclusive body that could hardly be further from "almost everyone."[22]

It is possible to make the case for some Roman engagement in the
international theory and practice of "popular sovereignty" (a hotly contested term in intellectual history) as early as the middle Republic, but even
case-studies of the more "radical" measures of the later Republic suggest
how much was lost and found in translation. If the dramatic date of
Polybius' analysis of the Roman state was 216 BCE (the immediate
aftermath of the Carthaginians' defeat of Rome at the Battle of Cannae),
he was in fact writing his history shortly before Tiberius and Gaius
Sempronius Gracchus were tribunes of the people (in 133 and 123–122
BCE respectively), brothers generally remembered in antiquity as dangerous radicals. Ancient accounts of the Gracchi hint at the intersection
between theory and practice. Plutarch significantly twins their biographies
with those of the mid- to later third-century Spartan revolutionaries Agis
and Cleomenes, whose activities had stimulated debates in Stoic philosophy around equality, justice, and private property. Blossius of Cumae,
prominent in Stoic circles of the Hellenistic Mediterranean, was remembered as an associate of Tiberius and, depending on the perspective of the
author, either encouraged him to be a champion of the people or propelled
him toward reckless criminality. Among his overtly "popularist" measures,
Tiberius' bill to redistribute to the Roman people illegally occupied public
land in 133 BCE, along with his intention of taking literally the terms of

---

[22] Champion 2007; Thornton 2013; see now Cartledge 2016, chapter 15.

Attalus III of Pergamum's bequest of his kingdom to the Roman people by distributing it to citizens in lots, suggest appeal to notions of social justice, equality, and common property. His brother Gaius proposed a new extortion law to replace existing procedures according to which senatorial governors were tried by their senatorial peers. The elaborate procedures of the new law suggest an appeal to ideological principles including transparency, with the people's role idealized as (to quote A. N. Sherwin-White) "a watch-dog," the "passive force of public opinion." They carefully distinguish *equites* eligible for extortion juries from holders of senatorial office, barring fathers, brothers, or sons of senators from these juries, doubling penalties for those convicted. and giving provincial prosecutors incentive by rewarding successful ones.[23]

In each case, we can see particular modifications according to later Hellenistic interpretations of social justice and democracy, and specifically Roman translations. Tiberius' bill was a revival of an earlier law and allowed occupation of public (!) land up to a shockingly large 500 *iugera* (with additional amounts for the possessor's children), while Gaius' rigorously selected equestrian juries were wholly indistinguishable from senators at this period in terms of wealth or social class. The composition of juries would be a major point of controversy in the late Republic, but Gaius Gracchus' early attempt to define the *equites* as a class would contribute to the progressive definition and hardening of *ordines* idealized as more or less hereditary social groups (although efforts to uphold this idealization betray the fact of considerable mobility in practice). If the Gracchi were remembered as radicals in the late Republic and early Empire, their applications are astonishingly undemocratic by the standards of fifth-century Athens and positively conservative by the standards of earlier Hellenistic Stoicism associated with Zeno and others.[24]

The fact that both the theory and practice of democracy were moving targets in a Hellenistic world of which Rome was a part adds to the difficulty of interpreting notices of direct interference by Roman officials in the political environments of its subjects. There are occasional such notices in addition to Pausanias' claim about Mummius' actions in Achaea

[23] For "popular sovereignty" in the middle and later Republic, the strongest case is put by Millar 1986; 1989. Millar's arguments have been strongly contested: see e.g., North 1990; Cartledge 2016, chapter 15. For recent scrutiny of the term "popular sovereignty" in pre-modern contexts, see Bourke and Skinner 2016.
[24] Democratic ideals of the Gracchi: Sherwin-White 1982, esp. 21; Nicolet 1983; Crawford 1996, 1; Erskine 2011, chapter 7; public land: see now Roselaar 2010, chapter 5.

in 146. The most significant examples concern a Roman magistrate arranging for the selection of councilors, selecting them directly himself, or making a point of handing this responsibility back to the community itself. In 167, in Livy's account of the settlement of Macedon, the Macedonians' selection of their own annual magistrates is one of the indications of freedom that L. Aemilius Paullus explicitly announces, along with their retention of land and cities and maintenance of their own laws (45, 29, 4). The selection of what Livy translates as "senators," juxtaposing the Latin term with the Greek "synhedri," takes place at a meeting of the Macedonians' council. Although no details are given about the process of selection, the expulsion of all the king's associates and officers at the same meeting gives a pragmatic sense of the actual constraints under which this was conducted (45, 32, 1–7). In an earlier episode of Livy, Flamininus is made to intervene directly in the affairs of Thessaly in 194, after the Battle of Cynoscephalae (197). During Flamininus' tour of the Macedonian kingdom that will leave behind settled conditions in the Greek mainland, he finds in Thessaly an unhealthy situation engendered by a combination of Macedonian monarchy and innate Thessalian tendencies. Specifically, they are unable to hold elections, assemblies, or councils without descending into riot. Flamininus' solution is to appoint "senate (*sic*) and *iudices* mostly on the basis of *census* (*sic*), and [make] more powerful the part of the community to whom it was more advantageous for everything to be secure and peaceful" (Livy 34, 51, 6).

Livy's gloss on Flamininus' actions seems very Augustan in its celebration of the wholesome effects of restoring society to its proper order, as we shall see in the next section of this chapter. There is, however, no good reason to distrust the fundamental point about Flamininus making direct appointments on the basis of what from a Roman perspective was *census* ("property assessment" in this context, one facet of a "reckoning"). Direct intervention of this kind is rare in the context of Roman rule. The principle of local communities and particularly their leaders acting with the blessing of Rome is the more usual response, anticipating the insidious development of imperial institutions and practices (e.g., tax collection, embassies, "imperial cult," Roman citizenship) that draw the local elites closer to the Roman center and allow them to capitalize on that proximity. Livy's delineation of the remedial nature of Thessalian society and character suggests unusual circumstances, which would also account for the intervention of Mummius in Achaean affairs in 146, an episode similar to that of Flamininus' action in Thessaly insofar as it involved property qualifications as a criterion of appointment to office. If Thessaly is an instance of crisis management, the treatment of Achaea is also a punitive act.[25]

The parallel Latin-Greek vocabulary pairings in these accounts – senators and *synhedri*, *census* and *timēmata* – hint at the complex processes of conceptual translation at the imperial interface. These processes took place in a highly pressurized environment, whether or not via direct intervention on the part of Roman officeholders. However, as we have already seen, these particular conceptual encounters were superimposed on longer and deeper processes of political and social change within the Hellenistic *poleis*. For example, if a *polis*' entitlement to elect its own officers can be singled out as part of a "freedom" that is granted rather than assumed, in the curious new universe of super powers, it is salutary to remember that deciding appointments by lot was a hallmark of the classical democratic polis as delineated by Aristotle: election was the mark of an oligarchy (*Pol.* 4, 9, 1294b8). Anna Heller's careful study of changes in the selection and expectations of councilors and officeholders in Greek *poleis* between the second century BCE and the second century CE suggests the subtlety of engagement with a model of Roman *ordines* as more or less permanent social groups, with the senate as the top *ordo*, its membership restricted to the highest census class, generally to ex-officeholders, and for life. For one thing, a shift in terminology from *boulē* to *synedrion* to refer to the council, and *perhaps* implying a conceptual shift, had already taken place in some Hellenistic *poleis* before the "coming of Rome." More profoundly, there are numerous indications of a considerable variety of practice between *poleis* even in the "high" Empire, as suggested by Pliny the Younger's letter to Trajan proposing to simplify a multitude of practices in his province, Bithynia-Pontus, including no entry fee for councilors and different fee amounts from city to city, by setting a single amount for every city (Trajan refuses) (*Ep.* 10, 112–13). More generally, any movement toward more strictly hierarchical social and political practices is tangled up with different ideologies of power, such as the sense of a contract between officeholders and people that renders office to some extent conditional.[26]

Somewhat ironically, given Pausanias' gloss on Mummius' actions as "putting down democracies," Roman political intervention in the affairs of Greek cities of the second century BCE seems to have been framed as

---

[25] Livy's gloss: Derow 1972; for the interesting and not unrelated trajectory of Roman constitutions of new and refounded cities, see Chapter 2.
[26] cf. Ferrary 1987–1989; Kallet-Marx 1995, 65–76; Heller 2009.

averting "tyranny." The question of where Roman interests end and genuine fears begin is unanswerable. Livy's account of Flamininus' intervention in Thessaly follows his earlier reversal of the infringements on freedom by Philip V's sponsorship of the cronies of his "faction" (a very strong word in Latin), a slippery condemnation of the Spartan "tyrant" Nabis combined with an apology for not actually removing him, and a sermon to the assembled Greeks at Corinth on the need for them to use with moderation the freedom granted by Rome (34, 48–50). Given the pervasiveness of the rhetoric of Roman liberation, it is important to acknowledge the tightening of the net in the course of the second century, with the Roman presence shifting the endemic, comparatively minor instability of *stasis* to which *poleis* were prone toward a more profound change in the ecology of local politics. Roman "resolutions" of local situations involved not only judgments and occasional direct political interventions, but also witch-hunts that resulted in the murder or exile of opponents and suspected opponents of Rome and the potential creation (in the short-term) of something approximating a modern one-party state. Polybius' own story vividly evokes the ugly mixture of suspicion, pressure, ingratiation and denunciation at the interface between Rome and local communities.[27]

The link between anti-Roman activity and the sort of revolutionary behavior associated with tyranny became more overt in Roman imperial ideology. It is in the background of the letter written by the praetorian proconsul Q. Fabius Maximus Servilianus in 144/3 to the archons, *synedrion* and *polis* of Achaean Dyme which praised the actions of a local citizen, Cyllanius, a neat illustration of the reactive nature of Roman government even in the policing of anti-Roman activities. Cyllanius had uncovered and denounced the "disturbance" of one Sosus of Dyme, together with some *sunhedri*, which included the burning of public records (*perhaps* aiming at the cancellation of debts), and the establishment of laws contrary to the *politeia* given by the Romans in their settlement of Achaea in 146, which had probably included property-class-based magistracies and council membership, and contrary to the "freedom" of the Greeks established by the Romans (ll. 9–10). There is a fascinating fusion of expectations here: hints of long, conservative traditions of portraying demagoguery as dangerous revolution that might also be expected to

---

[27] Polyb. 24, 8, 9–9, 15 and 10, 3–6 with Derow 1989, 299–300.

appeal to Rome, and the unflinching representation of the Romans being on the right side of history, as anti-tyranny freedom-fighters.[28]

The identification of Romans as anti-democratic, and the portrayal of the "coming of Rome" in terms of class warfare, was demonstrably a route available to its enemies. This is both distilled in Pausanias' Mummius "putting down democracies" in 146 and overt in the speech that Livy puts into the mouth of the Spartan Nabis in 195 BCE, giving Flamininus a lesson in the fundamental differences between Roman and Spartan socio-political organization (and contributing in the process to the long myth-history of Sparta). You Romans, says "Nabis," distinguish cavalry and infantry on the basis of *census*, and "want the few to excel in wealth, and the plebs to be subjected to them," whereas Lycurgus arranged Spartan society on the basis of an *equality* of fortune and rank, without the sort of concentration of power in the hands of the few represented by the Roman senate (34, 31, 17). While this is of course essentially a piece of creative writing in the virtuoso Roman tradition of enemy ventriloquy, it nicely spells out the possibility of construing difference as politically "opposite," a strategy that could be just as attractive as uncovering versions of democracy everywhere one looked. The construction of political difference as both "opposite" and deeply unfavorable could be instrumentalized effectively in many different ways. In his defense in 59 BCE of L. Valerius Flaccus on a charge of extortion during his governorship of the very wealthy province of Asia, Cicero discredited Flaccus' accusers not least on the basis of the disorderly conduct of the popular assemblies in the province and their empowerment of the "dregs of the state" as opposed to the "propertied and serious men." How different this was from Cicero's idealized version of a Roman assembly, with the people arranged neatly "by centuries and tribes, by *ordines*, classes and age-groups" (*Pro Flacco* 15–19)!

In this characterization, Cicero unwittingly hints at the continued vibrancy of the assembly in Asia, an important index if one is trying to quantify the "survival" of democratic politics in the *poleis*. There is nothing particularly partisan about the Romans preferring to deal with the propertied, as "leading men" were inevitably propertied even in the most radical of democracies in the ancient world. Roman "settlements" after military defeat and interventions in crises resulted in the exile or even death of many propertied individuals and families. Long-term patterns are subtler

---

[28] *Syll.* (3) 684; *RDGE* 43, tr. Bagnall and Derow 2003, 52, with Kallet-Marx 1995; cf. Champion 2007; compare Polybius' story (24, 11) of how Callicrates of the Achaean League taught the Romans how to manipulate the *stasis* endemic within Greek *poleis* in 180 BCE.

than the "class warfare" model would suggest. While there are no known cases of the Romans supporting a self-defined popular movement in any *polis* of the Greek world, careful prosopographical studies of the "leading men" of a number of *poleis* suggest the power of Roman backing and support of "friends" in creating centuries-long dynasties. It is of course not the case that Roman backing and support conferred dynastic invulnerability. As the local stories embedded in Strabo's *Geography* illustrate so well, Roman civil wars were important factors in the rise and fall of family fortunes, an ironic effect of the entwinement of imperial and local politics.[29]

## Brave New World

The critiques of Roman social and political ideals that we encountered in the previous section focused on property-based discrimination in eligibility for political office and in the assignment of political agency more generally. A series of Augustan measures would reinforce socio-specific notions of the importance of placement and order as never before, a powerful response to the fears of societal breakdown in terms of which the political disorder of the last decades of the Republic was experienced. These included emphasis on the census and Augustus' own role as censor, that quintessentially Roman overseer of the integrated social, economic and religious order of society, and top rung on the *cursus honorum*. A senatorial order was further delineated as, ideally, a hereditary caste, signaled by the financial support of old noble families, and by encouraging senators' sons to wear the insignia of senatorial membership in anticipation of their future entry. The introduction for the first time of a separate, higher property qualification for senators formally separated the order from that of the *equites*. The very considerable wealth signified by a *census* of one million sesterces was a necessary rather than a sufficient qualification, and the *princeps'* financial support of impoverished noble families underlined the fact that wealth in and of itself was not the point: rather, wealth was normally assumed to go hand in hand with social standing and, in practice, followed power and status rather than the other way around.[30]

Well-advertised Augustan legislation on adultery, marriage, and manumission suggest broader and, to modern eyes, more sinister concern with

---

[29] Absence of Roman support for popular movements: Briscoe 1967; Derow 1989, 310–11; continuity of "leading men": e.g., Gehrke 1993; Quaß 1993, 385–9.
[30] Brunt 1983; Nicolet 1984; Lendon 1997, 30–5; Brown 2012, 3–8.

keeping everyone in their place and enforcing the family unit, forbidding
intermarriage between the senatorial order and freedpersons, parading
caution in grants of the citizenship, and setting conditions on freeing
slaves, "in order to keep the people pure and unsullied by any influx of
foreign or servile blood" (Suet. *Aug.* 40, 3). The dignity of the Roman
citizen body was as a whole enhanced by extraordinary attempts to
enforce the wearing of the toga in the public space of the Forum (Suet.
*Aug.* 40, 5).[31]

Augustus' exceptional efforts to enact by legislation the sort of social
order that was normally limited to the utopian tradition of classical
antiquity also probably included a theater law passed in his own name in
either 22 or 19 BCE. The privilege of front-row seats for Roman senators
and chief magistrates dates back to 194 BCE, while eligibility for privileged
theater seating under the Lex Roscia of 69 BCE was set at a census of
400,000 sesterces, thus including *equites*. As far as we can see, the
Augustan law tightened up theater-seating rules and extended them to
gladiatorial and other shows. It established separate seating areas for
soldiers, married men, freeborn boys with their minders, toga-clad Roman
citizens, women, and Vestal Virgins, as well as senators, subdivisions of
senators, and *equites*. The vision of order that counters fears of societal
breakdown is manifested in these divisions that seek to enforce concerns
about sexual morality and muddling of distinct categories, some of which
are ancient (e.g., gender and age distinctions), some of which are recent
(e.g., *equites* as an *ordo* distinct from senators), and some of which are very
recent inventions of tradition, such as promoting the toga as "national
dress" for citizens, and separating soldiers from civilians. The distinctions
drawn by theater-seating legislation were static, freezing at the time of
performance the place that an individual held at that moment, a significant
artifice that clashed with well-advertised potential for mobility in Roman
society (especially crossing the line from slavery to freed status). Perhaps
precisely because it was so artificial, it struck a chord. The impulse to
differentiate expanded and became more intricate in the course of the first
century CE: particular divisions of *apparitores*, magistrates' attendants, were
given their rightful place, and privileged seating an honor detachable from
the office that had traditionally conferred it (a detachability that ultimately
followed the precedent of the *princeps'* tenure of tribunician or consular
power without the office itself).[32]

---

[31] E.g., Culham 1997; Severy 2003; Milnor 2005, 140–85; Mouritsen 2011.
[32] Rawson 1987; Galinsky 1996, 128–40.

Theater-seating designated in this intricate way was experienced as a quintessentially Roman practice. Tacitus tells an anecdote, typical of his interest in giving barbarian's-eye views of distinct features of Roman society, of Frisian ambassadors at the theater of Rome, unable to follow the show, but fascinated by the spectacle of the audience in their serried ranks (*Ann.* 13, 54). Intriguingly, this model of differential seating in the Roman theater seems to have played an important role in Roman reinter-pretations of Stoic philosophy. As we have seen, the radical emphasis on the redistribution of wealth that had characterized the teachings of Zeno between the late fourth and early third centuries BCE was already open to fundamental reinterpretation in the Hellenistic Stoa of the late third century. But in a Roman sociopolitical context, differential seating empha-sized not so much hierarchies and gulfs between groups, but the honor and dignity of a society in perfect balance, a comprehensive moral, social, and cultural package. One example is Pliny the Younger's famous reformu-lation of equality in a letter that purports to advise Calestrius Tiro on governing as proconsul of Baetica, but that reads more like a modern opinion piece, exhorting him to observe "discrimina ordinum dignitatum-que" ("distinctions of rank and honor"), since "nothing is more unequal than equality" (*Ep.* 9, 5, 1; 3).[33]

Theater-seating was, significantly, a concern of Roman and Latin town charters, where it was clearly important to articulate as exactly as possible their relationship with the Roman metropolis. The charter of the Caesar-ian colony of Urso in Spain contains detailed legislation on seating at shows, including special seats for decurions, local magistrates, and Roman magistrates, the separation of colonists from other groups at stage shows, and orchestra-seats reserved for Roman magistrates, senators or their sons at such shows, with stiff fines for contravening these rules. Differentiated theater- seating was very important for a self-consciously Roman town by the end of the Republic (Crawford 1996, 25, 125–7). More than a century later, the Flavian charter of the newly Latin towns of southern Spain explicitly upholds preexisting seating honors at the games as well as past or future laws, decrees, or rulings of the Roman people, senate, and emperors. In so doing, it finely calibrates what it is to be a Latin as distinct from a Roman town by prescribing a degree of autonomy for the

---

[33] Seating arrangements and Roman Stoicism: Erskine 2011, 105–10; individual patron-client relationships, both between ex-slave owners and freedmen and women, and between free persons of different socioeconomic status, were another important Roman institution that socialized a notion of appropriate and unequal place: Saller 1982; Wallace-Hadrill 1989a.

community (González and Crawford 1986, chapter 81). Outside towns of
Roman or Latin status, there is, as we would expect, little evidence of
Roman intervention. The main exception is response to a crisis, following
an incident at the Italian town of Puteoli (a town that of course had
Roman status by this time), when no-one gave up their seat for a late-
arriving senator. The response was heavy-handed: a universal *senatus
consultum* to command that space at the front of public shows anywhere
in the Empire should henceforth be reserved for senators (Suet. *Aug.* 44,1).
It is interesting, however, that when Polemon, the king of Pontus, was
enrolled among the friends and allies of the Roman people in 26 BCE, he
gave to senators the privilege of front seats in theaters throughout his
kingdom, voluntarily reproducing the first principle of the socio-specific
privilege-system associated with Roman rule (Cassius Dio 53, 25, 1).

In *poleis* of the Greek-speaking world, it can be hard, and is possibly
misguided, to seek to draw the line between local and specifically Roman
customs of theater seating. This problem is analogous to the more general
difficulty of drawing the line between independent local developments and
Roman influence in the political sphere. Localized criteria for privileged
seating may preexist the "coming of Rome" or be a "translation" of Roman
custom or a combination of both. Some developments are unquestionably
linked to the "coming of Rome," not least special seats for priests of the
imperial cult, one of the many features of Roman imperial culture that had
no preexisting, city of Rome models. More loosely, we observe the escalation of certain features after the "coming of Rome" that suggest broad
engagement with common, empire-wide ideas of designating privileged
status by differentiated theater seating, but we lack the means of tracing
direct influence. Thus, we see an increase in the number of seats reserved
for named individuals (including, but not restricted to, local magistrates
and priests). We also see a proliferation of group-based claims for privileged seating, notably dedicated seating for "voluntary associations" across
the empire, sometimes explicitly upheld by a grant of the authorities.
Examples include reserved seating for the copper-beaters, wineskin-makers
and jewelers at Bosra, the particularly good seats reserved for the Ascle-
pieum porters at Smyrna, and seating for the brotherhood of the *Dendro-
phoroi* at Vienne. The theater was one context in which the sub-elite
groups made particularly strenuous efforts to find privileged space in the
city. Elsewhere, we see them circumventing major elite spaces and contexts. Dedicated burial plots and complexes within the *necropoleis* that were
avoided by the elite in the high Empire are the most obvious example. As
Henrik Mouritsen has powerfully argued, the freedmen who are

overrepresented as creators and inhabitants of such plots and complexes were asserting ownership of the body that was denied to slaves as well as claiming space. Perhaps the most remarkable and innovative instance of claiming space is the case of the reserved latrines in Vedius' public gymnasium at Ephesus.[34]

The phenomenon of civic benefactors, honored by an appreciative public for their embellishment of the city, a generosity that was progressively linked to office in the form of election promises, or expectations or conditions of council membership, was not invented by Rome. On the contrary, the Republican city of Rome lagged behind others in Italy, not to mention the Greek *poleis*: private munificence was limited by a very different set of expectations about how buildings and monuments were funded, and was particularly focused on games. Once again, the charter of the Roman colony of Urso traces the specificity of *Roman* benefaction in all its peculiarity. Both the duumviri and aediles are instructed to put on games for the Capitoline triad, Venus and the other gods, and both the maximum amount of public funds and the minimum amount of their own funds that they are allowed to spend are specified (Crawford 1996, 25, 70–1), a detailed Roman sociopolitical lesson in the correct proportions of public and private.[35]

One of the most obvious signs of the major ideological shifts that encourage the development of dynastic monarchy at Rome is the dramatic increase in the scale of munificence: Julius Caesar's forum was a legendary feat of spending, allegedly reaching one hundred million sesterces (Suet. *Caes.* 26, 2–3; Pliny *N.H.* 36, 103). As we have seen, monarchy expanded vastly the pool of potential recipients for this discretionary spending as "liberality" became one of the most important virtues of the "good" emperor. This liberality was exercised in gifts of food or money that were neither means-tested nor regular. Grain tickets had to be deserved, or at least inherited from deserving family members, and regularity would detract from the spontaneity and surprise that were the point of the gift. Likewise, the short-lived alimentary schemes of the late first and early second century CE, in which the emperor actively encouraged the upper classes to follow his example, establishing a complicated system whereby

---

[34] Theatre-seating privileges: van Nijf 1997, 217–40 with Appendix 4; Sear 2006, 1–7; Ephesus latrines: Rogers 1991, 72.

[35] Rüpke 2006b, 40–1; for trajectories, ideologies, and practices of benefaction/euergetism in the Roman world, see Veyne 1992; Zuiderhoek 2009.

the interest paid on extra land acquired by the wealthy through mortgages paid for the keep of boys and girls in Italy, were not aimed at relief of the poor.[36]

The emperor and his family directly modeled benefaction by giving gifts to local communities as well as to the city of Rome. One early example of this is the magnificent city walls, barbarian-festooned gates, and towers of Saepinum in remote, Samnite Italy, which advertise the generosity of Tiberius in his own name and that of his dead brother Drusus, who built them "at their own expense" in 4 CE (*CIL* 9, 2443), probably to mark the settlement in the town of veterans of their own northern campaigns. Just as significantly, local elites superimposed their benefactions on those of the emperor and his family, one aspect of the striking location of power and status by association that we see frequently in the juxtaposition of statues of gods with statues of emperors and statues of local elites in the public spaces of imperial cities. The monumental version of Augustus' *Res Gestae* at Ancyra illustrates this phenomenon beautifully, in its juxtaposition of this archetype of benefaction reciprocated with honors with inscriptions that celebrate the benefactions of local priests of the imperial cult. Some of these gifts are self-consciously imperial, inspired by specific Augustan donations, and others suggest self-identification with Greek or Galatian traditions. The monarchy's monopolization of the city of Rome as a site of benefactions further encouraged the munificence and self-advertisement of the Roman citizen elite elsewhere: the juxtapositions were more distant and more virtual. The habit was boosted by the proliferation in the early imperial period of "Augustales," often freedmen able to use this public role to give lavishly and endorse themselves as if they were civic magistrates, a role denied to them by law.[37]

These superimpositions of local elites on imperial models suggest the sorts of questions raised about impostors in the discursive contexts of literary texts: does sitting on the king's throne or dressing up in the king's clothes make you "really" the king? The answer is always, "No," but you have to see the experiment through to arrive at that negative answer: there is a perceptible gap between the king and the impostor, but it may not be immediately obvious. In the case of superimpositions of local elites on imperial models, the proximity needs to be enough to draw on this

---

[36] Liberality: Noreña 2011, 82–92; grain: Erdkamp 2005; alimentary scheme: Duncan-Jones 1964; Garnsey 1968; Woolf 1990; Patterson 2006, 50–3.

[37] Saepinum: Matteini Chiari 1982, 51–68; Patterson 2006, 99; gods, emperors, local elites: Noreña 2011, 273 with n. 101; Ancyra: Cooley 2009, 7–13; self-advertisement outside Rome: Purcell 1983; Eck 1984; "Augustales": Ostrow 1990; Mouritsen 2005; Bruun 2014; Laird 2015.

particular association, but the distinction is important too: this is neither a case of self-effacing loyalty to the Roman center nor of "becoming Roman." The standing of local elites regularly draws simultaneously on other *loci* of power in individualized combinations, from the prestigious antiquity of the gods of Ephesus, drawn into a direct relationship with the newer powers of the Roman Empire in a sacred procession founded by C. Vibius Salutaris in 104 CE, to the early Tiberian arch of Gallic Saintes, given by C. Iulius Rufus of the Santones. The latter case is particularly interesting. While, as is not unusual in the northern provinces, the arch seems straightforwardly "Roman" in style rather than drawing on any identifiable local traditions, it invites parallels between the dynasty of C. Iulius Rufus and that of Tiberius. The arch is topped with a statue of Tiberius, flanked by Germanicus and Drusus, and an inscription makes clear their dynastic relationship and traces their genealogy to Julius Caesar. This dynastic emphasis echoes the official ideology of the early Tiberian age, but what is particularly of interest here is C. Iulius Rufus' emphasis on his own distinctive genealogy, the parallel strengthened by his important office of the imperial cult at Lugdunum. C. Iulius Rufus' genealogy is traced back to his great-grandfather, who bears the unmistakably "Gallic," and presumably locally famous, name of Epotsorovidius.[38]

## Knowing Your Place?

I conclude this chapter by considering briefly a famous inscription from Lanuvium, an ancient and esteemed Latin town in the Alban hills about twenty miles southeast of Rome. The inscription concerns a society (*collegium*) for the honoring of the goddess Diana and Antinous, the recently deceased lover of the emperor Hadrian, now a target of religious cult especially in Egypt and the eastern Mediterranean. The inscription, recently reedited and reinterpreted by Andreas Bendlin, commemorates a generous endowment by Lanuvium's patron and former *dictator*, Lucius Caesennius Rufus, promised on June 9, 136 CE, includes the *senatus consultum* authorizing the society and its activities on its foundation (or, perhaps, refoundation, harnessing Antinous to a preexisting society of Diana) in 133 CE, and sets out the society's *lex* (in this context "bylaws") explicitly as a contract for new members, detailing conditions of

---

[38] Impersonation: e.g., Herodotus 7, 12–19; Diodorus 34/5, 2, 16; 24 and 36, 7 for Eunus and Salvius, leaders of the Sicilian slave wars; Ephesus: Rogers 1991; Saintes: Woolf 2000, 126–30, with a more centralizing interpretation.

membership, conditions for the payment of expenses toward members' funerals, obligations and privileges of the society's officers, sequence of dinners, and prescribed conduct at these dinners.[39]

The inscription offers precious insights into the kinds of finely tuned and calibrated behaviors relating to wealth that have been the focus of this chapter, and into the complex processes of influence, change, and opportunism accompanying empire with which the book as a whole is concerned. Bendlin's rereading of the inscription has usefully refocused our attention so that we consider not only what is in it for the society's members, but what is in it for their patron, the senate and even the civic community of Lanuvium. The patron, senate, and the civic community of Lanuvium take the opportunity to endorse and celebrate a cult of Antinous that had been slow to gain ground in Italy and the western provinces, but that might reasonably have been expected to win imperial favor, a cult securely anchored to the antiquity and particular Latinity (in certain of her guises) of Diana. In doing so, they secure considerable benefits, not all of which feed-back directly into the imperial center: the patron and his family members hailed and commemorated in the established reciprocity of benefaction, their birthdays, along with those of Diana and Antinous, the only occasions feted by this particular calendar (taking the place of the imperial family who dominated the festival calendar of the Roman state) (col. 2, 11–13); the senate seen to perform its collective and important role in policing the security and upholding the order of the imperial world, a role enhanced and claimed from the early principate.[40]

At the same time, the members of the *collegium* also do more than simply feed off and nest neatly within an established imperial power system with fixed hierarchies. As Bendlin demonstrates, this is an unusual society, with no mention of an occupational focus and a rare interest in its bylaws in the particular issues raised by the presence of slave and freedmen members. The possibility that a significant proportion of its members were unfree or dependent on their former owners in legally enforceable ways might at first sight seem to detract from any benefits accrued by them. It is also important not to ignore the role that the patron, Lucius Caesennius Rufus, might have played in orchestrating events: here as elsewhere, the internalization of imperial institutions and vocabularies might have needed

---

[39] *CIL* 14, 2112 = *ILS* 7212 = *FIRA* 3, 35; Bendlin 2011, with extensive bibiography; cult of Antinous: Vout 2007, chapter 1; Jones 2010, chapter 7; for the trajectory of civic patronage in the western Empire, see Eilers 2002, 165–81.

[40] Cf. Chapter 5 for a full discussion of calendars and time in the Roman imperial world.

a bit of a push to take such a complex form (by the patron here, and by the governor in some other contexts).[41]

But the elaborate detail of the bylaws and the language of the document more generally are eloquent testimony to the claiming of privilege and differentiation on the part of individuals and, no less, on the part of the whole group, which substantially asserts itself like a tiny, self-governing, and exclusive citizenry. If the Lanuvium *collegium* is unusual among the myriad "voluntary associations" that are something of a viral phenomenon Roman Empire, with the clout of senate, patron and civic community behind it and to some extent even propelling it, it shares with them the ambition-feeding potential and fostering of small-scale peoplehood that participate in the dynamic force of the Roman Empire of the first to early third cents. CE, a minute version of cities and leagues.[42] Most obviously, we see the hierarchy of the chief official (*quinquennalis*), two additional officers with individualized titles (scribe and *viator*, probably "messenger"), and board of four rotating *magistri* of dinners (col. 2, 8–10, 14–16), the *quinquennalis* and *magistri* distinguished by their obligations, and the *quinquennalis*, scribe and *viator* by their dues and exemptions (col. 2, 17–22). The roles of the benefactors (*quinquennalis* and *magistri*) are suggested more fully by the contributions that they must make: wine, bread, four sardines a head, and hot water to mix with the wine for the dinners provided by *magistri*, and oil to be distributed by the *quinquennalis* at the public bath before the dinner on the birthdays of Diana and Antinous (col. 2, 30–2). The officers thus play the role of "real" local magistrates in their contributions of the currency of civic largesse: wine, bread and oil.

A concern for propriety runs through the bylaws and the document as a whole. It is manifest in the measures that achieve one of the society's major stated purposes, seeing to the appropriate "departure of the deceased" (col. 1, 15–16): the bylaws establish minutely the scope and limits of obligations and restrictions of what is owed to the dead, both in strictly financial terms (payment toward funerary expenses) and in social terms (handout of money at the funeral, representation of members at the funeral) (col. 1, 22-col. 2, 6). But it goes beyond that, and is rather a leitmotif of the society's more general self-regulation: in the stipulation

---

[41] Cf. Chapter 5, "Roman Days," for the initiative of the proconsul of Asia, P. Fabius Maximus, in choosing Augustus' birthday as the new New Year's Day for the *koinon* of Asia.

[42] See, especially, Noreña 2018 for a highly stimulating comparison of the dynamics of private associations within Roman and Han imperial contexts; cf. also Dench 2018.

that disrespecting the *quinquennalis* or other members, or disrupting the banquet in other ways, should be punished by a fine (col. 2, 23–8), and in the clause that states that the *quinquennalis'* extra rations are conditional on his probity, to encourage the good behavior of others (col. 2, 21–2). The self-identification of the society as a distinct and privileged community is underwritten by its invocation of the language of imperial prayer, by its alignment of "us, our families, our society" and its continued prosperity with that of the emperor and the imperial family (col. 1, 14–17), by the payment of a not negligible entry fee of 100 sesterces[43] (with the required amphora of "good" wine only enhancing the sense that all members are not just decurion-like but officer-ready in their preparedness for benefaction) (col 1, 20–1), by its endorsement by *senatus consultum* (col. 1, 10–13), and by the very fact of its inscribed bylaws, somewhat reminiscent of a town charter, but more explicitly concerned to model exemplary behavior.

As Bendlin correctly points out, the role of the society is not to replace that of family members, who would be responsible for the funerary arrangements. Nevertheless, the society uses the clout of its familiarity with the imperial center to address the particular concerns of its membership that have to do with unfree or dependent status. A clause prevents claims on the society by any creditor unless named by the deceased as their heir, and specifically by patron, patroness, master, or mistress (col. 1, 33–col. 2, 2), a reminder of and response to the serious downside to the reciprocal but asymmetrical relationships so characteristic of Roman society. There is provision for a symbolic funeral with a dummy of the deceased if the body of a slave-member is not released by the owner, and if there is no will (col. 2, 3–5), a poignant side-stepping of the fundamental condition of slavery. The elaborately constituted Lanuviate association of Diana and Antinous is hardly spontaneous, but nor does it merely feed an imperial machine without considerable benefit to the esteem and standing of its members.

---

[43] A month's wage for a contemporary legionary foot-soldier: see Speidel 1992.

# CHAPTER 4

# Force and Violence

## Emperor on the Edge

The Emperor Claudius' response to the requests made by the Greek and Jewish communities of Alexandria in 41 CE is unusual in its inclusion of several explicit "or else" clauses. The first stands out against the studied politeness that was the norm for such exchanges in the empire of letters (indeed, the Alexandrian requests were made on the back of the obligatory praise and honors for the new emperor): "and I tell you once and for all that unless you put a stop to this ruinous and obstinate enmity against each other, I shall be driven to show what a benevolent and kind ruler can be when turned to righteous indignation" (*P. Lond.* 6, 1912, ll. 79–82 = *CPJ* 2, 153 = *Sel. Pap.* 2, 212, tr. Hunt and Edgar 1934). After this exhortation not to fuel the violent troubles that had broken out between the Greek and Jewish communities of Alexandria under Caligula in 38 CE, reawakened more recently by Jewish riots on the death of Caligula, Claudius turns to the issue of further rights for each side. He refers the request for a *boulē* made by the Greek community to the prefect for investigation, reprimands them for their admission of non-citizens to the ephebate that qualified them for the Alexandrian citizenship, and exhorts them to allow the Jews to observe their customs. He orders the Jews not to press for further privileges, and specifically not to infiltrate the games at the Greek gymnasium, nor to admit fellow Jews into Egypt from Syria. He underlines these orders with a further, menacing "or else" clause: "I will by all means take vengeance on them as fomenters of what is a general plague infecting the whole world" (ll. 98–100).[1]

---

[1] For expected norms of emperors as alternatively more or less impartial judges or extenders of *indulgentia* in exchanges with cities, see Millar 1977, 410–47; 540–9; cf. Chaniotis 2003 for refusal of honors to other cities included in Aphrodisias' "archive wall" (see Figure 5). Harris 2001, chapter 10 for important contextualization of emperors' anger and its restraint.

This glimpse of the emperor's capacity to get angry is shocking and meant to be, the exasperated flip-side of the extraordinary benevolence that Claudius goes on to promise if everyone behaves. Both panegyric and everyday speech cultivated the expectation of benevolence, an optimistic way of characterizing the potential of a *princeps* to whom decision-making was increasingly delegated. The capacity to exercise that potential to frighten and enforce is generally the property of a "bad" emperor, although in Tacitus' dark, Thucydidean exposé of monarchy, it is an intrinsic part of the system itself, revealed particularly in the process of succession. The hasty dispatch of Agrippa Postumus on Augustus' death and Tiberius' immediate assumption of the role of commander-in-chief of the praetorian guard and armies make his hesitation in the senate an elaborate charade (Tac. *Ann.* 1, 6–7; 11–13).[2]

The situation in Alexandria was unusual, both in the intensity of its violence and in the structure of its community. In essence, the self-government of both the Greek and the Jewish communities of Alexandria was somewhat limited, especially in comparison with *poleis* of other regions in the Greek-speaking east. The prized Alexandrian citizenship was restricted to the Greek community. The Jewish community had a council and local officials with limited responsibilities. They held rights of residency in Alexandria but not the Alexandrian citizenship. Both communities were exempt from the poll tax paid by "Egyptians." Finally, both communities were peculiarly dependent on Rome, although in rather different ways: admission to the Alexandrian citizenship was overseen directly by the Roman emperor, while Jewish privileges had been directly granted by Augustus as a reward for services rendered to the Romans in the last years of the Ptolemaic kingdom. Claudius' anger is expressed as a just response to the violent and unreasonable behavior of the Greek and Jewish communities. The warning not to admit Jews from Syria hints at the fear of interconnected cells that characterizes Roman security concerns from the Bacchanalian affair of 186 BCE to officials' dealings with early Christian groups, and that meshes with the broader expectation that Roman Egypt is peculiarly prone to terrorism. But it is hard not to hold this intensified version of the profoundly uneven dispersal and withholding of honor and privilege that characterized Roman rule at least partly responsible for the Alexandrian situation, exacerbated by some serious errors of

---

[2] Tacitus and succession processes: Griffin 1996.

judgment on the part of the former prefect of Egypt, Flaccus, not to speak of Caligula.[3]

This rare glimpse of an emperor's anger underlines the specificity of the economy of violence that enforced Roman imperial power. Roman force and violence were not by any stretch of the imagination "only" symbolic, and I am committed in this chapter to emphasize their value and efficacy even (and perhaps especially) in the Empire of the Caesars: a slight hint of an older and more rigid periodization of Republican "war and law" imperialism versus "culture and *mores*" Empire lies buried just beneath the surface of the rather polite Empires that have proliferated in recent scholarship. On the other hand, the "Darth Vader" bottom-line Roman Empire of constant and horrific violence may be comfortingly distancing, and even useful (sometimes it really needs to be said that we do not like or endorse Roman modes of violent enforcement), but it does not explain very much. I am concerned to emphasize in this chapter the distinctive role- and rule-playing (and breaking) in which the Roman state and individual actors were involved along with, to a more limited extent, friends, subjects, and allies.[4]

## Imperial Economies of Violence

In Herodotus' early attempt to define how Croesus' subjection of Greeks to his *archē* ("rule" or "empire") infringed on their freedom in unprecedented ways, it is clear that violence is neither necessary nor sufficient to create an imperial relationship. The Cimmerians' smash and grab raid was not such a relationship, while Croesus' innovation is an ongoing relationship enacted variously by "friendship" or the payment of tribute (1, 6, 2–3). Nevertheless, as Herodotus follows the rise of the Persian empire, his account showcases the kinds of atrocities that went hand-in-hand with imperial power. His "barbarian" kings have a predilection for mutilation, imposing their will on bodies in the most memorable way, capped by occasional obscene sculptures created from human bodies. When Pythius the Lydian, an ancestral friend of the Persian king Darius, has given Xerxes, Darius' son, generous hospitality, he asks Xerxes to allow his eldest son to be left at home to look after him, rather than joining his army. Xerxes' angry response is to have the son cut in half and his ill-fated army

---

[3] Alexandria in 38 CE: Smallwood 1976, 220–56; Schwartz 1990, 77–89; Harker 2008, 9–47; 2012. Justifiable anger as key aspect of Claudius' image: Osgood 2011, 66–7.

[4] Darth Vader: Maier 2006, 8; for a usefully repulsive Rome, see most recently Morley 2010.

walk between the two halves of the body, a horrific violation of two of the most valued and sanctified relationships in Greek thought: guest-host and father-son (7, 38–40, 1).

While it is clear from this episode that such behaviors have undergone significant translation into a Greek understanding of arbitrary, tyrant-like behavior that breaks every human and divine rule, there is excellent textual and iconographic evidence of Achaemenid kings advertizing their capacity to punish violently by spectacular means. The most famous example is the Behistun monument of Darius, an assertive act of legitimation of the new king that advertises graphically his torture, mutilation, and execution of the "liar-kings" (in an upheaval dating to ca. 515 BCE). This violence is, importantly, part of a bigger picture: the fulfillment of justice and restoration of a world order overseen by the divine power of Ahura Mazda that includes the sponsorship and promotion of the obedient. In fulfillment of Herodotus' thesis of imperial relations as peculiarly fertile ground for transferring patterns of behavior, he offers oblique glimpses of the nascent fifth-century Athenian empire, concluding the dramatic events of his narrative with the Athenians' punishment of the Persian satrap Artaÿctes by nailing him to a board and leaving him hanging there to die, after witnessing them stone his son to death. While brutality is not the exclusive domain of "barbarians," there is something intrinsically brutal, and perhaps even barbaric, about imperial power (9, 120).[5]

These examples from the Achaemenid and Athenian empires introduce us to the stark economics of violence and brutality. As our own experience of ISIS tragically reminds us, occasional, horrific spectaculars terrorize effectively for longer with fewer resources and even casualties than the drip drip of conventional combat, especially when combined with effective, graphic advertisement. The question of where violence and brutality fit in with long-term ideologies of rule raises the problem of both sustainability and palatability. In ancient empires, one common scheme is an ideology of divinely ordained justice, such as we have seen promoted in the Achaemenid case. Elsewhere, we see denial or at least widely different representations of reality. The Parthenon frieze of fifth-century Athens portrays empire for a contemporary audience resident in or visiting Athens as a community, united in the worship of Athena, while later memory and reception in antiquity favor much darker visions of drag-netting islands, occupation, and economic oppression. In the evolving ideology

---

[5] Briant 2002, 204–54; Greek receptions of "barbarian" cruelty: Hall 1989, 158–9, cf. 79–84; Herodotus on Athens: Derow 1995; Moles 1996; 2002.

of kingship in the Hellenistic age, we see the stylization and heroization of righteous conflict, including hand-to-hand combat and worthy opponents, with a vast preference for displaying "barbarian" enemies over Greeks, and admiration for enemy bravery, especially in defeat and death. At the other extreme, we see the promotion of scientific, technological warfare that sets face-to-face combat at a psychological or even physical remove.[6]

A different variety of imperial economics of force and violence was also regularly practiced in efficiently securing manpower. While an enduring, traditional perspective held a citizen militia to be the heart and soul of the *polis*, both a symptom and an enactment of its idealized autonomy, for some ancient imperial powers the co-option of armed forces from subject peoples was a central mode of exercizing the imperial relationship and an ingenious approach to the potential problem of troublesome men of fighting age. Herodotus' heterogeneous parade of the Great King of Persia, its ethnic divisions marked by distinctive dress and weaponry, is a strange and magnificent spectacle framed by the contrasted implicit norm of the comparatively homogeneous citizen militia (7, 61–80). Within the rather different ideological norms of the Athenian empire, Thucydides sees the allies' avoidance of sending ships and preference for paying cash instead as a notable mechanism of their self-enslavement: any pretense of being Athens' allies as opposed to its subjects is lost in the process. Thucydides highlights one concrete problem from the subjects' perspective if they give cash rather than ships: they lose experience of war in the process, making real problems for themselves when the time comes to revolt (1, 99). This is an important insight into the delicate and complex balance of interests and risk in imperial situations that rely extensively on local infrastructures and motivation, a balance that is poorly maintained with disastrous effects in the Athenian empire.[7]

There were, of course, alternatives to mobilizing subject peoples, well deployed by the Hellenistic kings: the use of one's own citizenry (substantially still the practice of the Hellenistic kingdoms at war), typically supplemented by mercenaries. This was an attractive solution in terms of the ability to outsource military specialism, and to have supply match demand, although it came at a considerable ideological and economic cost:

---

[6] Economy of violence: Sahlins 2004; two faces of Athens: e.g. De Romilly 1963; Castriota 1992, 188–90; Constantakopoulou 2007, 125–34; Ma 2009; Hellenistic approaches: Chaniotis 2005, chs. 4 and 10.
[7] Idealized autonomy of the *polis*: Hall 2007.

sustaining "foreign" garrisons and their legitimate and illegitimate demands was deeply unpopular within the Greek cities.[8]

## The Roman Economy of Violence

There was considerable ideological investment on the part of Rome and its friends in the notion that the Roman state was consistently more violent and more successful in the use of force than any of its obvious historical or contemporary competitors. Rome's foundation stories are fraught with the destructive and generative forces of Mars and Venus, parents of its founding fathers, with rape and murder propelling early events as if written into its DNA. Their successes in warfare and conquest-based government are explicitly the Romans' "arts," their answer to Greek philosophical, fine, rhetorical and astronomical arts, in the famous words of Anchises to Aeneas in the underworld in the sixth book of Vergil's *Aeneid* (847–53). The Romans and their friends liked to think that their wars of conquest were fought by a "native" militia devoted to their homeland (e.g., Polybius 6, 52; Horace *Odes* 3, 6, 33–48). Dynasts and early emperors competed with Alexander the Great, continuing the raison d"être of his Hellenistic successors until the competition was well and truly over, with supremacy over the west as well as the east, unheard of peoples and places in submission, and Augustus recognized as king-maker *par excellence*. The Augustan peace was based on war to end all wars, with the end-result an unprecedented utopia.[9]

Perhaps the most readily quantifiable measure of Roman violence is the frequency with which the Romans went to war. This is the starting point of W. V. Harris' classic 1979 *War and Imperialism in Republican Rome, 327–70 BC*, a brilliant account of the state ecology that made going to war with great frequency in the Republic not only possible but highly desirable and even necessary. Since the publication of *War and Imperialism*, there has been some reevaluation of the world in which Rome emerged as an international power. In particular, the aggression, acquisitiveness, and expansionism of the Hellenistic successor kingdoms should not be played down. Nevertheless, after intense argument in the years immediately following its publication, Harris' thesis survives broadly unchallenged,

---

[8] Chaniotis 2005, 78–93; cf. Lendon 2007, a stimulating essay that to my mind overstates the contrast between Hellenistic and Roman systems.
[9] Rape and Roman origins: Arieti 1997; cf. Dench 2005; Rome's Alexander complex: Treves 1953, cf. Spencer 2002 (on Latin traditions); Augustan peace: Woolf 1993.

not least in its countering of theories of "defensive imperialism," the apologetic accounts that had proliferated in the nineteenth and earlier twentieth centuries, emphasizing Rome's prime motivation for going to war as the reluctant but genuine need to defend herself and its allies.[10]

In this section, I take the intense rhythm of warfare in the Roman Republic of the third to early first centuries BCE, along with Harris' extensive sociological explanation, as a given. The fits and starts of Roman expansionism in the early Empire are important symptoms of the changed conditions of monarchy, highlighting in turn the extraordinary rhythms of the last decades of the Republic. But I take equally seriously the performative and spectacular uses of violence and threats of violence. The Roman official or governor's role in enforcing justice physically (through threat or through action) was as much a part of his image as his sitting in judgment and fussing bureaucratically over his tablets. The expectation that subjects should be constantly aware of the coercive potential of Roman rule is suggested by the use in literary sources of the term *fasces* as a metonym for governors and even for empire itself. Just as important is the notion that violence and force were precious commodities, to be used and apportioned with care to avert a worse fate, institutionalized and personalized in due measure, an engagement with Rome's imperial legacy manifest in socio-specific ways, shaping and responding to its very particular political and social circumstances. Even the ancient celebrations of Roman force and violence with which we began this section marry them with generative powers and rebirth, or distance them from a more civilized present. Alternatively, such accounts idealize force and violence by comparison with a decadent present or foreign rival, or insist on the artfulness of violence. In hindsight, the fact that "defensive imperialism" could be argued for Rome at all, in combination with Harris' exposé of the extent to which warfare fueled Roman society, says something about the capaciousness of Roman claims of what counted as provocation, especially as they entered an international arena that appreciated the long-established inter-connection of justice and violence.[11]

In the domestic sphere, the escalation of violence in the late Republic was met with an increasing preoccupation with norms and rules as individual preeminence threatened to topple the state. We might think of the intensity of Sullan "constitutional" legislation, which established order on

---

[10] For a selection of responses to Harris 1979 soon after its publication, see Champion 2004b, chapter 1.
[11] Hellenistic bellicosity: Chaniotis 2005, chs. 1 and 4; Roman notions of provocation, Harris 1979, 171–254.

officeholding in general and the tribunate of the people in particular, the raison d'être of a regime built on violence. The dictatorship held by Sulla had historically been the epitome of last-resort forceful solution. Its extension from warfare against foreign enemies to domestic conditions with Sulla's own tenure was a significant innovation. Another example of this preoccupation with norms and rules was the vexed question of whether Cicero had committed treason or saved the state by executing the Catilinarian conspirators without trial in 63 BCE. Finally, we might emphasize the increasingly studied constitutionalism around the position of the triumvirs, insisted upon amidst atrocities of civil war and proscriptions.[12]

Octavian/Augustus' immediate ticket was vengeance against his adopted father's killers, and Augustus' establishment of multiple militarized bodies with responsibilities for keeping order in and around the city of Rome would pave the way for the emerging power of the praetorian prefect and ultimate concentration of forces within the city of Rome that would be one of Tacitus' major illustrations of the hardening of the monarchical system in the reign of Tiberius (*Ann.* 4, 2, 1 cf. 1, 7, 2). But the contemporary public discourse of the Augustan principate seems much more concerned with paternalism and self-restraint, even while insisting on Augustus' exceptionalism as a military commander. Examples include the slightly inaccurate, and therefore perhaps truthfully represented explanation for the division of provinces in 27 BCE that had the *princeps* relieving the senate and people of the bother of militarized provinces (Strabo 17, 3, 25; cf. Suet. *Aug.* 47). It takes Dio's retrospective account to attribute the Thucydidean motive of leaving the senators unarmed and unprepared for battle, neutering any threat to the monarchy (Dio 53, 12, 2–3 cf. 52, 27, 3–5). In 19 BCE (Dio 54, 11, 6), Agrippa refused a triumph, quietly anticipating the future monopoly of the imperial family on triumphs as well as modeling the *noblesse* of refusal that would characterize good monarchy from the principate of Augustus onwards.[13]

Throughout the Julio-Claudian era, the fear of a return to civil war was stoked, the continuation of the dynasty the only hope of forestalling it: the *Senatusconsultum de Cn. Pisone patre* insists on this (Potter and Damon

---

[12] Late Republican/triumviral violence, rules, and restraint: Millar 1973; Wiseman 1994, 357; Lintott 1999.

[13] Build-up and monopolization of force: Gilliver 2007; Rathbone and Alston 2007; ultimate dedication of the temple of Mars Ultor in 2 BCE as vengeance against the Parthians: Simpson 1977; refusing triumphs: Beard 2007, 288–301; refusal as keynote of Roman monarchy: Wallace-Hadrill 1982, 36–7.

1999, 45–9; cf. 12–15; 59–63). As the potentially terrifying power of the emperor became increasingly discussible, at least in theoretical or artistic contexts, the values of moderation and mercy (not at all coincidentally an advertised attribute of Julius Caesar) were loudly endorsed. Seneca's *De Clementia* preached in vain to a young Nero the righteous performance of justice and the judicial use of mercy rather than the exercise of crude power. The idealized persona of the emperor, performed repeatedly in correspondence that is in turn memorialized, is less the enforcer and more the corrector of injustice. On Trajan's Column, the princeps never bloodies his hands, leaving that task to the soldiers, while the predominant tendency is to blame the lowly or rogue (or preferably lowly *and* rogue: the agent of the tax collector or the imperial procurator) for cruelty and injustice, rather than the authority or system itself.[14]

Triumphs and the material repertoire that provided lasting monuments of their celebration are concerned primarily with the social and political frameworks in which citizens were involved, and centered on the city of Rome. Monuments that interpret and memorialize victory, enacting relationships between individuals and community, range from mid-Republican temples to the columns of Trajan and Marcus Aurelius. Outside Rome, from the later second century BCE, victories were advertised and memorialized much more broadly across the imperial landscape, in trophies that appropriated and adapted Hellenistic iconography and monumental forms. While trophies had traditionally asserted and monumentalized success in situ on the battlefield, Alexander the Great had marked the furthest extent of his expeditions by dedicating twelve altars in India (Arrian 5, 29, 1). We know of a number of Roman trophies from the late Republic through the early imperial period. Like roads, they suggest geographical ambitions, joining the dots to create a sense of imperial mastery. Notable monuments include: Pompey's in the Pyrenees after his defeat of Sertorius in 71 BCE, on either side of what would later be the Via Iulia Augusta, crossing from Gaul into Spain; Octavian's at Actium/Nikopolis, at the junction of "east" and "west" from an Italian perspective; the dedication by senate and Roman people to Augustus in 17 BCE at La Turbie, at the western edge of his campaigns, naming the forty-nine Alpine tribes he had conquered and his mastery "from the upper to the lower sea" (Pliny *NH* 3, 136); and Trajan's gigantic, one hundred foot diameter monument at Adamklissi, both a memorial to the Roman dead

---

[14] Acknowledgment of power of *princeps*: e.g. Griffin 1984; 2003; Trajan: Kampen 1995; Dillon 2006; blaming the lowly and rogue: van Nijf 2008.

and a celebration of the recovery of Moesia. In addition to signaling the imperial mastery of space, these monuments vividly depict imperial power, topped by the relevant *imperator* or cuirassed *genius* of the emperor, and portraying kneeling or seated bound barbarians in distinctive dress.[15]

As the Roman citizenship was expanded and Latin status became a distinctive stage in the hierarchy of privilege, the intricate relationship between Latin and Roman communities outside Rome and the Roman state itself became an urgent practical issue, as we saw in Chapter 2. The power to enforce, which was (along with justice) the primary attribute of an official, needed to be calibrated, so that we see in charters prescription of the number of lictors and attendants to accompany magistrates. In his evocation of the dangerous ambitions of Capua in the speech *On the Agrarian Law*, delivered before the Roman people at the beginning of 63 BCE, Cicero spells out the Capuan magistrates' insistence on being called praetors, rather than *duumviri* as in other colonies, and on being attended by lictors with the *fasces* rather than with axe-less *bacilla*, a freshly defined distinction in his day (*Leg. Agr.* 2, 93). On a grander scale, the articulation of monarchy and dynasty in terms of an ordained hierarchy of authority and command was manifest in unprecedented, explicit admonitions and observations. Notoriously, Livy ponders out loud the definition of *dux* as one who acts under his own auspices in relation to a contemporary dispute about the early Republican general A. Cornelius Cossus' eligibility for the *spolia opima*, a dispute in which Augustus himself had intervened with archaeological evidence (4, 20, 4–11). The Piso document spells out the hierarchy of the *imperium* of Piso in relation to that of Germanicus, and of the *imperium* of both of them in relation to Tiberius, to make clear the full horror of his insurrection (Potter and Damon 1999, 33–46). Dio casually analyzes observable differences between imperial legates and proconsular governors of provinces of the senate and Roman people (53, 13, 3–8).

The army is an institution in which questions about the apportionment of force and violence are played out in obvious ways: who fights, who commands, and whose army it is. In order to play up the contrast with the Carthaginian use of mercenaries, Polybius elides the very real differences between the Roman legions and the non-citizen Italian cohorts that made up the vast majority of the Republican army of overseas expansion. Thus,

---

[15] Triumph and triumphal monuments: Beard 2003; 2007; dedication of temples: Rawson 1990; Ziolkowski 1992; victory art: Hölscher 1967; 2003; Trajan's Column: Coarelli 2000; Davies 2000, 27–34; Koeppel 2002; Column of Marcus Aurelius: Davies 2000, 42–8; Scheid and Huet 2000; trophies: Formigé 1949; Charles-Picard 1957; Hölscher 1980; 2006.

he argues that Rome's troops fought for their homeland and their families, and that Italian bodies, inborn courage, and institutions to promote courage were all superior to those of their Phoenician/African counterparts (6, 52). In domestic contexts, varieties of nativism were emphasized in different contexts. One example is the powerful ideology of the citizen soldier, a model for elite behavior (Cato *Agr.* Preface 2; 4), a contrast with indulged, imported slaves in Gracchan rhetoric, showing the disparity of imperial enrichment (Plut. *T.Gracch.* 8, 7; 9, 4–5), or used to admonish the decadent present (Hor. *Odes* 3, 6, ll. 33–44). Another is the figure of a mosaic of troops differentiated by tribe (e.g., Ennius, *Ann.* 229 Sk.), perhaps a fragment of a more inclusive way of imagining Roman history. This strand would thicken considerably in the aftermath of the Social War of 91–89 BCE, because the notion of the deservedness of Rome's allies was crucial to the politics of political incorporation.[16]

Challenges to maintaining the ideal of Rome's army as a citizen militia were framed in antiquity in terms of supply, a problem that has so far eluded modern, empirical analyses of demography and patterns of settlement. The problem that the Romans perceived was addressed in different ways: by the Gracchan program, in the later second century BCE, of redistributing public land, increasing the number of propertied men eligible for the legions and by waiving the property requirement, in Marius' enrollment into the legions of formally property-less men (*capite censi/proletarii*), as consul in 107 BCE. The latter will have had little immediate effect, but over the longer term was one factor in changing the relationship between troops and the commanders on whom their post-service settlement depended. Some commanders were only too eager to find private means of funding to redress what they portrayed as overlapping public and private wrongs. Julius Caesar's account of his address to his soldiers on the public and private wrongs committed by the senate having him made a public enemy at the beginning of his civil war with Pompey (*BC* 1, 7), and Augustus' posthumous account of raising an army in 44 BCE "on my own initiative and at my own expense," the opening statement of his *Res Gestae*, are prime examples.[17]

The Augustan principate combined a regularization and institutionalization of the legions and auxiliary units with a marked personalization of

---

[16] Italian manpower: Brunt 1971; Ilari 1974; De Ligt 2007; cf. Dench 1995, chapter 2 and 2005, chapter 3 for ideologies of Italy.

[17] Modern challenges to ancient perception of problems in supply of troops: e.g Rathbone 1981; Rich 1983; De Ligt 2007 with extensive bibliography. De Blois 2007 on the interplay of private and state interests in the management of soldiers.

the role of commander-in-chief. A fixed length of service was set for legionaries (sixteen years with four years in reserve), fixed benefits were established, and their marriages and children born during their service ceased to be recognized in Roman law, a major factor in formalizing civilians and soldiers as separate categories. On the other hand, Augustus' personal role of commander is emphasized in the *Res Gestae*, where exceptional achievements are accomplished with "my soldiers," "my fleet" and "my army" (15, 26, 30). As we have seen, Augustus formally came to "take care of" most of the militarized provinces from 27 BCE, while triumphs came to be his and his family's to celebrate or refuse. His exceptionalism as commander-in-chief stunts the potential of others, and encourages further blurring of the line between individual preeminence and the state. We see this, above all, in the performances of personalized loyalty required of soldiers, including the repetition of oaths to his person and possibly even the circulation of the prototype of the festival calendar that survives from Dura Europus, heavy in equal measure on city of Rome festivals and celebrations of the imperial family. Tacitus' notice of Augustus leaving on his death a handwritten account of the number of "citizens and allies under arms", as part of a comprehensive inventory of the financial and human resources of state, beautifully conjoins the careful accounting and personalization of the principate (*Ann.* 1, 11–12). While this combination of institutionalization and very particular forms of personalization surely helped to ensure the length and success of the Augustan principate, it did not make his successors immune to army disloyalty. This is apparent in the mutinies that followed the death of Augustus, as well as in the senate's lavish and distinctly nervous praise of army loyalty in the Piso document after Piso's evident success in attempting some personalization of his own relationship with the army (ll. 53–7; 159–65; 172). We do not have to do much reading between the lines to see both the regime's dependence on military force and its potential vulnerability to it.[18]

## Embracing Roman Violence?

Rome's friends and subjects told their own, self-interested stories of Roman conquest and the maintenance of peace through force. Imperial receptions of Roman force and violence ranged from invested admiration to hostile rejection of Rome as a foreign body. In 1 *Maccabees* 8, an

---

[18] Augustan changes: Phang 2001; Gilliver 2007; Rathbone and Alston 2007, 162–3; 185–9; Dura-Europus festival calendar: cf. Chapter 5.

account is given of Rome's achievements, explaining why seeking an alliance against the Seleucids in 161 BCE might be attractive to the Judaeans. The writer revels in the destructive power of Rome alongside its political and ethical righteousness: its military accomplishment against the Gauls (who shared a reputation for deeply antisocial behavior right across the Greek-speaking world, a reputation on which the Attalids of Pergamon had capitalized so well), its crushing and humiliation of Hellenistic kings. As a small state in a volatile world, it might prove very attractive to be on the right side of a power that was able to secure its will through force.[19]

Polybius' treatment of the capture of the Carthaginian stronghold of New Carthage in Spain in 209 BCE, under the command of Scipio Africanus, is offered as a largely admiring type-scene of Roman imperial behavior, with perhaps just a hint of distance. The "Roman custom" identified by Polybius in such circumstances is to kill relentlessly, sparing none, cutting dogs in half and dismembering other animals before a tightly organized and choreographed pillaging by men assigned to the task, the spoils shared with total integrity (10, 15–17, 5). This intentional and highly disciplined spectacle of terror that leaves no room for hot-headedness implicitly classes Romans as an ethical model for Greeks in dispassion and trustworthiness, but also hints obliquely at barbarian-ness, albeit the kind that would bisect dogs and dismember animals rather than the kind that would, like Herodotus' Xerxes, bisect people.[20]

Livy's account of Antiochus IV Epiphanes introducing gladiatorial spectacle to his subjects was almost certainly told also by Polybius, and reads like a parable of the naturalization of specifically Roman forms of violence. When his Syrian subjects initially reacted to this unaccustomed mode of violent entertainment with fear rather than with pleasure, the Seleucid king got them accustomed to the idea by alternating versions in which the gladiators only wounded each other with ones in which they went for the kill. The result was that he encouraged in "most of the young men an enthusiasm for arms" and went from importing the gladiators from Rome to producing them at home (probably: the text is lacunose at this point) (41, 20, 10–12). The story, with its schematic representation of "Greeks" and "Romans," and choice of a single, foundational moment for

---

[19]  *1 Maccabees*: Millar 1997; Attalids and Gauls: Nachtergael 1977; Mitchell 2003.
[20]  Ancient accounts of Roman violence in warfare: Harris 1979, 263–4; Ziolkowski 1993; Polybius' location of the Roman character within the traditional binary scheme: Erskine 2000; Champion 2004a, 148–8.

the introduction of gladiatorial spectacle to the eastern Mediterranean, seems unlikely to be literally true. It is interesting that even Roman versions of gladiatorial games were sometimes imagined to have been Etruscan imports or at least mediated by the Etruscans, just as the *fasces* and other regalia were thought to be Etruscan (e.g., D.H. *Ant. Rom.* 3, 61; Florus 1, 5, 6), a suggestive categorization of these distinctively ritualized forms of violence as being at one remove from "us." Livy tells his story of Antiochus IV's socialization of his Syrian subjects within the context of the king's mad, exuberant restlessness, manifest also in enthusiastic "Roman" charades such as his topsy-turvy performance of playing a Roman magistrate and seeking votes for election. While the story has a distinctively Augustan logic of cultures as styles to play with, it also has a slightly different, second century BCE one: this is an era of active construction of "Greek" and "Roman" behaviors with two sources of power, authority and rulership style hanging in the balance.[21]

The late Republican ideology of imperial relationships hinted at violence in the absence of empire, with taxation the price of security from both internal and external troubles (e.g., Cicero *Q. fr.* 1, 1, 34). While, as we have seen, in the first century CE, monarchy is advertised as the only thing keeping the world from the horrors of civil war, at the same time we see the enthusiastic local embrace of the emperor's violence against outsiders, violence that brings glory as well as guaranteeing the continuation of peace. An inscription commemorates a gift made in 4 CE by the future emperor Tiberius in his name and that of his dead brother Drusus, to Saepinum in Samnite southeast Italy, of a magnificent array of towers and gates to grace their new town walls (*CIL* 9, 2443). The gates were decorated with bound, captive Germans, an appropriate reference to the pair's German campaigns. For a comparatively new city, the splendid walls, towers, and gates are highly symbolic, suggesting that to visit is to enter urbanity and civilization, and to leave outside the forces of barbarism and violence, including the everyday risk of bandits. The Samnites had not so long ago been considered ferocious and uncivilized "barbarians," formidable enemies of Rome in its fourth- to third-century BCE conquest of Italy before taking up arms against Rome again, terrifyingly, in the Social War of 91–89 BCE. But now they had been Roman citizens for

---

[21] Antiochus IV: cf. Polyb. 30, 25, 1; Edmondson 1999; Mann 2010; Etruscan origins or influence on Roman games, cf. the similar ancient and modern theory of Campanian origins: Welch 2007, 11–18; third to second century "Greek" versus "Roman" behaviors: Scheid 1995; "Greek" versus "Roman" behaviors in Augustan logic: Wallace-Hadrill 1998.

several generations, and the gift drew them further into a worldview in which shared barbarian common enemies were kept at bay by the imperial regime.[22]

If the towers and gates of Saepinum are a worthy gift to the city on the part of the imperial dynasty, we see elsewhere examples of local initiative to display their special relationship with the imperial center, underwritten by violence against others. To be on the right side of the emperor's sword was every bit as worthy of boasting about as being on the right side of the emperor's pen. In the second story of the south portico of the Sebasteion complex at the "free and immune" city of Aphrodisias, labeled reliefs emphasize the military might of Claudius over a personification of Britannia and of Nero over a personification of Armenia. These are highly stylized portraits, evoking Greek heroic antecedents, such as Achilles and Protesilea, rather than a visual narrative of contemporary warfare, but there is no doubt about the emphasis on military rather than civilian attributes. The emperors are half nude, wearing a military cloak, and their suggestive poses over the slumped female personifications of Britannia and Armenia, breasts and bodies revealed where their clothes part, make clear the act of subjection.[23]

The trophies of Pompey in the Pyrenees and Augustus in the Alps that we considered in the previous section were answered by a series of twelve locally dedicated arches in Gallia Narbonensis, mostly of Augustan date. The dedicators of the arches were also involved in the intensive building of the urban infrastructure of which these arches are an integral part. The decorative schemes favor exaggerated versions of the tendrils and fruit garlands associated with the Augustan iconography of peace, as well as bound barbarian prisoners. These bound barbarian prisoners seem to be generic, rather than offering some sort of cautionary tale of what has happened to "us" in the process of pacification, and what might happen to "us" if we misbehave. They perhaps combine smug celebration of what recently happened to neighbors with more general advertisement of the benefits of being on the right side. Interestingly, such monuments are no longer built in the second century CE, marking a particular moment in the articulation of imperial identity in Gallia Narbonensis.[24]

The trouble with nourishing a constant backdrop of threat and terror is that it is not always as neatly containable as one might hope. For local peoples of the empire, the sort of confidence in being on the right side of

[22] Saepinum: Matteini Chiari 1982, 57–8; Whittaker 1997; Samnites: Salmon 1967; Dench 1995.
[23] Smith 1987; Sion-Jenkis 2009.    [24] Küpper-Böhm 1996, esp. 121–6; Woolf 1998, 75–6.

Roman enforcement that is suggested by a gory passage from an ancient schoolbook in which the (to modern readers) awful spectacle of the governor meting out punishment is just part of a normal day, is not the whole story. The terrible prospect of that force and violence being turned against oneself came out in nightmares. Artemidorus' interpretations tackle dreams of crucifixion, being burned alive, thrown to the beasts and other, more mundane forms of Roman punishment (*Oneir.* 2, 49–54; cf. 1, 35; 40). Even if hierarchies of privilege, both (at least formally) of legal status and increasingly of social status, might give the more fortunate some reassurance that they were in their waking lives unlikely to face the gruesome deaths reserved for outlaws, the hapless, and the hopeless, it was acknowledged that enormous power over others came with the risk of great harm to oneself. Nero's nightmares of being surrounded and trapped by statues of subject peoples of the world who had come to life (Suet. *Nero* 46, 1) are an extreme version of the association of fear with "bad" emperors that runs through ancient accounts of imperial power, a fear that was, according to ancient logic, the likely companion of an *oppressive* slave-master.[25]

Most of the more alienated reactions to Roman force and violence occur in the presence of soldiers, especially in the province of Judaea as depicted in Jewish and early Christian texts, where interactions with the Roman imperial power are typified by heavy-handed militarism. This is nicely illustrated by an episode in the Gospels of Mark and Luke where Jesus encounters a man possessed by a demon, and asks its name. The man replies, "My name is Legion: for we are many" (Mark 5:9; cf. Luke 8:30). At "Legion's" own request, this company of demons is sent into a huge herd of pigs that throw themselves into the sea and drown. The impact of a Roman army of occupation is obvious in this vivid Judaean nightmare. The Greek *Legeōn* only very slightly Grecizes the Latin noun *legiō*, and the demons' choice of pigs as the animal to possess is beautifully appropriate: unclean animals for the Jews, but the meat most readily associated with Roman citizen legionaries.[26]

Outside the peculiarly tense situation of Judaea, relationships between army units and local peoples have been characterized in recent decades along a spectrum that ranges from very considerable integration of

[25] Nightmares: Shaw 2003; school text: Dionisotti 1982, 104–5; status and punishment: Garnsey 1970 with, now, Lavan 2016; Nero: Edwards 2003; fear and the master-slave relationship: nicely complicated in McKeown 2007; cf., for imperial relationships, Lavan 2013.
[26] "My name is Legion": Fuhrmann 2012, 232; Latin as a register of power in the New Testament: Millar 1995; phenomenon of linguistic interference: Adams 2003, chapter 4.

soldiers within civilian life to the army as a "total institution," its members occupying a behavioral and psychological space wholly separate from that occupied by civilians. While there will of course have been different degrees of friction, integration and separation according to context and circumstances, soldiers' space in relation to that of civilians is perhaps most accurately generalized as reflecting and responding to an "institutional identity" or "occupational community" somewhere in the middle of the spectrum. Soldiers and civilians did, of course, interact, but the nature of that interaction tended to be conditioned both by the particular roles played by and expected of soldiers as enforcement agents of the Roman state and by broader self-identification by soldiers as a distinctive community.[27]

We can flesh out this characterization by beginning with what soldiers typically *did* beyond warfare. Individual soldiers and army units were, along with the governor and his immediate staff, by far the most readily identifiable agents of the Roman state, as well as being by far the biggest and best organized ready-made work force available empire-wide. In addition to deployment in warfare, they were employed in garrisons focused on surveillance, security, and any potentially volatile situation (how far their presence was in fact preventative and how far it exacerbated things is, of course, debatable). Military personnel attended governors as well as imperial procurators charged with the care of the emperor's properties. In the case of centurions, their role as enforcers within the military sphere can spill over into civilian concerns with security and public order as well as with everyday law and order (especially in less urbanized areas). Military units were also engaged in other direct interventions of the Roman state, such as the building of roads, aqueducts, bridges, and other infrastructures, including occasionally, perhaps, civic buildings (as in the remarkable case of Waldgirmes, discussed in Chapter 2, "Frontiers").[28]

In terms of the interrelated questions of where soldiers were and who they were in relation to local communities, there was inevitably a considerable degree of economic codependence between military and civilian communities, whether military units were stationed within or immediately outside preexisting towns, as they frequently were in the Near East, with

---

[27] Considerably integrated: Alston 1995; "total institution": Shaw 1983; "institutional identity": Pollard 2000, 78; "occupational community": Haynes 2013, 10–20; for self-identification as a community of soldiers, see e.g., Macmullen 1984; James 1999; Stoll 2001.

[28] Soldiers' tasks off the battlefield: Alston 1995; Goldsworthy and Haynes 1999; Pollard 2000; Adams 2007, 222–4; centurions: Millar 1981b; Alston 1995, 86–96; Fuhrmann 2012, 186–238.

its highly developed urban infrastructure (e.g., Dura Europus, Bosra, and Zeugma), or in purpose-built camps or stations (e.g., Vindolanda on Hadrian's Wall or Vindonissa in Switzerland). Army units relied heavily on modest-scale local production even for the basic supplies that were funded by the state, and soldiers regularly supplemented and customized these basic provisions. The presence of army units with considerable needs and desires could result both in exploitative requisitioning and in lucrative entrepreneurial activity that thrived in this unusually cash-rich environment, including long-distance trade (e.g., of wine, olives, and olive oil from Italy, Spain, and Greece to camps on Hadrian's Wall and in Switzerland), vendors and taverners, manufacturers and repairers, and sex workers. When military units were not stationed in cities, "camp village" communities typically clustered in the vicinity of camps or forts, inhabited by people who occupied the considerable gray zone between soldiers and civilians, including veterans who settled in the vicinity, contractors, traders and tradespeople, and the families of soldiers. Sometimes, these "camp villages" became so established that they formed the basis of future towns (e.g., Wroxeter and Exeter) or even colonies (e.g., Colonia Ulpia Traiana/ Xanten).[29]

The existence of these communities raises the difficult question of the extent to which the Roman army was an "inbred" organization or, at the other extreme, an agent of widespread *legal* integration (at least: this is one area in which the looseness of the term "Romanization" tends to assume that legal, social, and cultural integration are more or less interchangeable), since auxiliaries between the age of Claudius and 140 CE were granted Roman citizenship after twenty-five years of service, and their wives and children born during their service legally recognized. On the basis of studies of inscribed tombstones from North Africa, it has been argued that the percentage of soldiers born to military families peaked at around 34 percent in the second to third centuries CE for legionaries, with a presumably somewhat lower rate for auxiliaries. Such a percentage would fit with sustainability calculations based on both the size of the pool available and mortality rates for soldiers. The majority of soldiers were therefore recruited from outside military families, and we have only occasional glimpses of how such recruitment might have been organized. We also have very little means of establishing the typical ethnic and geographical mix of units, although we hear of both ethnically diverse

[29] Garnsey 1989, 246–8; Herz 2007; Kehne 2007; Rathbone and Alston 2007, 165–73.

auxiliary recruits sent to units and some "ethnic units" that consistently recruited from the same region.[30]

Walter Scheidel's close study of the status of the women whose established relationships with legionaries are attested by their memorialization of the dead men on tombstones offers some of the most illuminating insights into the nature of military communities and their interactions with others. The vast majority (about 90 percent) of the women attested have Roman names, suggesting that they were either Roman citizens or at least "hopefully Roman," presumably a social desideratum for a legionary's partner. Within this group, a high number seem to have been freedwomen of the soldiers. Soldiers forming partnerships with women who had been their property, together with increasing evidence for sex workers in the presence of army camps and forts, enhance the impression of soldiers being at one remove from the more integrative social fabric of local communities.[31]

The nature of the typical interface between soldiers and civilians conditions and limits local receptions of institutions and behaviors associated with the Roman state: we certainly should not view the army in traditional terms as an instrument of "Romanization," in the sense of a generally applicable model of civilization. Soldiers performed a very particular kind of engagement with the central Roman state, notably in their heavily meat-based diet (with considerable variation according to where they were based, and to some extent between legionaries and auxiliaries) and targeting Latin even in Egypt, where Greek was the predominant "imperial language" of the army. At the fort of Mons Claudianus in Egypt, the unit used Latin passwords written in Greek letters, such as "Phortouna," "Konkordia," and "Saloutis imperat(oris)": the mismatch between letters and language signals the effort of hitting the desired register. Their distinctiveness was visible also in their particular enthusiasm for baths and gladiatorial spectacle as well as in their clothing. The Roman army had no uniforms in the modern sense, and individual customization as well as regional variation played important roles, but in any particular time and

---

[30] "Inbreeding": Shaw 1983; marriage, children, legal status: Phang 2001; Haynes 2013, 57–8; 83–4; recruitment questions: Speidel 2007; Haynes 2013, 125–6.

[31] Scheidel 2007 for demography of legionaries' partners: cf., for prostitution: Cuvigny 2003, 374–98; Haensch 2012; for the phenomenon of hopeful Roman status in army contexts, cf. the assumption by non-citizen auxiliaries of Roman names, their unfamiliarity suggested by awkwardness around them, e.g. in spelling out praenomina in full: e.g. *P. Oxy.* 7, 1022 = *CPL* 3; Haensch 2012; Haynes 2013, 97–102.

place there was a broad consensus about what constituted appropriate army clothing and equipment.[32]

The story told by Mark and Luke of the demon named Legion works through the separateness of Roman soldiers from the modest Judaean protagonists with whom the Gospels are largely concerned. It can be compared with the story in Acts of the Apostles of the baptism of Cornelius, the centurion (10–11), a major test for the apostles in a text that narrates in multiple ways the passage of early Christianity from a Jewish sect to a potentially universal church. Other contexts offer different perspectives on the place of Roman military forces within local imaginations, including their allure and efficacy. From the second century CE, the Egyptian gods Horus (Figure 1), Bes, and Anubis, the originally Commagene god known after the annexation of Syria as Iuppiter Dolichenus, and various Palmyrene gods begin to appear wearing the Roman military uniform of an emperor or high-ranking officer. The efficacy of Roman power at its most forceful is drawn into the divine sphere in its local idiom. In another, particularly challenging case that we mentioned in Chapter 2, the Hatrenes, who lived on the Parthian/Sasanian side of the eastern frontier of the Roman empire and had a complicated relationship with both sides, worshipped the Roman legionary standard as a divinity named Samya, perhaps a transliteration into Aramaic of the Greek word for standard, *sēmeion*. This example vividly illustrates the fact that recognizing the might and efficacy of Roman force does not necessarily entail loyalty to Rome.[33]

## One Direction (Armed Forces)?

The Roman state did not, or at least did not routinely disarm its subjects, as some imperial powers have done, enacting their monopoly on violence in this most directly institutional of ways. Rather, it relied substantially on the forces of subjects, allies, and friends to keep the peace within their own communities and to contribute actively to the bigger project of imperial expansion and peacekeeping by supplying individual soldiers or even whole units and commanders. This heavy reliance raises important questions about the particular risks and benefits to Rome particularly in the

---

[32] Critique of army's role in "Romanization": Haynes 2013, 21–2 with bibliography; diet: King 1999; Haynes 2013, 181–3; language: Adams 2003, 393–6; baths: Pollard 1996, 52–3; Bidwell and Hodgson 2009; amphitheaters: Welch 2007, 27–8; 79–82; Coleman 2010, 664–5; dress: James 1999; Haynes 2013, chs. 15–16.

[33] Gods in Roman military armor: Kantorowicz 1961; Speidel 1978; Frankfurter 1998, 3–4; Stoll 2001, 187–7; Samya: Andrade 2013, 1–2 with bibliography.

potential division of loyalty. We might see insistence on loyalty rituals within the legionary and auxiliary units of the army, particularly the repeated oath of loyalty to the emperor, partly as a response to the risk associated with heterogeneity of origins and command. We might also see them as a response to the more general risk inherent in highly trained forces led nominally by the emperor, but interacting on an everyday basis with highly capable and sometimes very ambitious commanders and, just as importantly, with peers in tightly knit groups. As such, the army makes an excellent case-study of how (and how far) such imperial rituals were internalized, and how they were reproduced.[34]

Polybius' insistence on the homegrown nature of the Roman army in contrast to the mercenary forces on which the Carthaginians relied blurs the fact that the bulk of Rome's fighting forces in the late fourth to early first centuries BCE were raised through individual alliances with Italian peoples made during the middle Republican wars of conquest in the peninsula. These alliances were maintained through the annual provision of men according to a formula contained in the treaty, known in the late second century BCE as the *formula togatorum* (*CIL* $1^2$, 2, 585, ll. 21; 50 = Crawford 1996, 2), who served in their own units with their own commanders. Polybius was well aware of this arrangement (e.g., 6, 21, 4–5; 26; 34, 1–4), but was contributing to a "nativist" ideology of Italy and Italians that we see emerging elsewhere in the second century BCE, encouraged by the dynamics of Rome's increasingly "global" (in terms of the contemporary visual field) empire. Rome's gradual differentiation between the way it exercised imperial power overseas and in Italy, and the grassroots identification of international Italian traders as *Rhomaioi* can be seen as two very different symptoms of the same process.[35]

From the perspective of the Roman state, there were huge advantages in distracting large numbers of men of fighting age from banditry and other kinds of trouble-making in external wars. From the perspective of Italian peoples, things were more complicated. One traditional modern version of the causes of the Social War of 91–89 BCE points to the exploitation of allied military forces as "sacrifice troops" and allied communities more generally as economically disadvantaged by the same imperial processes that enriched Rome. There is, however, no evidence for allied troops being mobilized in more dangerous situations than the Roman legions, while

---

[34] Disarmament: Brunt 1975.
[35] Italy: Dench 2005, chapter 3; Harris 2007; Prag 2013; *Rhomaioi*: Hatzfeld 1919, 238–45, cf. Gabba 1973, esp. 239–45.

there is substantial evidence for the enrichment of individual Italians and Italian communities, particularly through trade with the eastern Mediterranean in the long second century. In addition, a recently discovered Oscan dedication in the name of Lucius Mummius, on a statue base in the Temple of Apollo at Pompeii, reading "l mummis l kusul" ("Lucius Mummius, son of Lucius, consul"), has been identified as one of a number of local dedications of the spoils of Corinth, clustering in Italy and the Greek world after the city was sacked in 146 BCE, suggesting direct gains for Italian communities from Roman imperial campaigns.[36]

More recent accounts have taken on board much more fully such evidence of distinct economic prosperity in the course of the long second century on the part of allies such as the Oscan-speaking peoples of central and southern Italy, not least through international business connections fostered and strengthened by Roman mastery of the Mediterranean. Coupled with this economic prosperity, we see a strong sense of self-direction and worth in, for example, the Pompeian dedication of spoils. Like other Italian examples, it is much more carefully executed than examples from the Greek world, and seems to be less orchestrated, perhaps reflecting a genuine acknowledgment on both sides of the contribution of Italian troops to Rome's overseas campaigns, as well as a distinctiveness reflected in the Oscan language. We can also see this sense of self-direction and worth in the slogan, "no victory without or against the Marsi" (Appian BC 1, 46, 203). If the Marsic tribe is recast as a military unit through participating in Rome's wars, there is a heavy hint of the potentially ambiguous loyalty of such a unit. Such loyalty was tested to its limits in the Social War, a war that, according to this interpretation, reflected exasperation at the gap between prosperity, self-direction, and worth on the one hand, and legal and imperial status vis-à-vis Rome on the other.[37]

The Romans did not systematically raise troops outside Italy in fulfillment of treaties: this is one of several ways in which their relationship with, and management of Italy begins to look very different from that with overseas peoples. Nevertheless, there is no hard and fast distinction between Roman behavior within and outside of Italy. The story of the unit of hired Campanians under the command of Decius told by ancient authors in the run up to the outbreak of the First Punic War in 264 BCE

---

[36] Italians units as "sacrifice troops": Salmon 1967, 307–10; Pompeian inscription: Martelli 2002; Pobjoy 2006, 55.

[37] Economic/cultural status versus legal status: Wallace-Hadrill 2008, 137; 143. Italian dedications compared with Greek counterparts: Yarrow 2006; Social War slogans: Dench 1995, 129.

illustrates the range of manpower arrangements available to Rome and the possible advantages of fuzziness around authority and initiative. The story is told in connection with the account of the Mamertini, Oscan-speaking former mercenaries of Agathocles, ruler of Syracuse, who had gone rogue after his death and occupied the Greek city of Messana at the extreme northeastern tip of Sicily. In doing so, they were apparently inspired by the example of Decius and the Campanians, who had initially been looking after Rhegium (at the tip of south Italy just across the straits of Messana) in the service of Rome, but who had allegedly taken it upon themselves to occupy the city. The Romans had responded, but belatedly, by having the unit, along with its leader, beheaded, making for considerable embarrassment when the Mamertini, beleaguered in Messana by Hiero of Syracuse, appealed to Rome for help on the grounds of kinship (Polyb. 1, 6, 8–10; cf. DH *Ant. Rom.* 15, 5). These complicated stories locate Roman practices within international practices and geopolitics, and eloquently depict the fuzzy distinction between protectors, friends and occupiers, and the fragile control of states over bands, sometimes to the advantage of the hiring state, and sometimes not. Ancient traditions on the Mamertini suggest that their identity as a group was experienced as ethnogenesis, complete with a foundation myth that interweaves Greek and central Italian motifs (Festus 105 L.). These issues of self-determination recur in the history of "Roman" forces through to the fall of the western empire.[38]

In the course of Rome's Republican expansion, there is some evidence for the ad hoc raising of local troops, notably in mountain areas of Spain, a transitional stage of overseas imperial management that addresses the problem of controlling difficult populations while extracting much-needed human resources. There is also growing evidence for encouraging or allowing local communities to maintain their own militias. In Sicily, local garrisons, including a substantial force two hundred strong at Eryx, provided security that worked in the interests of Rome as well as those of the individual communities. The self-aggrandizement of at least one of the unit officers, technically subordinate to a Roman quaestor but referring to himself as a *chiliarchos* and suppressing any mention of his subordination, underlines the desirable fuzziness of authority on a day to day basis.[39]

---

[38] South Italy: Purcell 1994; ethnogenesis of the Mamertini: Dench 1995, 55–6; 185–6; 211–12; Crawford 2007.
[39] Spain: Vervaet and Ñaco del Hoyo 2007; Sicily: Prag 2007; *chiliarchos*: IG 14, 355, 55–6 cf. Mommsen's comment at *CIL* 10, 7258, with Prag 2007, 84.

From around the end of the second century BCE, regular use was made of specialist troops recruited at least initially from particular regions: the early recruitment of light-armed divisions of Ligurians and Thracians looks forward to the more extensive Roman use of foreign cavalry units, Balearic slingers, Cretan archers, and other auxiliary divisions from the late Republic. There is intriguing evidence for the recruitment of ready-made local forces: local nobles' raiding bands on horseback, royal armies, or other local militias. While we should not imagine the composition of auxiliary units over time in overly rigid ethnic terms, there were considerable benefits in continuing and fostering social bonds and hierarchies, and considerable dangers in disrupting them. The Batavian revolt of 69 CE under Vitellius was sparked off by a mishandled draft that encouraged suspicions of sexual abuse. The speech attributed by Tacitus to C. Iulius Civilis, leader of the revolt, condemns the undermining of the social fabric of local society and, not insignificantly, the delegation of the draft to subordinate Roman officials (*Hist.* 4, 14).[40]

The Roman army (including citizen legionaries as well as non-citizen auxiliaries) was the body most subject to state-level intervention not least at the level of its ritual life and, especially if we interpret the Dura Europus calendar as something *issued*, specifically religious observances. The effects are not always what we might expect, especially the further we zoom in. The religious life of soldiers, especially as performed in private dedications, reveals a great deal about the ways in which institutions and behaviors were internalized or transposed, as well as about social and geographical horizons and affinities. Despite any expectation that we may have of military units and individual soldiers tending to reproduce and maintain a religious community closely associated with the Roman state, soldiers prove to be little different from other groups in the Roman empire in their tendency to carve out and foster a living and evolving kind of peoplehood through their religious worship. One of the most striking examples of this is the regional cult of the *Matronae*, the "Mothers" adopted by the soldiers of Legio I Minervia at Bonn, and carried along the Rhine by them. More tantalizing still is evidence for reinterpretation of rituals closely associated with the particular varieties of "imperial cult" in which soldiers' lives were particularly immersed. Veterans in Syria made a dedication to the "genius of the oath," as if forgetting that the oath was tied to the person of the emperor rather than being a self-standing entity with a *genius* of its own. A graffito

---

[40] Haynes 2013 for auxiliaries, esp. chs. 8, 9 and 10 for caution about "ethnic soldiers" and 109–19 for the advantages of co-opting ready-made armed units.

scribbled by a Dacian auxiliary cavalryman called Dida at Al-Muwayh in Egypt celebrating five months in arms at the station garbles and personalizes the dedication "pro salute imperatoris" ("for the well-being of the emperor") as "pro salutem imperatore feliciter" ("for the well being of the emperor, yay!"). The soldiers' oath and the most basic formulas associated with the "imperial cult" could be experienced not so much as part of a world-wide matrix of rituals expressing loyalty to the emperor, but rather as detachable ends in themselves.[41]

Ancient commentators reflected deeply on the risks and benefits to a ruling state or individual associated with arming and not arming different constituencies. When Dio, in the dialogue he crafts between Agrippa and Maecenas at the foundation of the Augustan principate, attributes to "Maecenas" a penetrating vision of the hard realities of power, he reveals the benefit of keeping the most vigorous and capable men of empire occupied in warfare on behalf of the Roman state. In addition to bringing Rome the obvious advantages of mobilizing energetic soldiers, it prevents them from turning to banditry (52, 27, 5), a powerful reminder of the much broader ecology of violence within the Roman imperial space, with banditry arguably both the antithesis of state-sponsored violence and at the same time the mirror of state-sponsored violence and a co-dependent of the imperial state.[42]

The insight that Dio offers on disarming senators (an overly literal interpretation of Augustus' reservation of militarized provinces for himself, since of course he was reliant on senatorial legates), on the other hand, is that it makes them less effective rebels (53, 12, 3). This is an obvious echo of Thucydides' analysis of the Athenians' allies' self-enslavement when they resolve to send money rather than manning ships (1, 99). Empire by "enslavement" of the variety that Thucydides attributes to the Athenian empire might, according to this analysis, have avoided the particular risks of going it alone that Rome experienced in the case of former allies and friends: the Social War, the Batavian revolt, and the Palmyrene "empire." On the other hand, "enslavement," or at least loss of liberty, was precisely invoked as a cause of both the Social War and the Batavian revolt, underlining the importance of maintaining a sense of self-direction in this delicate balance of affairs. More positively, we see Polybius' attribution of

---

[41] Matronae: Haensch 2001; army and religion in general: Stoll 2001; 2007; Haensch 2012; *genius* of the oath: *AE* 1924, 135 with Haynes 2013, 220–2; Dida's graffito: *AE* 1996, 1647 with Stoll 2001, 220, Haynes 2013, 216–17.

[42] Banditry: Shaw 1984.

greater self-motivation for those ("Romans") fighting for their own children and homeland, who can never stint their anger, and stay heart and soul in the battle, in contrast to the Carthaginian mercenaries (6, 52, 7). We might extend this "backs against the wall" self-motivation to a more everyday self-determination reflected in the examples we have seen of self-aggrandizement, group reinforcement through the imperial experience, and distinctly idiosyncratic articulation of efficacious rituals and formulas, all of which arguably contribute to the dynamism of warfare and enforcement in the Roman empire.[43]

## One Direction (Civilian Spheres)?

The messages of force and violence that enforced and underlay Roman imperial rule were heard loudly and clearly. At times, they were reproduced faithfully, with local communities identifying themselves as loyal imperial insiders, as we saw in the locally sponsored and built triumphal monuments of Narbonese Gaul. Elsewhere, the efficacy and impressiveness of Roman cultures of force and violence were claimed even more obviously for the local subject, as in the monument to C. Cartilius Poplicola in Ostia (Figure 3) that we discussed in Chapter 1, "Reproducing Roman Power," its eight pairs of axeless *fasces* going as far as anyone dared in asserting the Augustus-like exceptionalism of a local magistrate.

In other cases, distinctive Roman cultures of force can seem to have seeped into local consciousness so far that they are reinterpreted in new and sometimes surprising ways. The Latin name of the goddess Victoria began to make inroads on Macedonian Nikē in Rome and its imperial contexts from the third century BCE, and was loaned into the local Italian languages of Rome's allies. In one striking example, she appears as the subject of a private dedication in Oscan, "Vikturrai" ("to Victoria") in the late second-century BCE Samnite temple at Pietrabbondante, a tantalizing hint of the potential local significance of drawing down the imperial efficacy of the Roman Victoria. Centuries later, Mars and Victoria are, for obvious reasons, much represented deities in military contexts in the frontier province of Roman Germany, but they are also regularly represented in civilian contexts. Both deities appear on the second-century CE Obernburg tombstone of a local couple with non-Roman names, Girisonius and

---

[43] Cf. modern analyses of the sapping conditions of slavery and profoundly unequal societies: esp. Scott 1985, 29 for "foot dragging, dissimulation, false compliance, pilfering, feigned ignorance, slander, arson, sabotage, and so forth."

Bibulla, who are shown enjoying a feast. The fact that Girisonius is portrayed wearing a toga suggests that the couple's feast is self-consciously Roman-style, presumably to convey its elegance and fanciness. Mars and Victoria appear on the sides of the stele, holding inscribed shields. The surviving part of Victoria's shield reads, "mem[oriam] pietat[e]," presumably "a memorial through piety." We might interpret Girisonius and Bibulla's monument as appropriating the essence of Victoria's power and efficacy, perhaps above all her association with specifically Roman power, but harnessing it to the preservation of individual memory.[44]

As we observed at the beginning of this chapter, the tone of conversations that constitute much of the government of the early Empire is generally polite with an emphasis on positive outcomes. The emperor is modeled as one who should correct the behavior of subordinates, and one whose beneficence is expected and hoped for. Any hint of enforcement is the exception, so that the emperor's Claudius' exasperated "or else" in his response to the Alexandrians in 41 CE is deeply unsettling amidst an upbeat norm. Subjects used to the formulas of imperial beneficence and omnipotence capably picked them up and used them within their own rhetoric, as they addressed emperor or governor in their petitions. In the early second-century CE province of Arabia, Babatha insisted that she lived in the "most blessed times of the governorship of Iulius Iulianus' when she complained that her son's guardians had spent too stingy a proportion of the interest on his assets on his upkeep (*P. Yadin* 15, ll. 10–11; ll. 26–7). As is the case in grander imperial panegyric, the continued blessedness of the times is silently dependent on the successful outcome of her complaint. Real-life Roman imperial actors and audiences were skilled in the subtleties of hearing and speaking "doublespeak." Certainly, Babatha's "dossier" suggests an individual very willing to try to use to her advantage the Roman governor's judicial capacities, as well as any other means available to her. Their find-spot, however, in the "Cave of the Letters" in the Judaean desert, with more than twenty skeletons nearby, should prevent us from getting too carried away in an optimistic reading of imperial empowerment: it is a reasonable assumption that Babatha herself was ultimately caught up with fatal consequences in the "or else" of Roman government around Masada.[45]

---

[44] Pietrabbondante: Poccetti 1979, 16; Nike/Victoria: Hölscher 1967; Samnite *Vikturrai*: Prosdocimi 1989, 529; Stek 2013, 346; German Victoria: Kousser 2006.

[45] Imperial blessings: Nutton 1978; "doublespeak" in literary contexts: Bartsch 1994; Babatha: Lewis, Yadin, Greenfield, Yardeni, Levine 1989; Yadin, Greenfield, Yardeni, Levine 2002; Bowersock 1991; Goodman 1991; Isaac 1992.

The Thracian villagers of Skaptopara who petitioned the young Emperor Gordian III in 238 CE laid out their "or else" clause explicitly, when they sought a solution to their complaints of harassment by soldiers from two army camps nearby, as well as by governors and procurators taking advantage of hot springs in the vicinity. In bringing their complaints to the emperor, the villagers remind him of his own formulaic wishes, that the villages should "in your most happy and everlasting times ... be inhabited and prosper" (ll. 11–13 tr. Hauken 1998, cf. ll. 100–1), as "you have on many occasions stated in your rescripts" (ll. 14–15, tr. Hauken 1998). The villagers emphasize their abject condition, suitable recipients of the emperor's beneficence, but the petition also contains the unmistakable threat that they will abandon their village and cease to pay the taxes that have helped to sustain the present, blessed imperial state (ll. 91–9 cf. ll. 15–17). There is a nicely ironic play here on the "tit for tat" imperial line that local taxes funded the security provided by Roman troops, but there is also perhaps just a hint of something more menacing between the lines. In part, the villagers' response might evoke the general, and realistic fear of what might happen when people abandoned or were shut out of the structures of society: they might become bandits (or "terrorists," if we want to be less quaint and evoke in our own terms the threat of the excluded turning on "us"). More specifically, Gordian III's grandfather and father, Gordian I and Gordian II, had come to short-lived power earlier that year during a tax rebellion against Maximinus Thrax (*SHA Gord. Tres* 7, 2–4). Contemporaries were well aware of the incendiary potential around the payment of taxes.[46]

For all this, both the rarity of such "or else" clauses and the mildness of the threat are indications of the preciousness and the perilousness of the currency of violence in the Roman Empire, especially from the subjects' perspective. The villagers muster their strength in numbers and cohesion in an almost *polis*-like collective appeal, although they are significantly reliant on Aurelius Purrus (sic), soldier of the tenth praetorian cohort named "Pia Fidelis Gordiana," and fellow-villager, as their advocate. They use all the bargaining power available to them, for which there are considerably more channels available than the passive aggression of the "weapons of the weak" in other, more recent societies. At the same time, they are surely also acutely aware of their vulnerability to imperial enforcement. The constraints of the villagers' empowerment are invisible, but

---

[46] Skaptopara petition: *IGBulg* 659; *AE* 1994, 1552; Hauken 1998, 5; Ando 2007a, 374–5. Ironies of "blessings" discourse: Fuhrmann 2012, 168.

might be compared with the situation in the micro-society of the Roman arena, with the audience of largely humble individuals empowered collectively to affect life and death decisions or make demands on an emperor or express discontent openly. This empowerment, however, is both temporary and conditional, constrained by the very architecture of spectacle buildings, "a giant trap for the unruly," in the words of Kathleen Coleman.[47]

In an empire that ran so effectively on the potential to enforce its will, with occasional spectacular displays of violence and enough small, everyday incidents of lowly officials throwing their weight about to make that potential very real, just a whisper of a threat was normally enough to correct aberrant action. In such a climate, the most powerful weapon of all was defiance, which is perhaps one reason why set speeches of Roman enemies were so prominent in imperial historiography, and why the figure of the violently anti-establishment pirate/bandit was such an intoxicating literary type. Most challenging of all was defiance in the face of death and punishment. This included the voluntary suicides of prominent Roman individuals that signaled the intolerable tyranny of emperors who were profligate with the economy of violence. But most spectacular of all were martyrdom traditions that made heroes of the victims of public executions staged to humiliate and discourage in horribly creative ways, always referring back to the crucifixion of Jesus, the punishment of a common criminal. Perpetua, facing her death in the arena, even dreams of being transformed into a naked man pitched in part athletic, part gladiatorial combat against a diabolical "Egyptian" (10, 6–7), as punishment becomes conquest and death victory.[48]

---

[47] Typically distant dealings of villagers with the emperor or governor: Mitchell 1999; "weapons of the weak": Scott 1985; empowerment of the arena: Hopkins 1983, 1–30; Wiedemann 1992, 160–70; Fagan 2011, chapter 4; "giant trap": Coleman 2010, 662.

[48] Speeches of Roman enemies: Adler 2011; literary pirates/bandits: Winkler 1980; Shaw 2004; suicide: Edwards 2007, 113–43; creativity and humiliation of public executions: Coleman 1990; Perpetua: Robert 1982; Shaw 1993; Perkins 1995, 104–23.

# CHAPTER 5

# *Time*

## Roman Days

[F]or this reason, with good luck and for (our) salvation, it has been
decreed by the Greeks in Asia that the New Year's first month shall
begin for all the cities on the ninth day before the Kalends of
October, which is the birthday of Augustus; in order that each time
the day might correspond in each city, (the Greeks) shall use the
Greek day along with the Roman; they shall make the first month –
(called) "Caesar," as previously decreed – begin with the ninth day
before the Kalends of October, the birthday of Caesar.

Laffi 1967 VI, 49–56 tr. Sherk 1984, 101

Probably in 8 BCE, the *koinon* (provincial council) of Asia, acting on the
initiative of the Roman proconsul, P. Fabius Maximus, decreed that the
province would henceforth celebrate its New Year's Day on Augustus'
birthday, our September 23. We know about this from fragments of
multiple copies of a dossier of documents relating to the change, including
the proconsul's decree and two decrees of the *koinon*. P. Fabius Maximus
was the winner of a competition established by the *koinon*, on the suggestion of an earlier proconsul, L. Volcacius Tullus, to propose a means of
honoring Augustus. He claimed that this new New Year's Day was
particularly fortuitous, as it corresponded more or less to the day on which
magistrates entered office in the various *poleis* of the province. The point is
clearly being pushed here to create a sense of a continuum of local past and
present centered on Rome, one example of the characteristic fusions and
juxtapositions of Roman imperial culture. Great care was taken to publi-
cize this change, and to aim for synchronicity across the province. The
proconsul's letter, a delicately calibrated mixture of deference to the
magnificence of Augustus' achievement, regard for local specificity, and
instruction mode, ends with the "suggestion" that the *koinon* should pass a
decree approving the change, and that he will issue orders that the decree

be inscribed and set up on a stele in the temple of Roma and Augustus in Pergamum, with his own edict "in both languages."

As the wording of the extract quoted above demonstrates, this innovation was an explicit engagement with the "Roman" calendar of the metropolis. The first decree of the *koinon* carefully details the change from the Macedonian lunar calendar to the Julian solar calendar, borrowing into the Greek text the untranslatable Latin vocabulary of "intercalation" and "kalends," signaling the socio-specific timekeeping of the Roman center. The calendar of Asia would start its year in the renamed, honorific month "Kaisar," followed by a list of traditional, Macedonian names – Apellaios, Audnaios, Peritios, Dystros, and so on – the beginning of each month recomputed with reference to the Roman kalends. These elaborate changes generated a second decree of the *koinon*, hinting at the problems experienced by individual *poleis* in coordinating their magistrates' entry to office on this new New Year's Day, and detailing a schedule for elections to ensure that everything happened on time. The designation of "Roman" days with which the reckoning of days familiar to the "Greeks" of the Asian *koinon* is to be aligned highlights both the concern to reproduce metropolitan practices and the distance between "us" and "Roman." In Roman Italy, enormous energy had similarly been expended on the calendar between the dictatorship of Caesar and the early principate as a locus of contemporary identity in both its technical brilliance and its continuation and recreation of a quintessentially Roman past and annual rhythm. But in Rome, of course, in contrast to the magistracies of Asia, consulships had since 153 BCE been taken up on the New Year's Day that is still commemorated in our own calendars, January 1.[1]

The complex correspondence of "Greek" with "Roman" days and the delicate balance between the authority of the proconsul and that of the *koinon* articulated in the dossier anticipate the central questions of this chapter: how modes of timekeeping configure the relationship between local peoplehood and the Roman state, creating distance or identity between "us" and "them"; the degree to which modes of timekeeping distinctive to the Roman state or centered on the Roman monarchy are either naturalized within local idioms or maintain their foreign presence; and the plurality of such "Roman" modes of timekeeping.

---

[1] Dossier: Laffi 1967 with Dreyer and Engelmann 2006, 175–82 for a new fragment from Metropolis; 8 BCE: Stern, 2012, 275–6.

## Imperial Interventions

The Near Eastern and Mediterranean empires that belonged to the broad imperial tradition in which Rome emerged did not micromanage the temporal sphere of their subjects in the manner of certain other imperial powers, such as the Qing dynasty from the seventeenth to the early twentieth century, which circulated each year more than two million copies of an official, centralized calendar translated into local languages, threatening anyone who made unofficial copies with decapitation. Nor should we expect the degree of synchronization encouraged both by colonial powers and by local internalization of the scientific coordination of time as a modernist ideal in the industrial age. But ancient Near Eastern and Mediterranean empires did purposefully disrupt and reconfigure local time, superimposing rhythms of their own. This was enacted via demands for regularized, coordinated "gifts," tribute, or levies, and by reckonings and reviews of the people that might be associated with these demands, but could also be regularly independent of them. It was also enacted in imperial festivals, in making the king's body a walking calendar linking disparate centers of empire by his stylized processions, and in assertions of official, imperial state means of reckoning months and days and counting years (by regnal years or, in the case of the Seleucids, by a single era). These temporal disruptions and impositions regularly have an impact on consciousness that goes beyond the immediate interaction between imperial power and constituents. One observable outcome is that imperial methods of time-reckoning lose their sociopolitical specificity and become *the* official and efficient way of doing things. For example, in the *koinon* of Asia dossier discussed at the beginning of this chapter, Macedonian months, a legacy of Seleucid rule, have become blandly "Greek" at the interface with the new "Roman" system.[2]

The Romans excelled at such received methods of mastering time, and went beyond them. Occasional spectacular acts of twinning destructions or foundations in a single consular year would commemorate the reach of Roman imperial power in time as well as space, embedding themselves in local consciousness by creating major turning points in local civic histories. The fates of Carthage and Corinth, both destroyed in 146 BCE, advertised

---

[2] Qing calendar: Smith 1991, 74–83; modern synchronization and coordination of time: Gell 1992, 306–13; Ogle 2015; Near Eastern and Mediterranean empires: Samuel 1972, 245–6; Smarczyk 1990; Sherwin-White and Kuhrt 1993, 130–1; Briant 2002, 186–95; Clarysse and Thompson 2006, vol. 2, 10–12; 18–20; Kosmin 2014, 142–80; 2018.

the stark bottom line of Roman *imperium* as power to exact obedience in the two distinct geographical spheres traditionally available for imperial ambition, their twinned status only emphasized by Caesar's refoundations exactly a century later. Ultimately, Julius Caesar, in his major calendar reform of 45 BCE co-opted "alien wisdom" from Egypt in the person of Sosigenes, an Alexandrian Greek expert (Pliny *NH* 18, 211). Through the reform, he mastered time itself, creating a 365-day year that was aligned with the solar year and required only a single, intercalated leap-year day in place of an entire intercalated month on an *ad hoc* basis, a regularization that, with a small Augustan tweak in 8 BCE, rendered the future predictable in an unprecedented way. Within two generations, the empire-wide shift to the solar calendar was so marked that exceptions seem very deliberate, somewhere between distinct preference for an alternative and resistance. Stern would place Athens, the Roman province of Macedonia, and Odessus in Moesia Inferior in the first category, and the Jewish and Gallic (Coligny) calendars (which we will discuss later in the chapter) in the second.[3]

According to Greek and Roman ethnographical thought, time-reckoning and temporal rhythms are one recurrent feature of the *nomoi, nomima,* or *mores* ("customs") that delineate and characterize peoplehood: Herodotus' Egyptians celebrate festivals not just once a year but very often (2, 59), and Caesar's Gauls reckon time by nights rather than days (*BG* 6, 17). Within this discourse, *nomoi, nomima,* or *mores* will very occasionally be changed by direct imperial intervention, especially if they run counter to the security interests of the imperial power, so that Croesus entreats Cyrus to tame his Lydians from rebelliousness by making them a nation of lyre- and harp-players and shopkeepers rather than warriors (Herod. 1, 155), and Tacitus' Agricola infamously settles down the Britons by encouraging them to turn their energies away from their bellicose tendencies and toward rhetoric competitions and building zeal (*Agr.* 21). In fact, the intervention of Tacitus' Agricola is calculating but indirect, a psychological ruse that disguises the reality of power relations, the enslavement of Britons through pleasures. Change is more frequently imagined as loosely accompanying contact rather than instigated directly by imperial powers. Obliterating the *nomoi, nomima,* or *mores* characteristic of peoplehood is

---

[3] Corinth and Carthage: Purcell 1995. 138–9; Julius Caesar's calendrical reforms: Feeney 2007, 196–201; avoidance of solar calendar: Stern 2012, chapter 6. There are now serious doubts about the earlier theory of Augustus' construction of a monumental time complex revolving around his own person, a huge sundial in the Campus Martius with an obelisk as pointer that cast its shadow on the Ara Pacis on his birthday: Heslin 2007 should be read against Buchner 1982.

not something that Near Eastern and Mediterranean imperial powers traditionally set out to do: for the Achaemenid empire, the most important imperial model before Rome, the mastery of peoples variegated by cultural traits was a crucial aspect of the self-image that it promoted.[4]

The Roman empire also maintains and sponsors peoplehood, but we should ask whether its active reconfiguration or constitution of peoples, by settlements, such as L. Aemilius Paullus' of Macedonia in 167 BCE, giving laws, provincial *formulae*, or charters, has consequences for modes of timekeeping. The increasingly homogeneous calendar of the *koinon* of Thessaly, closest to the calendar of the city of Larisa, a favored political and cult center of the League, raises questions about Roman intervention when the Thessalian League was reorganized and constituted as part of T. Quinctius Flamininus' settlement of 196 after the Second Macedonian War. But this comparative homogenization was a long and uneven process, making direct Roman intervention unlikely.

A clause in the much later, Caesarian charter of the Roman citizen colony of Urso (founded in 44 BCE), in which decisions about the festival calendar are specifically delegated to Urso's magistrates (Crawford 1996, 25, 64), might add further weight to the argument against direct Roman intervention and hint at a more general theory of the division of responsibilities. In the case of the *koinon* of Thessaly, formal and informal Roman encouragement of the prominence of Larisa might well have helped to enhance the prestige of her calendar among fellow league members, but that is a rather different proposition from direct Roman intervention in the calendar. The Flavian Tabula Irnitana, conferring Latin status on the Baetican town of Irni in the very different sociopolitical landscape of the later first century CE, contains a clause on the absolute avoidance of juridical business on a day "which it is appropriate to have or regard as a feast-day or in the category of festivals because of the worship of the Imperial house" (92, tr. Crawford, González and Crawford 1986), with the threat of invalidating action if such a holiday is not observed. Even if the calendar has taken on a rather different politics of loyalty, dominated by imperial festivals, infringements are policed by and punished within the community.[5]

The single probable example of direct imposition of the city of Rome calendar beyond the city of Rome is the so-called *Feriale Duranum*, a festival calendar found on papyrus in Dura Europus on the border between

---

[4] Achaemenid empire: Kuhrt 2002.
[5] Thessaly: Graninger 2011, chapter 3; Urso and Irni: Rüpke 2006b; 2008.

the Roman and Sassanian empires dating to ca. 224–35 CE, probably belonging to an auxiliary unit of the Roman army stationed there, the *Cohors xx Palmyrenorum*. The calendar reproduces city of Rome festivals with some minor curation: the Magna Mater festival is omitted, for example, and some additions pertaining particularly to the army (a festival for honorable discharge in January and a Rose Festival of the standards in May) have apparently been made. The calendar suggests a studied and particular kind of Roman state identity performance that contrasts markedly with the vibrant cultural and religious life of the Palmyrene unit that we observe in other contexts, such as inscriptions and graffiti in the Palmyrene dialect of Aramaic and participation in Palmyrene cults. If the Roman state calendar was indeed extended to the army as a whole, this measure can perhaps be understood as part of the Augustan introduction of fixed and graded terms of service and discharge, creating a professional, standing army. In this case, the lightly curated Roman state calendar figures the army as a direct franchise of the Roman state, a unique position within the Roman Empire.[6]

## The Impact of Roman Time

If, as we have seen, direct Roman intervention in local modes of time-keeping is very rare, there is a large gray area that might count as indirect intervention. Tacitus' particular version in *Agricola* 21 of the sorts of ancient parables told about imperial behavior and experience acknowledges this gray area, grasping at the psychological complexity of imperial relationships, including the role of the governor with his own baggage of norms, obligations and desires, and everything that is projected onto him within the operation of "soft" imperial power. The heavy presence of the two Roman governors in the dossier of the Asian *koinon*, with the past governor establishing the competition, the present governor winning it, and the whole affair focused on honoring Augustus rather than changing local norms, is an excellent real-life example of this dynamic.

The character of Roman imperial structures only compounds this fuzziness. In a few cases, such as the census, imperial structures are detachable from local governance with reasonable clarity, but they are more often embedded within local structures, as is generally the case with taxation, or available as one possible option alongside others, such as the

---

[6] *Feriale Duranum*: Fink, Hoey and Snyder 1940; Koßmann 2008; Rüpke 2011, 120; horizons of the Palmyrene unit in Dura Europus: Millar 1993, 448–52; Pollard 2000.

governor's assizes as a venue for legal disputes. In addition, from the early
first century BCE, in anticipation of the "impact of monarchy" proper after
Actium, Roman governance articulated in terms of state Roman institutions increasingly co-exists with the virtual embodiment of the Roman
state by individual dynasts. This progression is neatly illustrated by the
broad trajectory of the Roman "imperial cult" in the Greek-speaking east:
abstractions of Roma and the senate are overshadowed and eventually
eclipsed by individuals commemorated in festivals even before the formal
divinization of Julius Caesar. The everyday confusion that this produced
on many levels about the reach and authority of the Roman state is
beautifully illustrated both by Pliny the Younger's question to Trajan
about the applicability of Roman pontifical law in Bithynia-Pontus *and*
the emperor's response as Pontifex Maximus, a one-man authority on the
issue, advizing Pliny to make judgments, like his predecessors, on a case-
by-case basis (Pliny *Letters* 10, 68–9).[7]

   In view of this range of articulations of Roman authority, it is helpful to
imagine local engagement with modes of marking time associated with the
Roman center on a sliding scale. At one end of such a scale, we would find
modes of marking time that are tied most tightly to the specificity of the
Roman *res publica* and the topography of the city of Rome, notably the
Roman state calendar, at first sight the least translatable and movable of
institutions. The most basic example that survives from the mid-first
century BCE, the Fasti Antiates Maiores from the Roman colony of
Antium, designate the rhythm of days for business, political, and legal
activity, interspersed with different categories of holidays and other days
on which specified kinds of business are to be avoided. The calendar forms
a highly distinctive and heavily encoded pattern, with its days annotated
with obtuse abbreviations and tersely tagged as foundation anniversaries of
specific, city of Rome temples. At the other end of such a scale, we would
find modes of marking time that are most obviously translated or translatable into local terms of understanding and belief, the furthest removed
from the specificity of Roman state and Roman topography. The most
obvious example of this is what we might think of as "Caesar time" and its
antecedents: counting by the emperor's regnal years, eras initiated by
specific acts of Roman liberation or provincial eras. At various points in
the middle, we might place consular dating or dating by the emperor's
office, especially the *tribunicia potestas*, reckoning systems that are imbued
with Roman institutional insistence on annual office, but that are

----

[7] "Impact of monarchy": Millar 1984; imperial cult: Mellor 1975; Price 1984; Mileta 2008.

somewhat more detachable from the specific topography and frameworks of the city of Rome. As we shall see, a dating system's place on the scale does not determine the degree of impact as we might expect, with the most movable and translatable modes having the greatest impact: if anything, the reverse is true.[8]

The Roman calendar had been the focus of veneration and self-conscious reflection on socio-specific traditions since at least the second century BCE. The calendrical *fasti* had first been monumentalized in the 180s in M. Fulvius Nobilior's temple of Hercules Musarum ("Hercules of the Muses"), probably paired with consular *fasti*, a list of eponymous consuls that might have been inspired by the lists of eponymous magistrates, priests, and honored citizens that were a familiar aspect of the landscape of the Greek *polis*. These early second-century BCE calendrical *fasti* were probably the first to include temple foundation dates and anniversaries, inscribing within them the topography and history of Rome, and particularly her imperial character, since these temples were dedicated by generals successful in her wars of expansion. If these early calendrical *fasti* were indeed paired with consular *fasti* (an argument made on the grounds that such pairings are familiar in later examples, including the *Fasti Antiates*), the monument juxtaposed the rhythm and meaning of days with the organization of the past and its implicit relationship to the present and the future. Between Caesar's calendrical reform and the early principate, the calendar was increasingly dominated by festivals commemorating significant events relating to the emperor and his family. An Augustan monument at the eastern end of the Forum included consular *fasti* (the so-called *Fasti Capitolini*) from the beginning of the Republic down to 13 CE, but with notable additions that include a countdown from Romulus' foundation of the city of Rome and, at the end of the document, the years of Augustus' holding of *tribunicia potestas*, as well as, ultimately, those of Tiberius' holding of the same power. It paired these with triumphal *fasti* that further intertwined monarchy with the traditional institutions of the *res publica*, blurring the line between Republic and monarchy by starting with the triumph of the first king, Romulus, and ending in 19 BCE, suggesting the end of that particular history.[9]

---

[8] *Fasti Maiores Antiates*: Degrassi 1963, 1; Feeney 2007, 184–5; Rüpke 2011, 6–8.
[9] The calendar and Roman identity: Beard 1987; Laurence and Smith 1995–1996; M. Fulvius Nobilior: Gildenhard 2003; Rüpke 2011, 87–108; Feeney 2007, 169–70; Greek lists: Hedrick 2006, chapter 3; Battistoni 2011, esp. 176–7; Augustan monument: Wallace-Hadrill 1987; Feeney 2007, 172–89.

At first sight surprisingly, monumental calendar complexes that closely mirrored the city of Rome format in all its bewildering specificity were extremely popular for a few decades between the late first century BCE and the early first century CE. Fragments of some fifty examples survive, their provenances ranging from Brixia in Transpadane Italy to Tauromenium in eastern Sicily, an Augustan colony, but the vast majority cluster in Rome and neighboring parts of central Italy. Rüpke has highlighted the "uselessness" in practical terms of such calendars outside the city of Rome. In only rare examples are local practices or resonances even visible. The *Fasti* of the originally Latin city of Praeneste were embellished with an extensive commentary by Verrius Flaccus, tutor to Augustus' grandsons, and a two-day public festival for the internationally renowned (and architecturally magnificent) Praenestine temple and oracular center of Fortuna Primigenia was added to the otherwise strictly city of Rome roster of festivals. Tauromenium's localism is manifested in a rather different way in her Roman calendar: the ancestrally Greek community's mode of reckoning and naming of months maintains a shadowy presence in the Latin and otherwise wholly city-of-Rome rubric.[10]

In certain other cases, the consular list that is often twinned with the calendar invites a local response in the form of a mirroring list of the community's own officials. For example, the monument of the *vicomagistri*, sub-elite para-magistrates of a ward of the city of Rome, inscribes the first six months of calendrical *fasti* above consular *fasti* from 43 BCE (the date of Augustus' first consulship) on one side, and, on the other side, the second six months above a list of the four annual officials of this ward, beginning in 7 BCE when they were put in charge of the *Lares Augusti* by Augustus. In the monument set up by the *collegium* of the imperial household of Antium, the concept of officialdom has been interpreted even more comprehensively than it had been in the case of the *vicomagistri*, giving the names and job titles of the slave officials each year after the names of the consuls of Rome. When the Roman calendrical *fasti* were simply reproduced or embellished with a local flourish, and when the consular *fasti* were juxtaposed with a local list of officials, or consular names alternated with those of local officials, the essential authenticity of the Roman format and its accurate reproduction are the point, not

[10] Degrassi 1963, nos. 17; 60; Rüpke 2008, 23; 2011, esp. 139; 141; cf. Coarelli 1987, 35–84 for Fortuna Primigenia. The comparative geographical and juridical restrictiveness of monumental calendar finds (Taormina, the only non-Italian example, was a Roman calendar) may say something about an internalized perception of what is within reach, cf. the restriction of "double documents" that reproduce or imitate Roman official forms to the "hopefully Roman": Meyer 2004, 187–91.

unlike the local reproductions of selected details of the Forum Augustum. The local community pays homage to the sanctified, quintessentially Roman tradition and at the same time harnesses the power and prestige that come with it to their own group and its hierarchies.[11]

It was also possible for the form of either the Roman calendrical or the consular *fasti* to be internalized so completely that the model is obscured. The remarkable Coligny calendar from Gaul is difficult to date, but probably belongs to the high to late Roman Imperial period. Fragments of a second, apparently similar calendar found at Villards d'Héria about twenty miles to the east of Coligny hint at the possibility of a broader phenomenon. Scholars have tended to characterize it in two opposite ways: as an authentic "Druidic" survival, or as so Roman in form that it does not count as an example of locally distinct culture. But the point is surely that it is both: the form of the calendar, its Latin letters and very monumentalization recall those of the Roman calendrical *fasti*, but the language, content, and lunar reckoning of the calendar are markedly non-Latin and non-Roman, a monument to or a recreation of a very distinctive religious, social, and political culture. In this example, the metropolitan idea of monumental *fasti* has become fully naturalized in the monumentalization of local "authenticity."[12]

At the other end of the scale, the origins of what I am calling "Caesar time" can arguably be traced back to the beginning of the first century BCE, informed by a combination of supposedly Etruscan saecula, regnal dating, and messianic ideas of salvation and new beginnings that inform the increasingly individualized political face of Rome from the time of the dictatorship of Sulla onwards. While these broadly shared tendencies might be clear to us, "on the ground," especially in the rapidly changing political geography of the eastern Mediterranean between the age of Sulla and the principate of Augustus, there is a dizzying variety of localized new starts. Localized Sullan and Pompeian eras counting down from the "liberation" of the community from Mithridates or the Seleucids were in some cases still active hundreds of years later.[13]

*De facto* Augustan monarchy encouraged a proliferation of declarations of new beginnings. It was perhaps the very universality of the "impact of

---

[11] *Vicomagistri*: Degrassi 1947, no. 20; 1963, no. 12; collegium of imperial household at Antium: Degrassi 1947, no, 31; Wallace-Hadrill 2005; 2008, 245–8 for excellent discussions of these examples and the broad phenomenon.

[12] Coligny: Duval and Pinault 1986; Woolf 1998, 230n107; Monard 1999; Olmsted 2001; Rüpke 2011, 121; Stern 2012, 303–13.

[13] First-century BCE eras: Seyrig 1950; Leschhorn 1993, 416–32; Jones 2001; Luke 2014.

monarchy" that encouraged insistence on local resonance. As we have seen, the *koinon* of Asia dossier insists on the providential near synchrony of Augustus' birthday with local New Year's days and the entry of local annual magistrates to office. An inscription celebrating the erection of the Altar of the Numen of Augustus at Narbo in 11 CE prescribes the annual celebration of rites for Augustus' birthday, for the anniversary of his entry to his first consulship, and for the emphatically local anniversary of the *princeps'* reconciliation of the people to the decurions, to be commemorated on the day before the kalends of June (*CIL* 12, 4,333, col. 1; tr. Lewis and Reinhold 1990, vol. 1, 622). In marked contrast, regnal dating in Egypt that counts Augustus' reign immediately from the Egyptian New Year 30 BCE, used in documents as lowly as that detailing the lease of a red cow called Thayris in 26 BCE, suggests at the same time both complete rupture as a Roman monarch replaces the Ptolemaic dynasty, and complete fusion as "Roman" time so wholly continues the Ptolemaic system.[14]

Imperial interventions most familiarly mark themselves or are acknowledged in recommendations, decrees, edicts, honors, building inscriptions or milestones that signal their official status by a "date stamp," traditionally the quirky (to outsiders) Latin ablative absolute formula minus a verb, "with x and y consuls." From the beginning of monarchy, consular dating is often joined or replaced by a year reckoned by the number of times the ruling emperor has been saluted *imperator*, the number of times he has held the consulship and/or the annually renewed *tribunicia potestas*. The exceptionalism of the *princeps* is harnessed to traditional Roman state institutions, while these traditions are in turn updated to accommodate his extraordinary prominence: hailing him *imperator* is enumerated as if it were a political office, and in the case of the *tribunicia potestas*, power is abstracted from the office of tribune, while retaining the important popular overtones of the tribunate. The fact that the emperor's offices or honors become a principal means of dating neatly illustrates the progressively blurry line between the person of Caesar and the Roman state.[15]

Nevertheless, various indications suggest that consular dating would persist as the primary means of denoting an *official* date, a prime example of the "Republicanism" of the Roman "Empire of the Caesars" (whose members of course regularly held the consulship themselves in addition to patronizing the consulship). If such dating was standard in public inscriptions, it also appears in fits and starts in the much lowlier and normally invisible contexts of stamps on water pipes and bricks, including a

---

[14] Thayris the cow: Rea 1982; Millar 1984, 38–9.     [15] *Tribunicia potestas*: Lacey 1979.

remarkable bunching up of city of Rome brickstamps between 110 and 164 CE. Various explanations have been offered for this practice, but the most persuasive one is that this date stamp was a guarantee of quality and authenticity, perhaps reinforced at certain times by legislation along the lines of a modern Roman edict of 1821 that purported to be a revival of ancient practice. From the Tetrarchic period, consular dating begins to be found regularly in Egyptian documents outside of Roman public or legal contexts. The change is so dramatic that it probably follows a directive from Diocletian, as part of a larger push to integrate Egypt within Roman imperial systems.[16]

Consular dating had a considerable impact on the consciousness of the inhabitants of empire. In the Latin-speaking provinces, we see that consular dating is sometimes juxtaposed with dating by local magistrates or, more rarely, dating by local magistrates is given alone, reminding us of the different responses to Roman consular *fasti* that we have just considered. In the older Greek-speaking provinces of the empire, the system is rarely seen in epigraphic monuments, but rather more frequently in legal documents outside Egypt (where consular dating is avoided before the third century CE with the exception of Roman legal contexts), often in parallel with other systems of dating, including other methods that refer to the Roman center, such as "Caesar time."

Across the empire, consular dating was progressively used well beyond communications with imperial agents, and in documents and monuments that showed no particular interest in the imperial authorities, let alone loyalty to them. The use of consular dating in documents of the early second-century CE Babatha archive suggests how rapidly this method was received in the new province of Arabia as one by which to signal authority, at least by this attuned and proactive individual. Documents in the archive that use consular dating include Greek and Aramaic private contracts that do not engage in any direct way with Roman officialdom, such as the marriage contract of Babatha's stepdaughter Shelamzion and Judah Cimber, written in Greek with Aramaic statements by the male parties of the contract and witnesses' names also in Aramaic (*P. Yadin* 18), and Babatha's father's deed of gift to his wife Miriam, written in Aramaic (*P. Yadin* 7). Each of these documents piles consular dating up with other means of reckoning time (Roman and Babylonian/Macedonian days and provincial era in the former document, and regnal dating, provincial era

---

[16] Pipes and brickstamps: Bruun 1991, 36–7; Manacorda 1993; Pucci 2001; tetrarchy and consular dating in Egypt: Bagnall and Worp 2004, chapter 9; Salway 2008.

and Babylonian/Macedonian day in the latter), not unlike an ancient prayer or magical formula that covers all the possibilities, even at the risk of redundancy. Just as strikingly, Jewish inscriptions and graffiti in the city of Rome, and Christian funerary inscriptions and martyrdom accounts all use consular dating.[17]

A more detailed look at local receptions of consular dating reveals the effort it took to reproduce or (much more rarely) naturalize this mode of denoting time. The Latin formula was approximated in local languages, sometimes going so far as to reproduce also the even odder Roman means of designating the day of the month by counting backward from the Kalends, Nones, and Ides. The effects were felt already in the Oscan language in Italy in the second century BCE. An inscription from the territory of the Marrucini in the central Apennines dated a year by its chief magistracy, the *meddix tuticus*-ship, a singular office unlike the consular pairing, faithfully reproducing the truncated ablative absolute of the Latin formula: "m(edíkúd) t(úvtíkúd) ni(umsiúd) dekitiúd mi(ínieís)" ("in the *meddix tuticus*-ship of Numsis Decitis son of Minis") (Sa 2, l. 1, Rix 2002). The effects are even more jarring when the dating system is not naturalized in this way. When reproduced in Greek, as it is in the dossier of the *koinon* of Asia, the dative stands in for the Latin ablative (instead of the genitive, which might be the more natural way to translate the idiom into Greek). If the Roman day of the month is given, it must be reproduced in an odd blend of transliteration and literal translation, since it is wholly alien to the local means of designating the day. In some contexts, giving consular dates will induce complete "code-switching," moving from the language of the major part of the document into Latin or Greek (the closest "imperial" language).[18]

Consular dating not only put a stress on language. It also put considerable stress on keeping up-to-date with the names of "ordinary" consuls (the two consuls who took up office on January 1 and who gave their names to that year) nominated or appointed each year, testing the speed and accuracy of communications with the Roman center, especially as the increasing practice of appointing suffect (replacement) consuls part way through the year encouraged doubt about the identity of the eponymous ones. We get occasional glimpses of the tough reality, in the considerable

---

[17] Babatha archive: Millar 1993, 19–20; 415–16; Jews and Christians: Salomies 1995, 275–6; Rüpke 2011, 155–6; prayer and magical formulas: Hickson 1993; Graf 1997, esp. chapter 7.
[18] "Latinization" of Italian political language: Langslow 2012, 297–8; pressures on Greek and code-switching: Sherk 1969, 14; Adams 2003, 390–3; 504.

variations in order and sometimes in the names themselves that are attested, or the occasional instance of giving up altogether and writing "*after* the consulships of consul x and consul y," x and y being the names of the ordinary consuls of the previous year.[19]

Modes of reckoning time suggest the considerable impact of the Roman imperial presence on local consciousness, whether Roman practices are comprehensively naturalized, as in the examples of the Fasti of the Coligny calendar and the *meddix tuticus*-ship of the Marrucini, or a distinctive Roman practice is framed as such (more or less literally in the case of monumental calendar complexes, or metaphorically by linguistic awkwardness or code-switching in the use of consular dates). Regnal dating in Egypt and elsewhere (including a swathe of Anatolia west of the Euphrates from "flat" Cilicia in the south to Pontus in the north, Palestine, Bosporus, and Chersonesus) is the exception that proves the rule, casting Roman monarchy within preexisting local modes of reckoning time, an extreme but salutary reminder of the possibility of competing platforms of authority in the Roman imperial world. The other examples highlight the manifest value of invoking the dialect of Roman officialdom, whether in elevating local displays of power and prestige, getting things done, or raising the stakes of the community. That value is arguably only enhanced when it draws fully on the authenticity of Roman officialdom, when the dating system is barely translatable, most jarring on the ear.[20]

## Past, Present, and Future

In this section, we move from questions about the Roman imperial impact on modes of marking time by days and years to questions about the Roman imperial impact on conceptualizing and telling the past and its consequences for the present and future. In the traditional thought of the ancient Mediterranean, questions and answers about peoplehood were inevitably referred back to origins. The expectations behind such questions and answers were relational from the earliest discursive examples we have in the Homeric poems. When characters in the *Odyssey* ask variations on the questions, "Who are you of men, and where are you from? Where are your city and your parents?" (e.g., *Od.* 1, 170), they are asking the individual to locate himself within a bigger picture comprehensible both

[19] Variations in consular dating in any given year: Salomies 1995; Egyptian compromises: Bagnall 2009, 183.
[20] Geography of regnal dating in Roman Empire: Howgego 2005.

to the questioner and to the audience. Within the geography of the *Odyssey*, does the character link in to the diaspora of Trojan War heroes, is he an ancestral guest-friend, or is he an outsider who might also be plying the seas, a Phoenician or Cretan with a distinctive set of not-us characteristics, or a stateless pirate? We can see this same relationality at the heart of early Greek mythologies that articulate "local" versions of "great" narratives, where even illustrious panhellenic centers like Olympia have idiosyncratically "local" versions.[21]

While this discourse is certainly capable of writing peoples out, it is also regularly inclusive, especially when compared with the starkly exclusive racial categories commonly employed in the nineteenth and twentieth centuries. The particular variety of ethnocentrism that we might associate with the Greek-speaking world writes foreign peoples into interconnecting remote pasts and even kinship relationships, often via wandering gods or heroes, with more or less emphasis on sexual and martial violence. Even if it expects the self-accounts of other peoples to follow familiar patterns of encounters and to feature translatable gods and heroes, it is capable of offering the flexibility to recognize that other peoples, their ways and gods might predate Greek peoples and have influenced them (as is particularly the case for the Egyptians and Phoenicians), and of leaving room for the less translatable traditions of other peoples. As Greek ways of thinking about the world and its interconnections come to dominate the Mediterranean and Near East, especially through the establishment of the Hellenistic kingdoms, we see instances of creative reception and spontaneous versions among local peoples, who find a place for themselves and for the particularities of their own pasts within these frameworks of "great" history. The assertive centralization of power in the kingdoms of the Ptolemies and the Seleucids encourages and even actively sponsors Greek language self-accounts of peoplehood in the form of Manetho's *Aegyptiaka* and Berossus' *Babyloniaka*.[22]

As we move into the second century BCE, the Romans were increasingly conceptualized as a central force in Greek language historical narratives that were no longer just "great" but purported to be universal, with considerable consequences for the relative placement of "Romans" and "us." Polybius is an implicated observer of the expansion of Roman power

---

[21] Phoenicians in the *Odyssey*: Winter 1995; early Greek mythologies: Price 2005; Clarke 2008 on the modern historiography of "great" and "local" narratives; cf. Whitmarsh 2010 for the Roman empire.

[22] Flexibility of ancient ethnographical and historical traditions: Dench 2005, esp. chs. 1 and 5; Clarke 2008; Moyer 2011; Skinner 2012; Dillery 2015.

and ambitions as what he calls the making of a "whole" (1, 2, 7). The geographically localized parts of this "whole" remain very visible in his work, and he joins them together with explicit purpose (e.g., 4, 28, cf. 1, 4; 3, 32). At best, the Romans are an ethical and behavioral model from which contemporary Greeks could learn a great deal, but at the same time they are foreign and aloof, unwilling to give the benefit of the doubt if they believe that an outsider like Polybius has committed sins of omission (6, 11, 3–8).[23]

In the *Geography* of Strabo, which we encountered in the first section of Chapter 1, the Polybian universe has grown so large that it needs to be overseen by a father-like individual, Augustus, whose successors will continue that role (7, 4, 2). Strabo's use of "we" and "our" refers alternately to a centralizing vision of a huge, Roman imperial project and to the very specific, notably his own Black Sea homeland and the urban intellectual circuit of Asia Minor. This partial self-identification with specific places chimes in with a concern throughout to highlight the smaller stories of peoples and places that get caught up in the conflicts and domination of successive, sometimes rival super-powers, of which Rome is the largest and greatest at least for now. Although Strabo's world and his work finally land smoothly in Augustan monarchy, there is exceptional bumpiness in recent memory, as well as the recognition of compelling alternatives, from Alexander the Great to Mithridates, and from various losers in the Roman civil wars to the Parthians, who remain very present on the borderlands even if their friendship to Rome is secured by keeping their children at Rome (16, 1, 28; cf. 16, 1, 16; 16, 1, 19).[24]

More than a century later, the formulation of Appian of Alexandria is quite different. He insists that he will write an exclusively "Roman" history, characterizing the narrative arc of each section of his work as moving from the beginnings of Roman warfare with each people to the "end of each *ethnos*" (Pref. 14). His depiction of his own trajectory mirrors this arc, as he is drawn into the Roman orbit: after reaching the highest place in his homeland, Alexandria, and pleading cases before the emperors, until such a time as the Romans consider him worthy of a procuratorship (Pref. 15), which we know from correspondence between Fronto and Antoninus Pius (Fronto, *ad Ant. Pium* 10 [van den Hout 1988, 168]) to

---

[23] Polybius' relative placement of himself, Greeks and Romans: Walbank 1974; Momigliano 1982; Millar 1987; Clarke 1999a, chapter 2; Erskine 2000; Champion 2004a.
[24] Clarke 1999a, chapter 5.

have been an honorary position. At the same time, his arrangement of his history, treating each theater of war or each protagonist separately, maintains the strandedness and plurality of this "Roman" history. Roman interventions do not result in a homogeneous present, but in reconfigurations of peoplehood. Perhaps the starkest example is when he makes Sulla declare that the Ephesians must pay five years' tax upfront, to pay the price for having supported Mithridates. In return, they will preserve their Greek *genos*, their *onoma* and their *doxa* (their "race," "name" and "reputation"): subscription (in a very literal sense) to the Roman Empire is the price for preserving their peoplehood (*Mithr.* 9, 62). Appian's Rome both swamps local pasts and reconfigures and underwrites peoplehood. Even if individuals such as Appian are deemed worthy of their honors, the Romans remain emphatically "them."[25]

Polybius, Strabo, and Appian, writing within a substantially common tradition of universal history, would respond differently to the question of whether Roman history is "our" history. For Appian, it is a totalizing past, but that does not make it "our" past, while Polybius and Strabo admit different degrees of self-identification. For all the variation in responses, there is a striking difference between all these adventures in writing Roman history and colonial/postcolonial histories of modern European empires, in which subjects or former subjects resist writing the "whole."[26]

Some decades before Polybius wrote his historical work, Roman authors had begun to write and sponsor their own collective literary pasts, monumentalizing them for an audience that was geographically much broader than the city of Rome population at which aristocratic family displays of illustrious deeds were normally aimed. There are analogies between Fabius Pictor's Greek language history of Rome (toward the end of the third century BCE) from Herakles to the Hannibalic War and the self-accounts of Berossus and Manetho, writing Roman distinctiveness into and superimposing it onto a "great," Hellenistic universe. Ennius' epic *Annales*, staking out the authority of the poet as distinct from political actor, promoted and perhaps even substantially invented the tradition of hoary Roman priestly annals, spruced up with a thoroughly Hellenistic reception of Homer, an excellent example of the dynamic reworking of "local" tradition. As soon as Roman literary versions of their origins and early history begin to emerge, they feature an often-fraught multi-ethnic

---

[25] Cuff 1983; Bucher 2000; Weißenberger 2002; Welch 2015.
[26] See Dench 2011 for further development of this argument.

dimension, imagined in terms of arrivals, cultural contributions, war, rape and inter-marriage.[27]

In parallel with these self-accounts and building on older intellectual traditions of the Mediterranean world, the Romans were actively involved in "kinship diplomacy" on a selective basis, an important way of brokering divisive imperial relationships as they rose to "world" power. As they became major arbitrators of privilege, prestige and power in the Mediterranean, intervening directly in post-conquest settlements, constitutions and boundary drawing, and as their imperial presence was more generally felt, both local pasts and, significantly, localized Roman pasts became currency. In one notorious case, Hellenized Lydian Sardis and Greek Smyrna emerged as finalists in a competition between Asian cities heard by Tiberius and the senate in 26 CE to house a temple of the imperial cult. While Sardis was able to claim both a role in the making of pre-Roman Italy (through settling "Tyrrhenia," i.e., Etruria) and in the colonization of the Peloponnese, she was trumped by the recognition of help proffered to Rome by Smyrna in recent, difficult times, including giving clothing from their own backs to Sulla's army (Tac. *Ann.* 4, 55–6). While Smyrna ultimately wins on loyalty, Sardis' claim of priority vis-à-vis Rome as well as "old" Greece suggests the continued potential to draw on sources of power and prestige that put Rome in her place.[28]

While this particular competition is played out before a Roman audience, other examples emphasize the importance of dynamics between neighbors or within a community itself. Aphrodisias' "archive wall" (Figure 5) records both Roman privileges conferred on the city itself and the denial of similar privileges to others. C. Vibius Salutaris' endowment of statues, a lottery and repeated procession at Ephesus linked a particular version of the city's origins with the Roman hotspot that the new part of the city created, re-ordered the relationship of origins and present, and affirmed the social, religious and political logic of the city.[29]

The promotion of distinctive local pasts was closely intertwined with imperial and colonial politics, sometimes based on thick, centuries-deep layers of "middle ground" negotiations with successive powers. This is certainly the case in Roman Egypt, where use of the Egyptian language in

---

[27] Aristocratic displays: e.g., Hölscher 1984; Flower 1996; Hölkeskamp 2005; early Roman historical writing: succinctly Beck 2007; Ennius: Gildenhard 2003; Rüpke 2006c; Elliott 2013; multi-ethnic roots of Rome: Dench 2005.

[28] Kinship diplomacy: Curty 1995; Jones 1999; Erskine 2001; Battistoni 2010; vibrant local Roman Republican histories: Jones 2001.

[29] Aphrodisias: Chaniotis 2003; Ephesus: Rogers 1991.

Figure 5   Detail of the so-called archive wall of Aphrodisias (on the north *parodos* of the
theater) displaying carefully selected imperial documents and correspondence that highlight
the city's privileged relationship with the Roman center. Third century CE.
Photo: Jonathan Blair/Getty Images.

public documents to demarcate a potent religious sphere continued even
while "Egyptians" were reimagined as a category excluded from the tax
privileges shared by Roman citizens and citizens of "Greek cities" in
Roman Egypt. "Punicity" was reclaimed in the Augustan era, Carthage's
erstwhile threat to Rome reimagined as a mostly tamed twin, her script and
language both sufficiently urbane and sufficiently alternative to be paired
with Latin in the building inscriptions of the magnificent monumental
rebuilding of Lepcis Magna. In parts of the north and west (especially
Gaul), it can be harder to spot, primarily because of the internalization of
value systems that struggle to compute local forms. Local languages and
shapes of gods are considerably buried in Latin and more familiar iconographies and materials, although hyphenated gods, the maintenance of
memory sites, and even re-appropriated "barbarian" dress and behavior,
suggest processes not dissimilar from those in provinces with longer
interconnected histories.[30]

---

[30]   Egypt: Moyer 2011; Adams 2003, 533–6; Jördens 2012; "Punicity": Davidson 1998; Quinn 2010;
Gaul: Woolf 1994; 1998; 2003; 2011; western Europe: Johnston 2017.

In certain contexts, that "local" that had been reclaimed, assigned, enhanced, or re-evaluated through messy imperial politics was aggressively asserted against Rome. The slogans *Italia* (in Latin)/*Viteliu* (in Oscan) used by the insurgent Italian allies in the Social War owed as much to a Roman political concept of *Italia* as to pre-Roman traditions, but as the aggressive Italic bull verus Roman wolf reverse of a famous rebel coin-type makes clear, they implied no friendliness toward, or even inclusion of Rome. When C. Iulius Civilis initiated the Batavian revolt of 69 CE by an ominous meeting in a grove, bound the participants to his purpose by a "barbarous rite" and "native curses," and displayed emblems of wild beasts brought out of the woods and groves (Tac. *Hist.* 4, 14; 15; 22), his version of "going native" surely owed a great deal to the kind of Roman ethnographic expectations that sponsored and shaped the identity of the Batavian auxiliaries. The rebel coinages of the Jewish War of 66–70 and of the Bar Kochba Revolt of 132–6, in their slogans (Hebrew script, new eras, "Israel," "Zion," or "Jerusalem," but never "Judaea"), iconography (e.g., pomegranates) and even their types (e.g., shekels) seem deliberately to exclude the Roman imperial model, and are also strikingly different from the compromises of local, Hasmonaean coinage. Even so, the emphasis in the iconography of the Bar Kochba coinage on buildings, notably the Temple, seems to recall the contemporary Roman enthusiasm for images of buildings on coins, underlining the role that deliberate avoidance rather than more passive survival plays in the choice of other features.[31]

And what of the future? The tradition of empire as a continuum suggested that the fall and end were written in to the experience of empire at its peak. Scipio Aemilianus' tears at the fall of Carthage were, as Polybius' account apparently spelled out, for the future fate of his own city, Rome (38, 21–2): the much older tradition narrated by Herodotus of Xerxes, the Persian king, weeping at the thought of the ephemeral lives of his army as he surveyed them in all their magnificence at the Hellespont, is just below the surface here (7, 44–6). From the moment when Roman ascendancy began to remodel empire, it demanded explanation and apology, inspired local attempts to draw down that power by redeploying symbols and practices associated with it, and provoked apocalyptic visions of her coming doom. The vulnerability and profound changes of the later Empire, and the eventual fall of Rome in the west in 476 CE, encouraged

---

[31] *Italia/viteliu*, the bull, and the wolf; Brunt 1965a, 98; Burnett 1998; Wallace-Hadrill 2008, 88–9; C. Iulius Civilis and the Batavians: Derks 1998; Derks and Roymans 2009; coins of Jewish War and Bar Kochba revolt: Goodman 2005.

intense interest in the Roman past, a model so overpowering that it became hard to resist, even if that meant thinking in Manichaean opposites. In Augustine's *City of God*, Rome's role as a mortal foil for the heavenly kingdom creates one of the most coherent accounts of Roman history ever written. Medieval kingdoms claimed continuity with the Roman empire even as they embraced "barbarian" identities, and even the postcolonial western world in recovery from the profits and losses of enthusiastic appropriation of an ancient imperial model asks anxiously, "are we Rome?"[32]

[32] Apocalypse: succinctly Frankfurter 1998; medieval kingdoms: Amory 1997; Halsall 2007; "Are we Rome?": e.g., Murphy 2007.

# Epilogue
## Becoming Roman?

We began this book by "talking" to Francis Haverfield, whose book, *The Romanization of Roman Britain*, written and intensively rewritten in the early years of the twentieth century, offers a stimulating and slightly distanced way into many of the major debates about change accompanying the Roman empire over the last century. Haverfield's eschewal of a top-down model of the Roman empire that would emphasize offices of the imperial state and the might of the Roman army anticipates a sophisticated, later twentieth-century emphasis on empire as a belief system based on widespread "buy in" on the part of Rome's subjects. In his insistence on change in language and things (e.g., clothing, jewelry, and dining wares) as proxies for processes and mental states, a bold and challenging statement within an educational context that so highly prized the study of ancient languages and literatures, he was also ahead of his time. He anticipated the emancipation of the archaeology of the Roman provinces from the study of Classics and from that of the "high" art focus of Classical Archaeology in post–World War II Britain, and its realignment with social scientific and scientific approaches to prehistoric archaeology.

The problematic aspect of Haverfield's analysis is his collapsing of the multiple, complex processes that make things proxies for ideas, and the narrowing of the scope of these ideas to diagnose a particular set of political sentiments, so that the adoption of Latin and what he described as "Roman," "classical," or "Mediterranean" "fashions" were indices of loyalty to the Roman empire on the part of "Romanized" individuals. The collapsing of multiple, complex processes to read political loyalty to Rome from things (and, indeed, focusing only or primarily on political loyalty to Rome when analyzing material culture) proved to be remarkably seductive, even in the face of increasing problematization of the concept of "Romanization." Replacing one catch-all term, Romanization, with another, e.g., globalization (and its situated counterpart, "glocalization"), shifts the imagery and associations, but continues to ignore the complexity of entangled phenomena that one is purporting to describe.[1]

For Haverfield, adoption of Latin and "Roman fashions" signaled a total, secular conversion made possible by the absence of racial barriers that, in his view, prevented "Asiatic" or "African" subjects of contemporary European empires from doing anything more than dressing up in western clothing.[2] An emerging sense of disappointment about the failure of contemporary European empires to achieve a desirable level of assimilation is answered by an idealized, significantly more successful Roman empire. This is not the only part of the contemporary debate about empire on which Haverfield's Roman Britain offers more or less direct commentary: elsewhere, he engages with arguments about the persistence and emergence of resistant nationalism. Thus, in Roman Britain, any remnants of the "Celtic" in Britain were vestigial, atavistic, style without political substance. Indeed, Haverfield was deeply suspicious of the Romantic view that pre-Roman "national" sentiments hung around to be marshalled on the fall of Rome.[3]

The distinctly end-of-history, tail-end of the twentieth century overtones of Greg Woolf's *Becoming Roman: The Origins of Provincial Civilization in Gaul* (1998), and Clifford Ando's *Imperial Ideology and Provincial Loyalty in the Roman Empire* (2000) are very different from those of Haverfield's account of the assimilation of Roman Britain.[4] There is no objective "coherent civilization" to which Woolf's Gauls are magnetically drawn, but the internalization of an imperial value system, *humanitas*, that allows both participation in the game of power and determination of its rules. The rhythmic rituals that bind Ando's individual subjects into the Roman imperial state represent a powerful and compelling account of structure and process that is entirely lacking when Haverfield reads loyalty to the Roman center from the adoption of "Roman" things.

Woolf's and Ando's analyses highlight the processes that contributed to the extraordinary success of the Roman empire in co-opting subjects within its systems, and even in making them insiders, an ability without parallel in any earlier or, it might plausibly be argued, any later imperial system. While each account emphasizes the localization of the phenomenon examined (value system or ritual), the Roman empire as a system or locus of power fully eclipses alternative or more immediate systems and loci of power. Ando makes explicit his aim to account for the longevity of

---

[1] See Woolf 2014 for excellent discussion of this complexity.     [2] Haverfield 1915, 20.
[3] Haverfield 1915, 23; cf. chapter 9.     [4] Cf. Fukuyama 1989; 1992.

the Roman empire rather than its ultimate collapse, and in general both accounts are searching for manifestations of assimilation over those of looking in different directions, looking out for oneself, or even outright resistance.[5]

This has to do partly with the splintering of modern approaches that we considered in the Introduction, and with the relegation of resistance to the less sophisticated, "evil empire" accounts that remain comparatively untouched by models of agency that complicate stark oppositions of "Romans" and "natives." Notions of anything less than the complete and coherent functioning of the Roman imperial state have become even more marginalized in recent accounts of the early, "high," or later Roman empire. This is partly because of a largely productive paradigm shift that identified "late antiquity" as a period of transformation rather than of "decline," the more traditional narrative's evocation of the quasi-biological trajectory of a political system.[6] It is also partly because of recent tendencies to turn (and in some cases return) to catastrophic and largely external causes of the fifth-century CE fall of the Roman empire in the west: plague, barbarian invasions, and climate change.[7]

In the Introduction to this book, I identified and criticized the conversion model that entered discussions of change accompanying empire in the Roman world in the nineteenth and early twentieth centuries, and that has arguably never entirely left them. This underlying conversion model has encouraged us to imagine change within the Roman empire at a local or individual level as a totalizing shift of being, as "becoming Roman." Liberation from this model allows us to appreciate the performative aspects of identity in the Roman empire, and, just as profoundly, the thinly stretched nature of Roman power, and its coexistence with competing systems of power and authority, along with the opportunism engendered by the Roman empire's substantial reliance on local states and groups.[8].

Recognizing that, even at the height of empire, Roman power was thinly stretched, coexisted with competing systems of power and authority, and fostered opportunism on the part of local states and groups, should encourage us to reintegrate within the appraisal of empire as a system the conditions most clearly visible in the making of empire, at its edges and in times of crisis. Such conditions become less exceptional and more

---

[5] Ando 2000, 1–15.   [6] Ando 2009; Rebenich 2009.
[7] E.g., Ward-Perkins 2005; Heather 2005; Harper 2017 emphasizes the Roman empire's structural facilitation of the spread of disease.
[8] Roman imperial identities as performative: Andrade 2013; Johnston 2017.

diagnostic of the way empire worked even at less fraught times. For the making of empire, this would include the play off in the later third to second centuries BCE between not just individual Hellenistic kings and Roman statesmen but between the concepts of kingship and the Roman Republic themselves, when the world seemed to hang in balance between two systems of rule. At the more local and material level, this is the world of Andrew Wallace-Hadrill's Samnites, whose distinctive selfhood, articulated through the Oscan language or polygonal masonry, is thrown into relief by the international ambition of their monumental complexes. A few decades later, this selfhood is harnessed to the efficacy and imperial might associated with Roman symbolism to deliver its crushing message in the rebel coinage of the Social War. It is also the world of the earlier tales told by and of Greg Woolf's "barbarians," like the foundation myth of Alesia, named after the wanderings ("*alē*") of Herakles' army, somewhere between Mediterranean ethnocentrism and the Gauls' autoethnography.[9]

At the edges of empire and in its crises, it is the world of Titus' siege of the Temple of Jerusalem turning into a holy war, or Brent Shaw's bandits, running now in parallel with the Roman state, now in cahoots with Roman authorities, or the periodically messy question of sovereignty along the Roman/Parthian-Sasanian fault-line.[10] As for the fall of the western empire, I would certainly not want to deny the complex geographical and cultural patterns of continuity and change in the later Roman empire, or to minimize the impact of catastrophic non-human agents such as plague and climate change, not to speak of "barbarian" movements and tribal coagulations set off at least in part by the faltering power of the Roman imperial system. But we can also see the emergence of "barbarian" federations within the Roman empire as sharing much in common with a long, familiar story of the risks and benefits of a fuzzy notion of who exactly was in control of troops nominally in the service of the Roman imperial state. If it was this service itself that, ironically, engendered grouphood, it is tempting to imagine, with Guy Halsall, the federation of Goths embracing a particular kind of "barbarian" identity formed self-consciously in opposition to Rome.[11]

But the greatest benefits of moving away from imagining the Roman empire as working through a totalizing shift of being, through "becoming Roman," are to be found, in my view, in the workings of the early and "high" Roman empire in more normal circumstances, following through

[9] Wallace-Hadrill 2008, 121–3; Woolf 2011, 19–21 on Diod. 4, 19, 1–2.
[10] Jos. *BJ*; Shaw 1984; Potter 2004, chapter 6.    [11] Halsall 2007, esp. chapter 3; chapter 14.

the consequences of the degree to which functions of state were delegated to, or more often simply assumed by, local agencies and institutions within the Roman empire. This is to imagine an altogether edgier and potentially more precarious empire than that of many late twentieth-century accounts, but, I would argue, a significantly more flexible, resilient, and dynamic one.

# Bibliographical Essay

## The Path Taken by This Book

The Introduction to this book functions as a broad bibliographical guide to the path taken and choices made within it, an exploration of the emergence of and changes within local political cultures of the Roman imperial world, alongside the emergence of, and changes within, the imperial culture of the Roman state. Haverfield 1915, focusing on material change in Roman Britain as an indication of assimilation within Roman imperial norms and as an index of loyalty to Rome, is a fascinating starting point for reflecting on twentieth-century debates. Woolf 1998, a study of the material and economic changes that accompany the Gauls' engagement with, and contribution to, the Roman imperial value-system of *humanitas* ("civilization") and Ando 2000, an exploration of the rituals that connect individuals within the empire to the imperial center, and thereby engender consensus, are essential starting points for understanding the Roman empire at the turn of the millennium and for possible ways forward in the twenty-first century. Sophisticated modern works that emphasize more ambivalence in the material record of the Roman provinces (especially the northern/western provinces) vis-à-vis Rome include Mattingly 1997 and Webster and Cooper 1996. For the Greek-speaking world, see Whitmarsh 2010.

## Deep Dives into Local Contexts

Although we have touched on a number of case-studies at the interface of Roman and local systems, a book of this scale cannot possibly do justice to the complexity of local situations. An updated and more integrated version of Fergus Millar's *The Roman Empire and its Neighbours* (1981a) would be possible now that the material understanding of a number of individual provinces is surfacing to the extent that it can be usefully synthesized, and such an undertaking would encourage a truly plural appreciation of Roman history. For now, readers keen to take a deep dive into the complexity of one or two provinces without remaining submerged and never resurfacing could usefully browse two recent "companions." Riggs (2012) for Roman Egypt, and Millett, Revell, and Moore (2016) for Roman Britain, offer helpful, very up-to-date introductions to contemporary debates and areas of interest in (according to the traditional binary thinking on the Roman empire) respectively a "Greek-speaking"/eastern and a "Latin-speaking"/northern/western province. Each region has yielded an unusual amount and quality of evidence: Egypt, because of the environmental conditions that encourage the survival of documentary papyri attesting to local and imperial systems; Britain, because of centuries of highly invested focus. Traditional arguments made about the unusualness (for different reasons) of each of these provinces raise questions about what, if anything, would qualify as a "normal" province, and usefully dissuade us from making overly broad generalizations on the basis of local specificity.

## Ideas and Things "From the Ground Up"

Haverfield's assertive and ahead of his time concern (1915) to read ideas and political affiliation from material culture collapses the gap between ideas and things and minimizes the complexity and enormity of distinguishing between intertwined processes that include trade and supply networks, the formation and articulation of taste, conscious and unconscious levels of appreciation, and ethnic/political sentiments and actions. In this book, I have tried to follow a single thread by focusing on "political cultures," but this thread is never easily separable from these other entangled issues. The task of building "bottom up" from things to ideas and from "culture" to "power" has been a central issue in the archaeology of the Roman provinces since Haverfield. This process has been increasingly problematized, and the complexity of the relationship between text-based narrative and material evidence recognized. Of many examples, see e.g., Halsall 1995 for the gap between texts and things, and 2007 for a stimulating, sophisticated "bottom up" approach to historical change between the late Roman Empire and Medieval kingdoms. Alcock 2001 is essential reading for the danger of focusing narrowly on elite contexts and processes. Dench 2004 highlights the problem of text-based narratives and their alternatives. Laurence 2012 offers an excellent overview of the different kinds of questions asked and approaches taken by archaeologists and ancient historians, very pertinent to the concerns of this book.

## Paths Not Taken: Religion

Questions of religion as an interface between local particularity and the Roman imperial center are integrated within the chapters of this book, from the Introduction which highlights Simon Price's *Rituals and Power* (1984) as a game changer in our understanding of the Roman empire *tout court*, to Chapter 5 "Time," with its analysis of festival calendars and other naturalizations of Roman imperial power. There is, however, much more to say about the intersection of the Roman empire and religious organization and experience. Among a number of highly stimulating recent contributions, see e.g., de Blois, Funke, Hahn 2006; Rüpke 2007; Ando 2008; 2013; and MacRae 2016.

# Bibliography

Adams, C. 2007, "War and Society," in Sabin, van Wees, and Whitby (eds.), vol. 2, 198–232.

Adams, C. and Laurence, R. (eds.) 2001, *Travel and Geography in the Roman Empire*, London and New York, NY.

Adams, J. N. 2003, *Bilingualism and the Latin Language*, Cambridge.

Ades, D., Benton, T., Elliott, D., and Whyte, I. B. (eds.) 1995, *Art and Power: Europe under the Dictators 1930–45*, London.

Adler, E. 2011, *Valorizing the Barbarians: Enemy Speeches in Roman Historiography*, Austin, TX.

Alcock, S. E. 2001, "Vulgar Romanization and the Dominance of Elites," in Keay and Terrenato (eds.), 227–30.

Alcock, S. E., Bodel, J., and Talbert, R. J. A. (eds.) 2012, *Highways, Byways, and Road Systems in the Pre-Modern World*, Chichester and Malden, MA.

Alcock, S. E., D'Altroy, T. N., Morrison, K. D., and Sinopoli, C. M. (eds.) 2001, *Empires: Perspectives from Archaeology and History*, Cambridge.

Alföldy, G. 1991, "Augustus und die Inschriften: Tradition und Innovation: Die Geburt der imperialen Epigraphik," *Gymnasium* 98, 289–324.

Alonso-Nuñez, J. M. 2002, *The Idea of Universal History in Greece: From Herodotus to the Age of Augustus*, Amsterdam.

Alston, R. 1995, *Soldier and Society in Roman Egypt: A Social History*, London and New York, NY.

Amory, P. 1997, *People and Identity in Ostrogothic Italy, 489–554*, Cambridge.

Ando, C. 1999, "Was Rome a *polis?*," *Classical Antiquity* 18, 5–34.

2000, *Imperial Ideology and Provincial Loyalty in the Roman Empire*, Berkeley, CA.

2006, "The Administration of the Provinces," in Potter (ed.), 177–92.

2007a, "The Army and the Urban Elite: A Competition for Power," in Erdkamp (ed.), 359–78.

2007b, "Exporting Roman Religion," in Rüpke (ed.), 429–45.

2008, *The Matter of the Gods: Religion and the Roman Empire*, Berkeley, CA.

2009, "Narrating Decline and Fall," in Rousseau (ed.), 59–76.

2011a, *Law, Language, and Empire in the Roman Tradition*, Philadelphia, PA.

2011b, "Law and the Landscape of Empire," in Benoist, Daguet-Gagey, and Hoët-van Cauwenberghe (eds.), 25–47.

2013, "Subjects, Gods, and Empire, or Monarchism as a Theological Problem," in Rüpke (ed.), 85–114.

Ando, C. and Rüpke, J. (eds.) 2006, *Religion and Law in Classical and Christian Rome*, Stuttgart.

Andrade, N. J. 2013, *Syrian Identity in the Greco-Roman World*, Cambridge.

Andreau, J. 1999, "Intérêts non agricoles des chevaliers romains (IIe siècle av. J.-C.-IIIe siècle ap. J.-C.)," in Demougin, Devijver, and Raepsaet-Charlier (eds.), 271–90.

Arieti, J. A. 1997, "Rape and Livy's View of Roman History," in Deacy and Pierce (eds.), 209–29.

Armitage, D. 2000, *The Ideological Origins of the British Empire*, Cambridge.

Astin, A. E., Walbank, F. W., Frederiksen, M. W., and Ogilvie, R. M. (eds.) 1989, *Cambridge Ancient History, Vol. 8: Rome and the Mediterranean to 133 BC* (2nd edn.), Cambridge.

Austin, M. M., Harries, J., and Smith, C. (eds.) 1998, *Modus operandi: Essays in Honour of Geoffrey Rickman*, London.

Avilia, F. and Jacobelli, L. 1989, "Le naumachie nelle pitture pompeiane," *Rivista di studi pompeiani* 3, 131–54.

Badian, E. 1958, *Foreign Clientelae (264–70 B.C.)* (reprinted with corrections 1984), Oxford.

1968, *Roman Imperialism in the Late Republic* (2nd edn.), Ithaca, NY.

1972, *Publicans and Sinners: Private Enterprise in the Service of the Roman Republic*, Oxford.

Bagnall, R. S. 2009, "Practical Help: Chronology, Geography, Currency, Measures, Names, Prosopography, and Technical Vocabulary," in Bagnall (ed.), 179–96.

Bagnall, R. S. (ed.) 2009, *The Oxford Handbook of Papyrology*, Oxford.

Bagnall, R. S. and Derow, P. S. (eds.) 2003, *The Hellenistic Period: Historical Sources in Translation* (2nd edn.), Malden, MA and Oxford.

Bagnall, R. S. and Worp, K. A., 2004, *Chronological Systems of Byzantine Egypt* (2nd edn.), Leiden and Boston, MA.

Baker, P., Forcey, C., Jundi, S., and Witcher, R. (eds.) 1999, *TRAC 98: Proceedings of the Eighth Annual Theoretical Roman Archaeology Conference (Leicester 1998)*, Oxford.

Bakker, E. J., de Jong, I. J. F., and van Wees, H. (eds.) 2002, *Brill's Companion to Herodotus*, Leiden and Boston, MA.

Bang, P. F. 2007, "Trade and Empire: In Search of Organizing Concepts for the Roman Economy," *Past and Present* 195, 3–54.

Barchiesi, A. and Scheidel, W. (eds.) 2010, *The Oxford Handbook of Roman Studies*, Oxford.

Barrett, J. C. 1997, "Romanization: A Critical Comment," in Mattingly (ed.), 51–64.

Bartsch, S. 1994, *Actors in the Audience: Theatricality and Doublespeak from Nero to Hadrian*, Cambridge, MA.

Battistoni, F. 2010, *Parenti dei romani: mito troiano e diplomazia*, Bari.

2011, "Time(s) for Tauromenion: The Pilaster with the List of the stratagoi (IG XIV 421) – The Antikythera Mechanism," *Zeitschrift für Papyrologie und Epigraphik* 179, 171–88.

Beard, M. 1987, "A Complex of Times: No More Sheep on Romulus' Birthday," *Proceedings of the Cambridge Philological Society* 33, 1–15.

2003, "The Triumph of the Absurd: Roman Street Theatre," in Edwards and Woolf (eds.), 21–43.

2007, *The Roman Triumph*, Cambridge, MA.

Beard, M., North, J., and Price, S. 1998, *Religions of Rome*, 2 vols., Cambridge.

Beck, H. 2007, "The Early Roman Tradition," in Marincola (ed.), 259–65.

Beck, H., Duplá, A., Jehne, M., and Pina Polo, F. (eds.) 2011, *Consuls and res publica: Holding High Office in the Roman Republic*, Cambridge and New York, NY.

Beck, H. and G. Vankeerberghen (eds.) 2018, *Citizens and Commoners in Ancient Greece, Rome, and China*, Malden, MA and Oxford.

Bénabou, M. 1976, *La résistance africaine à la romanisation*, Paris.

Bendlin, A. 2011, "Associations, Funerals, Sociality, and Roman Law: The Collegium of Diana and Antinous in Lanuvium (*CIL* 14.2112) Reconsidered," in Öhler (ed.), 207–96.

Benoist, S., Daguet-Gagey, A., and Hoët-van Cauwenberghe, C. (eds.) 2011, *Figures d'empire, fragments de mémoire : pouvoirs et identités dans le monde romain imperial (IIe s. av. n. è.–VI s. de n. è.)*, Villeneuve-d'Ascq.

Bergmann, B. and Kondoleon, C. (eds.) 1999, *The Art of Ancient Spectacle*, Washington DC, New Haven, CT and London.

Bhabha, H. K. 1994a, "Of Mimicry and Man: The Ambivalence of Colonial Discourse," in Bhabha 1994b, 85–92 (first published in 1984, 125–33).

1994b, *The Location of Culture*, London and New York, NY.

Bidwell, P. T. and Hodgson, N. (eds.) 2009, *The Roman Army in Northern England*, South Shields.

Bispham, E. 2006, "*Coloniam Deducere*: How Roman was Roman Colonization during the Middle Republic?" in Bradley and Wilson (eds.), 73–160.

2007, *From Asculum to Actium: The Municipalization of Italy from the Social War to Augustus*, Oxford.

Blagg, T. F. C. and King, A. C. (eds.) 1984, *Military and Civilian in Roman Britain: Cultural Relationships in a Frontier Province*, Oxford.

Blagg, T. F. C. and Millett, M. (eds.) 1990, *The Early Roman Empire in the West*, Oxford.

Bloch, H. 1958, "C. Cartilius Poplicola," in Squarciapino (ed.), 209–19.

Bodde, D. 1986, "The State and Empire of Ch'in," in Twitchett and Loewe (eds.), 20–102.

Bodel, J. (ed.) 2001, *Epigraphic Evidence: Ancient History from Inscriptions*, London and New York, NY.

Boedeker, D. and Raaflaub, K. A. (eds.) 1998, *Democracy, Empire, and the Arts in Fifth-Century Athens*, Cambridge, MA.

Boschung, D. 1993, *Die Bildnisse des Augustus (Pt. I. of Vol. II of Das römische Herrscherbild)*, Berlin.

Bourke, J. and Skinner, Q. (eds.) 2016, *Popular Sovereignty in Historical Perspective*, Cambridge.

Bowersock, G. W. 1965, *Augustus and the Greek World*, Oxford.

1969, *Greek Sophists in the Roman Empire*, Oxford.

1986, "Rostovtzeff in Madison," *American Scholar* 55, 391–400.

1991, "The Babatha Papyri, Masada, and Rome (Review of N. Lewis, Y. Yadin and J. C. Greenfield [eds.], *The Documents from the Bar Kokhba Period in the Cave of Letters: Greek Papyri; Aramaic and Nabatean Signatures and Subscriptions* and H. M. Cotton and J. Geiger [eds.], *Masada: The Yigael Yadin Excavations 1963-1965. Final Reports, Vol. II: The Latin and Greek Documents*," *Journal of Roman Archaeology* 4, 336–44.

2003, "Rostovtzeff's *Birth of the Roman Empire*, St. Petersburg (Petrograd) 1918," *Mediterraneo antico* 6, 613–24.

Bowie, E. L. 1970, "Greeks and Their Past in the Second Sophistic," *Past and Present* 46, 3–41.

Bowman, A. K. 1996, "Provincial Administration and Taxation," in Bowman, Champlin, and Lintott (eds.), 344–70.

Bowman, A. K., Champlin, E., and Lintott, A. (eds.) 1996, *The Cambridge Ancient History*, vol. 10: *The Augustan Empire, 43 BC–AD 69* (2nd edn.), Cambridge

Bowman, A. K., Garnsey, P. D. A., and Rathbone, D. (eds.) 2000, *The Cambridge Ancient History*, vol. 11: *The High Empire, AD 70–192* (2nd edn.), Cambridge.

Bowman, A. K. and Rathbone, D. 1992, "Cities and Administration in Roman Egypt," *Journal of Roman Studies* 82, 107–27.

Bradley, G. J. 2014, "The Nature of Roman Strategy in Mid-Republican Colonization and Road Building," in Stek and Pelgrom (eds.), 60–72.

Bradley, G. J. and Wilson, J.-P. (eds.) 2006, *Greek and Roman Colonization: Origins, Ideologies and Interactions*, Swansea.

Bradley, M. (ed.) 2010, *Classics and Imperialism in the British Empire*, Oxford.

Braund, D. 1984, *Rome and the Friendly King: The Character of the Client Kingship*, London and New York, NY.

(ed.) 1988, *The Administration of the Roman Empire (241 BC–AD 193)*, Exeter.

1996, "River Frontiers in the Environmental Psychology of the Roman World," in Kennedy (ed.), 43–7.

Breed, B. W., Damon, C., and Rossi, A. (eds.) 2010, *Citizens of Discord: Rome and Its Civil Wars*, Oxford.

Breeze, D. J. 2008, *Edge of Empire: Rome's Scottish Frontier: The Antonine Wall*, Edinburgh.

Breeze, D. J. and Dobson, B. 2000, *Hadrian's Wall* (4th edn.), London.

Briant, P. 2002, *From Cyrus to Alexander: A History of the Persian Empire*, tr. P. T. Daniels, Winona Lake, IN.

2010, *Alexander the Great and His Empire: A Short Introduction*, tr. A. Kuhrt, Princeton, NJ.

Briscoe, J. 1967, "Rome and the Class Struggle of the Greek States 200–146 B.C.," *Past and Present* 36, 3–20.

Broadhead, W. 2007, "Colonization, Land Distribution, and Veteran Settlement," in Erdkamp (ed.), 148–63.

Brodersen, K. 1995, *Terra cognita: Studien zur römischen Raumerfassung*, Hildesheim and New York, NY.

Brown, F. E. 1951, *Cosa I: History and Topography*, Rome.

1980, *Cosa, The Making of a Roman Town*, Ann Arbor, MI.

Brown, F. E., Richardson, E. H., and Richardson, L. 1960, *Cosa II: The Temples of the Arx*, Rome.

1993, *Cosa III: The Buildings of the Forum: Colony, Municipium, and Village*, University Park, PA.

Brown, P. 2012, *Through the Eye of a Needle: Wealth, the Fall of Rome, and the Making of Christianity in the West, 350–550 AD*, Princeton, NJ.

Brunt, P. A. 1965a, "Italian Aims at the Time of the Social War," *Journal of Roman Studies* 55, 90–109.

1965b, "Review of J. de Romilly, *Thucydides and Athenian Imperialism* and R. Syme, *Thucydides*," *The Classical Review* 15, 115.

1966, "The *fiscus* and Its Development," *Journal of Roman Studies* 56, 75–91.

1971, *Italian Manpower, 225 BC–AD 14*, Oxford.

1975, "Did Imperial Rome Disarm Her Subjects?," *Phoenix* 29, 260–70.

1978, "Laus imperii," in Garnsey and Whittaker (eds.), 159–91.

1983, "*Princeps* and *equites*," *Journal of Roman Studies* 73, 42–75.

1988a, *The Fall of the Roman Republic and Related Essays*, Oxford.

1988b, "The *equites* in the Late Republic," in Brunt, 144–93.

1990a, "Charges of Provincial Maladministration under the Early Principate," in Brunt, 53–95.

1990b, *Roman Imperial Themes*, Oxford.

Bruun, C. 1991, *The Water Supply of Ancient Rome: A Study of Roman Imperial Administration*, Helsinki.

2014, "True Patriots? The Public Activities of the *Augustales of Roman Ostia and the *summa honoraria*," *Arctos* 48, 67–91.

Bucher, G. S. 2000, "The Origins, Program, and Composition of Appian's *Roman History*," *Transactions of the American Philological Association* 130, 411–58.

Buchner, E. 1982, *Die Sonnenuhr des Augustus. Nachdruck aus RM 1976 und 1980 und Nachwort über die Ausgrabung 1980/81*, Mainz.

Burbank, J. and Cooper, N. 2010, *Empires in World History: Power and the Politics of Difference*, Princeton, NJ.

Burden, M. (ed.) 1998, *A Woman Scorn'd: Responses to the Dido Myth*, London.

Burgers, P. 1993, "Taxing the Rich: Confiscation and the Financing of the Claudian Principate (AD 41–54)," *Laverna* 4, 55–68.

Burnett, A. M. 1986, "The Iconography of Roman Coin Types in the Third Century BC," *The Numismatic Chronicle* 145, 67–75.

1998, "The Coinage of the Social War," in Burnett, Wartenberg, and Witschonke (eds.), 165–72.

2005, "The Roman West and the Roman East," in Howgego, Heuchert, and Burnett (eds.), 171–80.

Burnett, A. M., Wartenberg, U., and Witschonke, R. (eds.) 1998, *Coins of Macedonia and Rome: Essays in Honour of Charles Hersh*, London.

Burrell, B. 2003, *Neokoroi: Greek Cities and Roman Emperors*, Leiden and Boston, MA.

Burton, G. P. 1979, "The *curator rei publicae*. Towards a Reappraisal," *Chiron* 9, 465–87.

2000, "The Resolution of Territorial Disputes in the Provinces of the Roman Empire," *Chiron* 30, 195–215.

2004, "The Roman Imperial State, Provincial Governors and the Public Finances of Provincial Cities: 27 BC–AD 235," *Historia* 53, 311–42.

Burton, P. J. 2011, *Friendship and Empire: Roman Diplomacy and Imperialism in the Middle Republic (353–146 BC)*, Cambridge.

Butcher, K. 2003, *Roman Syria and the Near East*, Malibu, CA.

Butler, S. J. 2012, *Britain and its Empire in the Shadow of Rome: The Reception of Rome in Socio-Political Debate from the 1850s to the 1920s*, London and New York, NY.

Caballos Rufino, A. 2006, *El nuevo bronce de Osuna y la política colonizadora romana*, Seville.

2010, "Colonizzazione cesariana, legislazione municipale e integrazione provinciale : la Provincia Hispania Ulterior," in Urso (ed.), 63–84.

Cahn, H. A. and Simon, E. (eds.) 1980, *Tainia: Roland Hampe zum 70. Geburtstag am 2. Dezember 1978*, 2 vols., Mainz.

Cairns, F. and Fantham, E. (eds.) 2003, *Caesar against Liberty? Perspectives on His Autocracy (Vol. 11 of Papers of the Langford Latin Seminar)*, Leeds.

Callagerin, L. and Réchin, F. (eds.) 2009, *Espaces et sociétés à l'époque romaine: entre Garonne et Èbre, actes de la table ronde de Pau (janvier 2007): hommage à Georges Fabre*, Pau.

Cameron, A. and Kuhrt, A. (eds.) 1993, *Images of Women in Antiquity* (2nd rev. edn.), London.

Campanile, E. and Letta, C. 1979, *Studi sulle magistrature indigene e municipali in area italica*, Pisa.

Campbell, B. 2000, *The Writings of the Roman Land Surveyors: Introduction, Text, Translation and Commentary*, London.

2012, *Rivers and the Power of Ancient Rome*, Chapel Hill, NC.

Capogrossi Colognesi, L. and Gabba, E. (eds.) 2006, *Gli statute municipali*, Pavia.

Carratelli, G. P. (ed.) 1989, *Italia omnium terrarum parens: La civiltà degli Enotri, Choni, Ausoni, Sanniti, Lucani, Brettii, Sicani, Siculi, Elimi*, Milan.

Carter, J. B. and Morris, S. P. (eds.) 1995, *The Ages of Homer: A Tribute to Emily Townsend Vermeule*, Austin, TX.

Cartledge, P. 2016, *Democracy: A Life*, Oxford.

Cartledge, P., Garnsey, P. D. A., and Gruen, E. S. (eds.) 1997, *Hellenistic Constructs: Essays in Culture, History, and Historiography*, Berkeley, CA.

Cartledge, P. and Harvey, D. (eds.) 1985, *Crux: Essays Presented to G. E. M. de Ste Croix*, Exeter.

Cartledge, P. and Spawforth, A. 2002, *Hellenistic and Roman Sparta: A Tale of Two Cities* (2nd edn.), London and New York, NY.

Casson, L. 1989, *The Periplus Maris Erythraei: Text with Introduction, Translation, and Commentary*, Princeton, NJ.

Castriota, D. 1992, *Myth, Ethos, and Actuality: Official Art in Fifth-Century BC Athens*, Madison, WI.

Catalano, P. 1978, "Aspetti spaziali del sistema giuridico-religioso romano. *Mundus, templum, urbs, ager*, Latium, Italia," *Aufstieg und Niedergang der römischen Welt II* 16.1, 440–553.

Champion, C. B. 2004a, *Cultural Politics in Polybius's Histories*, Berkeley, CA.

(ed.) 2004b, *Roman Imperialism: Readings and Sources*, Malden, MA and Oxford.

2007, "Empire by Invitation: Greek Political Strategies and Roman Imperial Interventions in the Second Century BCE," *Transactions of the American Philological Association* 137, 255–75.

Chaniotis, A. 2003, "The Perception of Imperial Power in Aphrodisias: The Epigraphic Evidence," in de Blois, Erdkamp, Hekster, de Kleijn, and Mols (eds.), 250–60.

2005, *War in the Hellenistic World: A Social and Cultural History*, Malden, MA and Oxford.

Charles-Picard, G. 1957, *Les trophées romains. Contributions à l'histoire de la religion et de l'art triomphal* de Rome, Paris.

Clarke, K. 1997, "In Search of the Author of Strabo's *Geography*," *Journal of Roman Studies* 87, 92–110.

1999a, *Between Geography and History: Hellenistic Constructions of the Roman World*, Oxford.

1999b, "Universal Perspectives in Historiography," in Kraus (ed.), 249–79.

2001, "An Island Nation: Re-Reading Tacitus" *Agricola*," *Journal of Roman Studies* 91, 94–112.

2008, *Making Time for the Past: Local History and the Polis*, Oxford.

Clarysse, W. and Thompson, D. J. 2006, *Counting the People in Hellenistic Egypt*, 2 vols., Cambridge.

Coarelli, F. 1987, *I santuari del Lazio in età repubblicana*, Rome.

1988, "Colonizzazione romana e viabilità," *Dialoghi di archeologia* (ser. III) 6, 35–48.

1992, "Colonizzazione e municipalizzazione: tempi e modi," *Dialoghi di Archeologia* (ser. III) 10, 21–30.

2000, *The Column of Trajan*, tr. C. Rockwell, Rome.

Coleman, K. M. 1990, "Fatal Charades: Roman Executions Staged as Mythological Enactments," *Journal of Roman Studies* 80, 44–73.

2010, "Spectacle," in Barchiesi and Scheidel (eds.), 651–70.

Constantakopoulou, C. 2007, *The Dance of the Islands: Insularity, Networks, the Athenian Empire, and the Aegean World*, Oxford.

Cooley, A. E. (ed.) 2009, *Res gestae divi Augusti: Text, Translation, and Commentary*, Cambridge.

Cornell, T. J. 1993, "The End of Roman Imperial Expansion," in Rich and Shipley (eds.), 139–70.

Cornwell, H. 2015, "The King Who Would Be Prefect: Authority and Identity in the Cottian Alps," *Journal of Roman Studies* 105, 41–72.

Cottier, M. et al. (eds.) 2008, *The Customs Law of Asia*, Oxford.

Cotton, H. M. 1993, "The Guardianship of Jesus Son of Babatha: Roman and Local Law in the Province of Arabia," *Journal of Roman Studies* 83, 94–108.

Crawford, M. H. 1969, *Roman Republican Coin Hoards*, London.

1977, "Review of H. J. Mason, *Greek Terms for Roman Institutions: A Lexicon and Analysis*," *Journal of Roman Studies* 67, 249–50.

1978, "Greek Intellectuals and the Roman Aristocracy in the First Century BC," in Garnsey and Whittaker (eds.), 193–207.

1985, *Coinage and Money under the Roman Republic*, London.

1990, "Origini e sviluppi del sistema provinciale romano," in Momigliano and Schiavone (eds.), 91–121.

1995, "La storia della colonizzazione romana secondo i Romani," in Storchi Marino (ed.), 187–92.

1996, *Roman Statutes*, London.

1998, "How to Create a municipium: Rome and Italy after the Social War," in Austin, Harries, and Smith (eds.), 31–46.

2006, "From Poseidonia to Paestum via the Lucanians," in Bradley and Wilson (eds.), 59–72.

2007, "The Mamertini, Alfius and Festus," in Dubouloz and Pittia (eds.), 273–9.

Creighton, J. D. 2000, *Coins and Power in Late Iron Age Britain*, Cambridge.

2006, *Britannia: The Creation of a Roman Province*, London and New York, NY.

Creighton, J. D. and Wilson, R. J. A. (eds.) 1999, *Roman Germany: Studies in Cultural Interaction*, Portsmouth, RI.

Crook, J. A., Lintott, A., and Rawson, E. (eds.) 1994, *The Cambridge Ancient History, Vol. 9: The Last Age of the Roman Republic, 146–43 BC* (2nd edn.), Cambridge.

Cuff, P. J. 1983, "Appian's *Romaica*. A Note," *Athenaeum* 61, 148–64.

Culham, P. 1997, "Did Roman Women Have an Empire?" in Golden and Toohey (eds.), 192–204.

Cunliffe, B. (ed.) 1988, *The Temple of Sulis Minerva at Bath, Vol. 2: The Finds from the Sacred Spring*, Oxford.

Curty, O. 1995, *Les parentés légendaires entre cités grecques: catalogue raisonné des inscriptions contenant le terme syngeneia et analyse critique*, Geneva.

Cuvigny, H. (ed.) 2003, *Praesidia du désert de Bérénice, Vol. 1: La route de Myos Hormos : l'armée romaine dans le désert oriental d'Égypte*, Cairo.

Dandelet, T. J. 2014, *The Renaissance of Empire in Early Modern Europe*, Cambridge.

Davidson, J. 1998, "Domesticating Dido: History and Historicity," in Burden (ed.), 65–88.

Davies, P. J. E. 2000, *Death and the Emperor: Roman Imperial Funerary Monuments from Augustus to Marcus Aurelius*, Cambridge.

Dávila, A. 2016, *El mall: The Spatial and Class Politics of Shopping Malls in Latin America*, Oakland, CA.

De Blois, L. 2007, "The Military Factor in the Onset of Crises in the Roman Empire in the Third Century AD," in De Blois and lo Cascio (eds.), 497–507.

De Blois, L., Erdkamp, P., Hekster, O. J., de Kleijn, G., and Mols, S. (eds.) 2003, *The Representation and Perception of Roman Imperial Power. Proceedings of the Third Workshop of the International Network Impact of Empire (Roman Empire, c. 200 BC–AD 476), Netherlands Institute in Rome, March 2002*, Amsterdam.

De Blois, L., Funke, P., and Hahn, J. (eds.) 2006, *The Impact of Imperial Rome on Religions, Ritual and Religious Life in the Roman Empire. Proceedings of the Fifth Workshop of the International Network Impact of Empire (Roman Empire, 200 BC–AD 476), Münster, June–July 2004*, Leiden and Boston, MA.

De Blois, L. and lo Cascio, E. (eds.) 2007, *Impact of the Roman Army (200 BC–AD 476): Economic, Social, Political, Religious, and Cultural Aspects. Proceedings of the Sixth Workshop of the International Network Impact of Empire (Roman Empire, 200 BC–AD 476), Capri, March–April 2005*, Leiden and Boston, MA.

De Blois, L. and Rich, J. (eds.) 2002, *The Transformation of Economic Life under the Roman Empire. Proceedings of the Second Workshop of the International Network Impact of Empire (Roman Empire, c. 200 BC–AD 476), Nottingham, July 2001*, Amsterdam.

De Callataÿ, F. 2005, "The Graeco-Roman Economy in the Super Long-Run: Lead, Copper, and Shipwrecks," *Journal of Roman Archaeology* 18, 361–72.

De Lange, N. R. M. 1978, "Jewish Attitudes to the Roman Empire," in Garnsey and Whittaker (eds.), 255–81.

De Ligt, L. 2007, "Roman Manpower and Recruitment during the Middle Republic," in Erdkamp (ed.), 114–31.

De Ligt, L., Hemelrijk, E. A., and Singor, H. W. (eds.) 2004, *Roman Rule and Civic Life: Local and Regional Perspectives. Proceedings of the Fourth Workshop of the International Network Impact of Empire (Roman Empire, c. 200 BC–AD 476), Leiden, June 2003*, Amsterdam.

De Ligt, L. and Northwood, S. (eds.) 2008, *People, Land, and Politics. Demographic Developments and the Transformation of Roman Italy 300 BC–AD 14*, Leiden and Boston, MA.

De Romanis, F. and Tchernia, A. (eds.) 1997, *Crossings: Early Mediterranean Contacts with India*, New Delhi.

De Romilly, J. 1963, *Thucydides and Athenian Imperialism*, tr. P. Thody, Oxford.

Deacy, S. and Pierce, K. F. (eds.) 1997, *Rape in Antiquity: Sexual Violence in the Greek and Roman Worlds*, London.

Degrassi, A. (ed.) 1947, *Fasti consulares et triumphales, Inscriptiones Italiae*, vol. 13: *Fasti et elogia*, fasc. I, Rome.

  (ed.) 1963, *Fasti anni Numani et Iuliani, Inscriptiones Italiae*, vol. 13: *Fasti et elogia*, fasc. II, Rome.

Demougin, S., Devijver, H., and Raepsaet-Charlier, M.-T. (eds.) 1999, *L'ordre équestre : histoire d'une aristocratie : IIe siècle av. J.-C.-IIIe siècle ap. J.-C.: actes du colloque international (Bruxelles-Leuven, 5–7 octobre 1995)*, Rome.

Dench, E. 1995, *From Barbarians to New Men: Greek, Roman, and Modern Perceptions of Peoples of the Central Apennines*, Oxford.

  2003, "Beyond Greeks and Barbarians: Italy and Sicily in the Hellenistic Age," in Erskine (ed.), 294–310.

  2004, "Samnites in English: The Legacy of E. Togo Salmon in the English-Speaking World," in Jones (ed.), 7–22.

  2005, *Romulus' Asylum: Roman Identities from the Age of Alexander to the Age of Hadrian*, Oxford.

  2011, "Roman Imperial Pasts," in Benoist, Daguet-Gagey, and Hoët-van Cauwenberghe (eds.), 487–502.

  2018, "Race," in Noreña (ed.), 201–221.

Derks, T. 1998, *Gods, Temples and Ritual Practices: The Transformation of Religious Ideas and Values in Roman Gaul*, Amsterdam.

Derks, T. and Roymans, N. (eds.) 2009, *Ethnic Constructs in Antiquity: The Role of Power and Tradition*, Amsterdam.

Derow, P. S. 1972, "Review of J. Deininger, *Der politische Widerstand gegen Rom in Griechenland 217–86 v. Chr,*" *Phoenix* 26, 303–11.

  1979, "Polybius, Rome, and the East," *Journal of Roman Studies* 69, 1–15 (republished in Derow 2015, 125–50).

  1989, "Rome, the Fall of Macedon and the Sack of Corinth," in Astin, Walbank, Frederiksen, and Ogilvie (eds.), 290–323 (republished in Derow 2015, 47–82).

  1995, "Herodotus Readings," *Classics Ireland* 2, 29–51.

  2015, *Rome, Polybius, and the East*, ed. A. Erskine and J. C. Quinn, Oxford.

Dickenson, C. P. and van Nijf, O. M. (eds.) 2013, *Public Space in the Post-Classical City. Proceedings of a One Day Colloquium Held at Fransum (July 2007)*, Leuven.

Dillery, J. 2015, *Clio's "Other" Sons: Berossus and Manetho*, Ann Arbor, MI.

Dillon, S. 2006, "Women on the Columns of Trajan and Marcus Aurelius and the Visual Language of Roman Victory," in Dillon and Welch (eds.), 244–71.

Dillon, S. and Welch, K. E. (eds.) 2006, *Representations of War in Ancient Rome*, Cambridge.

Dionisotti, A. C. 1982, "From Ausonius' Schooldays? A Schoolbook and Its Relatives," *Journal of Roman Studies* 72, 83–125.

Dirven, L. 2011, "Religious Frontiers in the Syrian-Mesopotamian Desert," in Hekster and Kaizer (eds.), 157–73.

Dirven, L. (ed.) 2013, *Hatra. Politics, Religion and Culture between Parthia and Rome, Oriens et Occidens,* vol. 21, Stuttgart.

Disraeli, B. 1847, *Tancred, or the New Crusade,* London.

Domingo Gygax, M. 2016, *Benefaction and Rewards in the Ancient Greek City: The Origins of Euergetism,* Princeton, NJ.

Doyle, M. W. 1986, *Empires,* Ithaca, NY.

Dreyer, B. and Engelmann, H. 2006, "Augustus und Germanicus im ionischen Metropolis," *Zeitschrift für Papyrologie und Epigraphik* 158, 173–82.

Dubouloz, J. and Pittia, S. (eds.) 2007, *La Sicile de Cicéron: lectures des Verrines : actes du colloque de Paris (mai 2006),* Besançon.

Dubuisson, M. 1985, *Le latin de Polybe: les implications historiques d'un cas de bilinguisme,* Paris.

Dueck, D. 2000, *Strabo of Amasia: A Greek Man of Letters in Augustan Rome,* London and New York, NY.

Dueck, D., Lindsay, H., and Pothecary, S. (eds.) 2005, *Strabo's Cultural Geography: The Making of a kolossourgia,* Cambridge.

Duindam, J., Harries, J., Humfress, C., and Hurvitz, N. (eds.) 2013, *Law and Empire: Ideas, Practices, Actors,* Leiden and Boston, MA.

Duncan-Jones, R. P. 1964, "The Purpose and Organization of the *alimenta,*" *Papers of the British School at Rome* 32, 123–46.

1982, *The Economy of the Roman Empire: Quantitative Studies* (2nd edn.), Cambridge.

1994, *Money and Government in the Roman Empire,* Cambridge.

Duval, P.-M. and Pinault, G. (eds.) 1986, *Recueil des inscriptions gauloises, Vol. III: Les calendriers de Coligny (73 fragments) et Villards d'Heria (8 fragments),* Paris.

Eck, W. 1984, "Senatorial Self-Representation: Developments in the Augustan Period," in Millar and Segal (eds.), 129–67.

(ed.) 1999, *Lokale Autonomie und römische Ordnungsmacht in den kaiserzeitlichen Provinzen vom 1. bis 3.* Jahrhundert, Munich.

2000, "Provincial Administration and Finance," in Bowman, Garnsey, and Rathbone (eds.), 266–92.

2004, *Köln in römischer Zeit: Geschichte einer Stadt im Rahmen des Imperium Romanum,* Cologne.

Eder, W. (ed.) 1990, *Staat und Staatlichkeit in der frühen römischen Republik: Akten eines Symposiums, 12.-15. Juli 1988, Freie Universität Berlin,* Stuttgart.

Edmondson, J. C. 1999, "The Cultural Politics of Public Spectacle in Rome and the Greek East, 167–166 BCE," in Bergmann and Kondoleon (eds.), 77–95.

Edwards, C. 1996, *Writing Rome: Textual Approaches to the City,* Cambridge.

2003, "Incorporating the Alien: The Art of Conquest," in Edwards and Woolf (eds.), 44–70.

2007, *Death in Ancient Rome,* New Haven, CT.

Edwards, C. and Woolf, G. (eds.) 2003, *Rome the Cosmopolis,* Cambridge.

Eigler, U., Gotter, U., Luraghi, N., and Walter, U. (eds.) 2003, *Formen römischer Geschichtsschreibung von den Anfängen bis Livius: Gattungen, Autoren, Kontexte*, Darmstadt.

Eilers, C. 2002, *Roman Patrons of Greek Cities*, Oxford.

Elliott, J. 2013, *Ennius and the Architecture of the Annales*, Cambridge.

Erdkamp, P. (ed.) 2002, *The Roman Army and the Economy*, Amsterdam.

2005, *The Grain Market in the Roman Empire: A Social, Political and Economic Study*, Cambridge.

(ed.) 2007, *A Companion to the Roman Army*, Malden, MA and Oxford.

Erskine, A. 2000, "Polybios and Barbarian Rome," *Mediterraneo antico* 3, 165–82.

2001, *Troy between Greece and Rome: Local Tradition and Imperial Power*, Oxford.

(ed.) 2003, *A Companion to the Hellenistic World*, Malden, MA and Oxford.

2010, *Roman Imperialism*, Edinburgh.

2011, *The Hellenistic Stoa: Political Thought and Action* (2nd edn.), Bristol.

Evans, J. D. (ed.) 2013, *A Companion to the Archaeology of the Roman Republican Period*, Chichester.

Ewald, B. C. and Noreña, C. F. (eds.) 2010, *The Emperor and Rome: Space, Representation, and Ritual*. Yale Classical Studies 35. Cambridge.

Fagan, G. G. 2011, *The Lure of the Arena: Social Psychology and the Crowd at the Roman Games*, Cambridge.

Feeney, D. C. 2007, *Caesar's Calendar: Ancient Time and the Beginnings of History*, Berkeley, CA.

Fentress, E. 2000a, "Frank Brown, Cosa, and the Idea of a Roman City," in Fentress (ed.), 11–24.

(ed.) 2000b, *Romanization and the City: Creations, Transformations, and Failures. Proceedings of a Conference Held at the American Academy in Rome to Celebrate the 50th Anniversary of the Excavations at Cosa, May 1998*, Portsmouth, RI.

(ed.) 2003, *Cosa, Vol. 5: An Intermittent Town: Excavations 1991–1997*, Ann Arbor, MI.

Fenwick, C., Wiggins, M., and Wythe, D. (eds.) 2008, *TRAC 2007: Proceedings of the Seventeenth Annual Theoretical Roman Archaeology Conference (London 2007)*, Oxford.

Ferrary, J.-L. 1987–1989, "Les Romains de la République et les démocraties grecques," *Opus* 6–8, 203–16.

1988, *Philhellénisme et impérialisme: aspects idéologiques de la conquête romaine du monde hellénistique, de la seconde guerre de Macédoine à la guerre contre Mithridate*, Rome.

Fink, R. O., Hoey, A. S., and Snyder, W. F. 1940, "The Feriale Duranum," *Yale Classical Studies* 7, 1–222.

Finley, M. I. 1973, *The Ancient Economy*, London.

1986a, "How It Really Was," in Finley 1986b, 47–66.

1986b, *Ancient History: Evidence and Models*, New York, NY.

1999, *The Ancient Economy* (updated with a foreword by I. Morris), Berkeley, CA and Los Angeles, CA.

Flower, H. I. 1996, *Ancestor Masks and Aristocratic Power in Roman Culture*, Oxford.

Formigé, J. 1949, *Le trophée des Alpes (La Turbie)*, Paris.

Frank, T. 1914, *Roman Imperialism*, New York, NY.

Frankfurter, D. 1998, *Religion in Roman Egypt: Assimilation and Resistance*, Princeton, NJ.

Frederiksen, M. W. 1965, "The Republican Municipal Laws: Errors and Drafts," *Journal of Roman Studies* 55, 183–98.

1984, *Campania*, London.

Freeman, P. W. M. 1997, "Mommsen to Haverfield: The Origins of Studies of Romanization in Late 19th-c. Britain," in Mattingly (ed.), 27–50.

2007, *The Best Training-Ground for Archaeologists: Francis Haverfield and the Invention of Romano-British Archaeology*, Oxford.

Frei-Stolba, R. and Gex, K. (eds.) 2001, *Recherches récentes sur le monde hellénistique : actes du colloque international organisé à l'occasion du 60e anniversaire de Pierre Ducrey (Lausanne, novembre 1998)*, Bern.

Fuchs, B. 2001, *Mimesis and Empire: The New World, Islam, and European Identities*, Cambridge.

Fuhrmann, C. J. 2012, *Policing the Roman Empire: Soldiers, Administration, and Public Order*, Oxford.

Fukuyama, F. 1989, "The End of History?," *The National Interest* 16, 3–18.

1992, *The End of History and the Last Man*, New York, NY and Toronto.

Gabba, E. 1958, "L"elogio di Brindisi," *Athenaeum* 36, 90–105.

1973, "Le origini della guerra sociale e la vita politica romana dopo l'88 a.C.," in Gabba, *Esercito e società nella tarda repubblica romana*, 193–345, Florence (first published in *Athenaeum* 32, 1954, 41–114, 293–345).

(ed.) 1974, *Polybe : neuf exposés suivis de discussions*, Vandœuvres.

1976, *Republican Rome, the Army, and the Allies*, tr. P. J. Cuff, Berkeley, CA.

Galinsky, K. (ed.) 1996, *Augustan Culture: An Interpretive Introduction*, Princeton, NJ.

2005, *The Cambridge Companion to the Age of Augustus*, Cambridge.

Gallina Zevi, A. and Humphrey, J. H. (eds.) 2004, *Ostia, Cicero, Gamala, Feasts, and the Economy: Papers in Memory of J. H. D'Arms*, Portsmouth, RI.

Galsterer, H. 2000, "Local and Provincial Institutions and Government," in Bowman, Garnsey, and Rathbone (eds.), 344–60.

2006, "Die römischen Stadtgesetze," in Capogrossi Colognesi and Gabba (eds.), 31–56.

Gargola, D. J. 1995, *Lands, Laws, and Gods: Magistrates and Ceremony in the Regulation of Public Lands in Republican Rome*, Chapel Hill NC.

Garnsey, P. D. A. 1968, "Trajan's *alimenta*. Some problems," *Historia* 17, 367–81.

1970, *Social Status and Legal Privilege in the Roman Empire*, Oxford.

1989, *Famine and Food Supply in the Graeco-Roman World: Responses to Risk and Crisis*, Cambridge.

2004, "Roman Citizenship and Roman Law in the Late Empire," in Swain and Edwards (eds.), 133–55.

Garnsey, P. D. A. and Whittaker, C. R. (eds.) 1978, *Imperialism in the Ancient World: The Cambridge University Research Seminar in Ancient History*, Cambridge.

Gehrke, H.-J. 1993, "Thisbe in Boiotien. Eine Fallstudie zum Thema "Griechische *Polis* und Römisches *Imperium*", *Klio - Beiträge zur Alten Geschichte* 75, 145–54.

Gehrke, H.-J. and Möller, A. (eds.) 1996, *Vergangenheit und Lebenswelt: Soziale Kommunikation, Traditionsbildung und historisches Bewusstsein*, Tübingen.

Gell, A. 1992, *The Anthropology of Time: Cultural Constructions of Temporal Maps and Images*, Oxford and Providence, RI.

Gettel, E. 2018 "Culture and Classics: Edward Burnett Tylor and Romanization." In E. Varto (ed.), 99–131.

Gibson, B. and Harrison, T. (eds.) 2013, *Polybius and His World: Essays in Memory of F. W. Walbank*, Oxford.

Gildenhard, I. 2003, "The 'Annalist' Before the Annalists: Ennius and His *Annales*," in Eigler, Gotter, Luraghi, and Walter (eds.), 93–114.

Gilliver, C. M. 2007, "Battle," in Sabin, van Wees, and Whitby (eds.), vol. 2, 122–57.

Gismondi, I. 1958, "Le architetture," in Squarciapino (ed.), 169–90.

Golden, M. and Toohey, P. (eds.) 1997, *Inventing Ancient Culture: Historicism, Periodization, and the Ancient World*, London and New York, NY.

Goldsworthy, A. and Haynes, I. (eds.) 1999, *The Roman Army as a Community: Including Papers of a Conference Held at Birkbeck College, University of London (January 1997)*, Portsmouth, RI.

González, J. and Crawford, M. H. 1986, "The *lex Irnitana*: A New Copy of the Flavian Municipal Law," *Journal of Roman Studies* 76, 147–243.

Goodman, M. 1989, "Nerva, the *Fiscus Judaicus* and Jewish Identity," *Journal of Roman Studies* 79, 40–4.

1991, "Babatha's Story (Review of N. Lewis, Y. Yadin and J. C. Greenfield [eds.], *The Documents from the bar Kokhba Period in the Cave of Letters: Greek Papyri; Aramaic and Nabatean Signatures and Subscriptions*)," *Journal of Roman Studies* 81, 169–75.

2005, "Coinage and Identity: The Jewish Evidence," in Howgego, Heuchert, and Burnett (eds.), 163–6.

Graf, F. 1997, *Magic in the Ancient World*, tr. F. Philip, Cambridge, MA.

Graham, M. W. 2006, *News and Frontier Consciousness in the Late Roman Empire*, Ann Arbor, MI.

Grandjean, C. (ed.) 2008, *Le Péloponnèse d'Epaminondas à Hadrien: Colloque de Tours, 6–7 octobre 2005*, Bordeaux.

Graninger, D. 2011, *Cult and Koinon in Hellenistic Thessaly*, Leiden and Boston, MA.

Griffin, M. T. 1984, *Nero: The End of a Dynasty*, London.

1996, "Tacitus, Tiberius and the Provinces," in Malkin and Rubinsohn (eds.), 33–57.

2003, "Clementia after Caesar: From Politics to Philosophy," in Cairns and Fantham (eds.), 157–82.

Gruen, E. S. 1984, *The Hellenistic World and the Coming of Rome*, Berkeley, CA.

Haensch, R. 1997, *Capita provinciarum: Statthaltersitze und Provinzialverwaltung in der römischen Kaiserzeit*, Mainz.

2001, "Inschriften und Bevölkerungsgeschichte Niedergermaniens: Zu den Soldaten der *legiones* I Minervia und XXX Ulpia Victrix," *Kölner Jahrbuch für Vor- und Frühgeschichte* 34, 89–134.

2012, "The Roman Army in Egypt," in Riggs (ed.), 68–82.

Hall, E. 1989, *Inventing the Barbarian: Greek Self-Definition through Tragedy*, Oxford.

Hall, J. M. 2007, "Polis, Community, and Ethnic Identity," in Shapiro (ed.), 40–60.

Halsall, G. 1995, *Early Medieval Cemeteries: An Introduction to Burial Archaeology in the Post-Roman West*, Skelmorlie.

2007, *Barbarian Migrations and the Roman West, 376–568*, Cambridge.

2009, "Beyond the Northern Frontiers," in Rousseau (ed.), 409–25.

Hanel, N. 2007, "Military Camps, Canabae, and Vici. The Archaeological Evidence," in Erdkamp (ed.), 395–416.

Hänger, C. 2001, *Die Welt im Kopf: Raumbilder und Strategie im Römischen Kaiserreich*, Göttingen.

Hanson, W. S. 2002, "Zones of Interaction: Roman and Native in Scotland," *Antiquity* 76, 834–40.

Harker, A. 2008, *Loyalty and Dissidence in Roman Egypt: The Case of the Acta Alexandrinorum*, Cambridge.

2012, "The Jews in Roman Egypt: Trials and Rebellions," in Riggs (ed.), 277–87.

Harper, K. 2017, *The Fate of Rome: Climate, Disease, and the End of an Empire*, Princeton, NJ.

Harris, W. V. 1971, "On War and Greed in the Second Century BC," *American Historical Review* 76, 1371–85.

1979, *War and Imperialism in Republican Rome, 327–70 BC*, (updated with new Preface in 1985), Oxford.

(ed.) 1993, *The Inscribed Economy: Production and Distribution in the Roman Empire in the Light of "instrumentum domesticum." The Proceedings of a Conference Held at the American Academy in Rome (January 1992)*, Ann Arbor, MI.

2001, *Restraining Rage: The Ideology of Anger Control in Classical Antiquity*, Cambridge, MA.

2007, "Quando e come l'Italia divenne per la prima volta Italia? Un saggio sulla politica dell''identità," *Studi Storici* 48, 301–22.

Harris, W. V. and Holmes, B. (eds.) 2008, *Aelius Aristides between Greece, Rome, and the Gods*, Leiden and Boston, MA.

178                          *Bibliography*

Hatzfeld, J. 1919, *Les trafiquants italiens dans l'Orient hellénique*, Paris.
Hatzopoulos, M. B. 1996, *Macedonian Institutions under the Kings*, 2 vols., Athens.
Hauken, T. 1998, *Petition and Response: An Epigraphic Study of Petitions to Roman Emperors, 181–249*, Bergen.
Haverfield, F. 1905, *The Romanization of Roman Britain* (1st edn.), London.
    1912, *The Romanization of Roman Britain* (2nd edn.), Oxford.
    1915, *The Romanization of Roman Britain* (3rd edn.), Oxford.
    1923, *The Romanization of Roman Britain* (4th edn., rev. by G. Macdonald), Oxford.
Haynes, I. 2013, *Blood of the Provinces: The Roman Auxilia and the Making of Provincial Society from Augustus to the Severans*, Oxford.
Heather, P. J. 2005, *The Fall of the Roman Empire*, London.
Hedrick, C. W., Jr. 2006, *Ancient History: Monuments and Documents*, Malden, MA and Oxford.
Hekster, O. and Kaizer, T. (eds.) 2011, *Frontiers in the Roman World. Proceedings of the Ninth Workshop of the International Network Impact of Empire (Durham, April 2009)*, Leiden and Boston, MA.
Heller, A. 2009, "La cité grecque d'époque impériale: vers une société d'ordres?" *Annales: Histoire, sciences sociales* 64, 341–73.
Herring, E. and Lomas, K. (eds.) 2000, *The Emergence of State Identities in Italy in the First Millennium* BC, London.
Herz, P. 2007, "Finances and Costs of the Roman Army," in Erdkamp (ed.), 306–22.
Herzog, T. 2015, *Frontiers of Possession: Spain and Portugal in Europe and the Americas*, Cambridge, MA.
Heslin, P. 2007, "Augustus, Domitian and the So-Called *Horologium Augusti*," *Journal of Roman Studies* 97, 1–20.
Hickson, F. V. 1993, *Roman Prayer Language: Livy and the Aeneid of Vergil*, Stuttgart.
Hingley, R. 2000, *Roman Officers and English Gentlemen: The Imperial Origins of Roman Archaeology*, London and New York, NY.
    2005, *Globalizing Roman Culture: Unity, Diversity and Empire*, London and New York, NY.
Hingley, R. and Hartis, R. 2011, "Contextualizing Hadrian's Wall: The Wall as 'Debatable Lands'", in Hekster and Kaizer (eds.), 79–95.
Hitchner, R. B. 2008, "Globalization *avant la lettre*: Globalization and the History of the Roman Empire," *New Global Studies* 2, 1–12.
Hobson, J. A. 1902, *Imperialism: A Study*, New York, NY.
Hölscher, T. 1967, *Victoria Romana. Archäologische Untersuchungen zur Geschichte und Wesensart der römischen Siegesgöttin von den Anfängen bis zum Ende des 3. Jhrs. n. Chr.*, Mainz.
    1980, "Römische Siegesdenkmäler der späten Republik," in Cahn and Simon (eds.), vol. 1, 351–71.
    1984, *Staatsdenkmal und Publikum; Vom Untergang der Republik bis zur Festigung des Kaisertums in Rom*, Konstanz.

2003, "Images of War in Greece and Rome: Between Military Practice, Public Memory, and Cultural Symbolism," *Journal of Roman Studies* 93, 1–17.

2006, "The Transformation of Victory into Power: From Event to Structure," in Dillon and Welch (eds.), 27–48.

Hoepfner, W. 2006, "Die griechische Agora im Überblick," in Hoepfner and Lehman (eds.), 1–28.

Hoepfner, W. and Lehmann, L. (eds.) 2006, *Die griechische Agora: Bericht über ein Kolloquium am 16. März 2003 in Berlin veranstaltet vom Institut für Klassische Archäologie der Freien Universität Berlin*, Mainz.

Hölkeskamp, K.-J. 2005, "Images of Power: Memory, Myth and Monument in the Roman Republic," *Scripta Classica Israelica* 24, 249–71.

2006, "Der Triumph: 'Erinnere Dich, dass Du ein Mensch bist,'" in Stein-Hölkeskamp and Hölkeskamp (eds.), 258–76.

2011, "The Roman Republic as Theatre of Power: The Consuls as Leading Actors," in Beck, Duplá, Jehne, and Pina Polo (eds.), 161–81.

Holliday, P. J. (ed.) 1993, *Narrative and Event in Ancient Art*, Cambridge.

Hopkins, K. 1978a, *Conquerors and Slaves*, Cambridge.

1978b, "Rules of Evidence (Review of F. Millar *The Emperor in the Roman World [31 BC–AD 337]*," *Journal of Roman Studies* 68, 178–86.

1980, "Taxes and Trade in the Roman Empire (200 BC–AD 400)," *Journal of Roman Studies* 70, 101–25.

1983, *Death and Renewal*, Cambridge.

2002, "Rome, Taxes, Rents and Trade," in Scheidel and von Reden (eds.), 190–230 [Originally published in *Kodai: Journal of Ancient History* 6–7 (1995/96): 41–75].

Horden, P. and Purcell, N. 2000, *The Corrupting Sea: A Study of Mediterranean History*, Oxford and Malden, MA.

Howgego, C. 2005, "Coinage and Identity in the Roman Provinces," in Howgego, Heuchert, and Burnett (eds.), 1–17.

Howgego, C., Heuchert, V., and Burnett, A. M. (eds.) 2005, *Coinage and Identity in the Roman Provinces*, Oxford.

Hoyos, B. D. (ed.) 2013, *A Companion to Roman Imperialism*, Leiden and Boston, MA.

Humfress, C. 2011, "Law and Custom under Rome," in Rio (ed.), 23–47.

2013, "Thinking through Legal Pluralism: 'Forum Shopping' in the Later Roman Empire," in Duindam, Harries, Humfress, and Hurvitz (eds.), 225–50.

Humm, M. 1996, "Appius Claudius Caecus et la construction de la *via Appia*," *Mélanges de l'école française de Rome* 108, 693–746.

Ilari, V. 1974, *Gli Italici nelle strutture militari romane*, Milan.

Innes, D., Hine, H., and Pelling, C. (eds.) 1995, *Ethics and Rhetoric: Classical Essays for Donald Russell on His Seventy-Fifth Birthday*, Oxford.

Isaac, B. 1990, *The Limits of Empire: The Roman Army in the East*, Oxford.

1992, "The Babatha Archive: A Review Article," *Israel Exploration Journal* 42, 62–75.

James, S. 1999, "The Community of the Soldiers: A Major Identity and Centre of Power in the Roman Empire," in Baker, Forcey, Jundi, and Witcher (eds.), 14–25.

Jehne, M. and Pina Polo, F. (eds.) 2015, *Foreign Clientelae in the Roman Empire: A Reconsideration*, Stuttgart.

Jewell, N. 2015, *Shopping Malls and Public Space in Modern China*, Farnham.

Jiménez, A. 2008, "A Critical Approach to the Concept of Resistance: New "Traditional" Rituals and Objects in Funerary Contexts of Roman Baetica," in Fenwick, Wiggins, and Wythe (eds.), 15–30.

2010, "Reproducing Difference: Mimesis and Colonialism in Roman Hispania," in van Dommelen and Knapp (eds.), 38–63.

Jördens, A. 2012, "Status and Citizenship," in Riggs (ed.), 247–59.

Johnston, A. C. 2017, *The Sons of Remus: Identity in Roman Gaul and Spain*, Cambridge, MA.

Jones, C. P. 1971, *Plutarch and Rome*, Oxford.

1978, *The Roman World of Dio Chrysostom*, Cambridge, MA.

1999, *Kinship Diplomacy in the Ancient World*, Cambridge, MA.

2001, "Memories of the Roman Republic in the Greek East," in Salomies (ed.), 11–18.

2010, *New Heroes in Antiquity: From Achilles to Antinoos*, Cambridge, MA.

Jones, H. (ed.) 2004, *Samnium: Settlement and Cultural Change. The Proceedings of the Third E. Togo Salmon Conference on Roman Studies*, Providence, RI.

Jones, S. 1997, *The Archaeology of Ethnicity: Constructing Identities in the Past and Present*, London and New York, NY.

Jongman, W. M. 2002, "The Roman Economy: From Cities to Empire," in de Blois and Rich (eds.), 28–47.

Kaizer, T. 2016, *Religion, Society and Culture at Dura-Europos*, Cambridge.

Kallet-Marx, R. 1995, *Hegemony to Empire: The Development of the Roman Imperium in the East from 148 to 62 BC*, Berkeley, CA.

Kampen, N. B. 1995, "Looking at Gender: The Column of Trajan and Roman Historical Relief," in Stanton and Stewart (eds.), 46–73.

Kantorowicz, E. H. 1961, "Gods in Uniform," *Proceedings of the American Philosophical Society* 105, 368–93.

Katzoff, R. and Schaps, D. (eds.) 2005, *Law in the Documents of the Judaean Desert*, Leiden and Boston, MA.

Keay, S. and Terrenato, N. (eds.) 2001, *Italy and the West: Comparative Issues in Romanization*, Oxford.

Kehne, P. 2007, "War- and Peacetime Logistics: Supplying Imperial Armies in East and West," in Erdkamp (ed.), 323–38.

Kellum, B. 2010, "Representations and Re-Presentations of the Battle of Actium," in Breed, Damon, and Rossi (eds.), 187–206.

Kennedy, D. L. (ed.) 1996, *The Roman Army in the East*, Ann Arbor, MI.

King, A. C. 1999, "Animals and the Roman Army: The Evidence of Animal Bones," in Goldsworthy and Haynes (eds.), 139–49.

Kiser, E. and Kane, D. 2007, "The Perils of Privatization: How the Characteristics of Principals Affected Tax Farming in the Roman Republic and Empire," *Social Science History* 31, 191–212.

Kissel, T. 2002, "Road-Building as a *munus publicum*," in Erdkamp (ed.), 127–60.

Koch, H. 1993, *Achämeniden-Studien*, Wiesbaden.

Koeppel, G. 2002, "The Column of Trajan: Narrative Technique and the Image of the Emperor," in Stadter and van der Stockt (eds.), 245–57.

Kolb, A. 2001, "Transport and Communication in the Roman State: The Cursus Publicus," in Adams and Laurence (eds.), 95–105.

2002, "The Impact and Interaction of State Transport in the Roman Empire," in de Blois and Rich (eds.), 67–76.

Kosmin, P. J. 2014, *The Land of the Elephant Kings: Space, Territory, and Ideology in the Seleucid Empire*, Cambridge, MA.

2018, *Time and Resistance in the Seleucid Empire*, Cambridge, MA.

Koßmann, D. 2008, "Römische Soldaten als Teilnehmer von Festen," in Rüpke (ed.), 133–52.

Koumoulides, J. T. A. (ed.) 1987, *Greek Connections: Essays on Culture and Diplomacy*, Notre Dame, IN.

Kousser, R. 2006, "Conquest and Desire: Roman Victoria in Public and Provincial Sculpture," in Dillon and Welch (eds.), 218–43.

Kraus, C. S. (ed.) 1999, *The Limits of Historiography: Genre and Narrative in Ancient Historical Texts*, Leiden and Boston, MA.

Kuhrt, A. 2002, *"Greeks" and "Greece" in Mesopotamian and Persian Perspectives*, Oxford.

Kuhrt, A. 2007, *The Persian Empire: A Corpus of Sources from the Achaemenid Period*, London and New York, NY.

Kuhrt, A. and Sherwin-White, S. 1991, "Aspects of Seleucid Royal Ideology: The Cylinder of Antiochus I from Borsippa," *Journal of Hellenic Studies* 111, 71–86.

Küpper-Böhm, A. 1996, *Die römischen Bogenmonumente der Gallia Narbonensis in ihrem urbanen Kontext*, Espelkamp.

Kurke, L. 1992, "The Politics of ἁβροσύνη in Archaic Greece," *Classical Antiquity* 11, 91–120.

1999, *Coins, Bodies, Games, and Gold: The Politics of Meaning in Archaic Greece*, Princeton, NJ.

Lacey, W. K. 1979, "*Summi fastigii vocabulum*: The Story of a Title," *Journal of Roman Studies* 69, 28–34.

Laffi, U. 1967, "Le iscrizioni relative all'introduzione nel 9 a.C. del nuovo calendario della Provincia d'Asia," *Studi classici e orientali* 16, 5–98.

Laird, M. L. 2015, *Civic Monuments and the Augustales in Roman Italy*, Cambridge.

Langslow, D. 2012, "Integration, Identity, and Language Shift: Strengths and Weaknesses of the '"Linguistic" Evidence,'" in Roselaar (ed.), 289–309.

Laurence, R. 2012, *Roman Archaeology for Historians*, London and New York, NY.

Laurence, R., Esmonde Cleary, S., and Sears, G. 2011, *The City in the Roman West, c. 250 BC–c. AD 250*, Cambridge.

Laurence, R. and Smith, C. 1995–1996, "Ritual, Time and Power in Ancient Rome," *Accordia Research Papers* 6, 133–151.

Lavan, M. 2013, *Slaves to Rome: Paradigms of Empire in Imperial Culture*, Cambridge.
　　2016, "The Spread of Roman Citizenship, 14–212 CE: Quantification in the Face of High Uncertainty," *Past and Present* 230, 1, 3–46.

Lendon, J. E. 1997, *Empire of Honour: The Art of Government in the Roman World*, Oxford.
　　2007, "War and Society," in Sabin, van Wees, and Whitby (eds.), vol. 1, 498–516.

Lenin, V. I. 1939, Imperialism, the Highest Stage of Capitalism: A Popular Outline, *rev. tr. (first published in 1917)*, New York, NY.

Lepik, A. and Bader, V. S. (eds.) 2016, *World of Malls: Architectures of Consumption*, Berlin.

Leschhorn, W. 1993, *Antike Ären: Zeitrechnung, Politik und Geschichte im Schwarzmeerraum und in Kleinasien nördlich des Tauros*, Stuttgart.

Lewis, D. M., Boardman, J., Hornblower, S., and Ostwald, M. (eds.) 1994, *The Cambridge Ancient History, Vol. 6: The Fourth Century BC* (2nd edn.), Cambridge.

Lewis, N. and Reinhold, M. 1990: *Roman Civilization: Selected Readings* (3rd edn.), 2 vols., New York, NY.

Lewis, N., Yadin, Y., and Greenfield, J. C. (eds.) 1989, *The Documents from the Bar Kokhba Period in the Cave of Letters: Greek Papyri; Aramaic and Nabatean Signatures and Subscriptions*, Jerusalem.

Liddel, P. and Fear, A. (eds.) 2010, *Historiae mundi: Studies in Universal History*, London.

Linke, B. and Stemmler, M. (eds.) 2000, *Mos maiorum: Untersuchungen zu den Formen der Identitätsstiftung und Stabilisierung in der Römischen Republik*, Stuttgart.

Lintott, A. 1993, *Imperium romanum: Politics and Administration*, London and New York, NY.
　　1999, *Violence in Republican Rome* (2nd edn.), Oxford.

Liu, X. 1988, *Ancient India and Ancient China: Trade and Religious Exchanges, AD 1–600*, Delhi.

Lloyd, G. E. R. 1966, *Polarity and Analogy: Two Types of Argumentation in Early Greek Thought*, Cambridge.

Lo Cascio, E. 2000, *Il princeps e il suo impero: studi di storia amministrativa e finanziaria romana*, Bari.

Loewe, M. 1986, "The Religious and Intellectual Background," in Twitchett and Loewe (eds.), 649–725.

Long, J. 1996, "Two Sides of a Coin: Aurelian, Vaballathus, and Eastern Frontiers in the Early 270s," in Mathisen and Sivan (eds.), 59–71.

Luke, T. S. 2014, *Ushering in a New Republic: Theologies of Arrival at Rome in the First Century BCE*, Ann Arbor, MI.

Luttwak, E. N. 1976, *The Grand Strategy of the Roman Empire from the First Century AD to the Third*, Baltimore, MD.

Ma, J. 2002, *Antiochos III and the Cities of Western Asia Minor* (2nd edn.), Oxford.

2003, "Kings," in Erskine (ed.), 177–95.

2009, "Empire, Statuses and Realities," in Ma, Papazarkadas, and Parker (eds.), 125–48.

2013, *Statues and Cities: Honorific Portraits and Civic Identity in the Hellenistic World*, Oxford.

Ma, J., Papazarkadas, N., and Parker, R. (eds.) 2009, *Interpreting the Athenian Empire*, London.

Maas, M. 2003, "'Delivered from Their Ancient Customs:' Christianity and the Question of Cultural Change in Early Byzantine Ethnography," in Mills and Grafton (eds.), 152–88.

MacMullen, R. 1984, "The Legion as Society," *Historia* 33, 440–56.

MacRae, D. 2016, *Legible Religion: Books, Gods and Rituals in Roman Culture*, Cambridge, MA.

Magie, D. 1950, *Roman Rule in Asia Minor: To the End of the Third Century after Christ*, Princeton, NJ.

Maier, C. S. 2006, *Among Empires: American Ascendancy and Its Predecessors*, Cambridge, MA.

Malkin, I. 2011, *A Small Greek World: Networks in the Ancient Mediterranean*, Oxford.

Malkin, I. and Rubinsohn, W. Z. (eds.) 1995, *Leaders and Masses in the Roman World. Studies in Honor of Zvi Yavetz*, Leiden.

Manacorda, D. 1993, "Appunti sulla bollatura in età romana," in Harris (ed.), 37–54.

Mann, C. 2010, "Gladiators in the Greek East: A Case Study in Romanization," in Papakonstantinou (ed.), 124–49 (first published in the *International Journal of the History of Sport* 26 [2009], 272–97).

Manning, J. G. 2010, *The Last Pharaohs: Egypt under the Ptolemies, 305–30 BC*, Princeton, NJ.

Marchand, S. L. 1996, *Down from Olympus: Archaeology and Philhellenism in Germany, 1750–1970*, Princeton, NJ.

Marincola, J. (ed.) 2007, *A Companion to Greek and Roman Historiography*, Malden, MA and Oxford.

Martelli, A. 2002, "Per una nuova lettura dell'iscrizione Vetter 61 nel contesto del santuario di Apollo a Pompei," *Eutopia* (nuova serie II) 2, 71–81.

Mason, H. J. 1974, *Greek Terms for Roman Institutions. A Lexicon and Analysis*, Toronto.

Mathisen, R. W. and Sivan, H. S. (eds.) 1996, *Shifting Frontiers in Late Antiquity*, Aldershot and Brookfield, VT.

Matijević, K. 2010, *Römische und frühchristliche Zeugnisse im Norden Obergermaniens. Epigraphische Studien zu unterer Mosel und östlicher Eifel*, Rahden.

Matteini Chiari, M. (ed.) 1982, *Saepinum: Museo documentario dell'Altilia*, Campobasso.

Mattingly, D. J. 2011, *Imperialism, Power, and Identity: Experiencing the Roman Empire*, Princeton, NJ.

(ed.) 1997, *Dialogues in Roman Imperialism: Power, Discourse, and Discrepant Experience in the Roman Empire*, Portsmouth, RI.

Mattingly, D. J. and Hitchner, R. B. 1995, "Roman Africa: An Archaeological Review," *Journal of Roman Studies* 85, 165–213.

Mayer, E. 2010, "Propaganda, Staged Applause, or Local Politics? Public Monuments from Augustus to Septimius Severus," in Ewald and Norena (eds.) (Yale Classical Studies 35), 111–34.

McDougall, J. and Scheele, J. (eds.) 2012, *Saharan Frontiers: Space and Mobility in Northwest Africa*, Bloomington, IN.

McLynn, N. 2003, "Seeing and Believing: Aspects of Conversion from Antoninus Pius to Louis the Pious," in Mills and Grafton (eds.), 224–70.

McKeown, N. 2007, *The Invention of Ancient Slavery?*, London.

Mellor, R. 1975, ΘΕΑ ΡΩΜΗ. *The Worship of the Goddess Roma in the Greek World*, Göttingen.

Meyer, E. A. 2004, *Legitimacy and Law in the Roman World: Tabulae in Roman Belief and Practice*, Cambridge.

Meyer-Zwiffelhoffer, E. 2002, Πολιτικῶς ἄρχειν: *Zum Regierungsstil der senatorischen Statthalter in den kaiserzeitlichen griechischen Provinzen*, Stuttgart.

Migeotte, L. 2008, "L'organisation de l'oktōvolos eisphora à Messène," in Grandjean (ed.), 229–43.

Mileta, C. 2008, "Die prorömischen Kulte der Provinz Asia als Brücke zwischen dem hellenistischen Herrscherkult und dem frühen Kaiserkult," *Altertum* 53, 111–23.

Millar, F. G. B. 1963, "The *fiscus* in the First Two Centuries," *Journal of Roman Studies* 53, 29–42.

1964, *A Study of Cassius Dio*, Oxford.

1973, "Triumvirate and Principate," *Journal of Roman Studies* 63, 50–67.

1977, *The Emperor in the Roman World: 31 BC–AD 337*, London.

1981a, *The Roman Empire and Its Neighbours* (2nd edn.) (with contributions by R. N. Frye and others), London.

1981b, "The World of the *Golden Ass*," *Journal of Roman Studies* 71, 63–75

1984, "State and Subject: The Impact of Monarchy," in Millar and Segal (eds.), 37–60.

1986, "Politics, Persuasion and the People before the Social War (150–90 BC)," *Journal of Roman Studies* 76, 1–11.

1987, "Polybius Between Greece and Rome," in Koumoulides (ed.), 1–18.

1989, "Political Power in Mid-Republican Rome: *Curia* or *comitium*? (Review of K. A. Raauflaub, *Social Struggles in Archaic Rome: New Perspectives on the Conflict of the Orders* and K.-J. Hölkeskamp, *Die Entstehung der Nobilität: Studien zur Sozialen und Politischen Geschichte der Römischen Republik im 4. Jhdt. v. Chr.*)," *Journal of Roman Studies* 79, 138–50.

1993, *The Roman Near East, 31 BC–AD 337*, Cambridge, MA.

1995, "Latin in the Epigraphy of the Roman Near East," in Solin, Salomies, and Liertz (eds.), 403–19.

1996, "Emperors, Kings and Subjects: The Politics of Two-Level Sovereignty," *Scripta Classica Israelica* 15, 159–73.

1997, "Hellenistic History in a Near Eastern Perspective: The Book of Daniel," in Cartledge, Garnsey, and Gruen (eds.), 89–104.

Millett, M., Revell, L. and Moore, A. (eds.) 2016, *The Oxford Handbook of Roman Britain*, Oxford.

Millar, F. and Segal, E. (eds.) 1984, *Caesar Augustus: Seven Aspects*, Oxford.

Mills, K. and Grafton, A. (eds.) 2003, *Conversion in Late Antiquity and the Early Middle Ages: Seeing and Believing*, Rochester, NY.

Milnor, K. 2005, *Gender, Domesticity, and the Age of Augustus: Inventing Private Life*, Oxford.

Mitchell, S. 1976, "Requisitioned Transport in the Roman Empire: A New Inscription from Pisidia," *Journal of Roman Studies* 66, 106–31.

1993, *Anatolia: Land, Men, and Gods in Asia Minor*, 2 vols., Oxford.

1999, "The Administration of Roman Asia from 133 BC to 250 AD," in Eck (ed.), 17–46.

2003, "The Galatians: Representation and Reality," in Erskine (ed.), 280–93.

2008, "Geography, Politics and Imperialism in the Asian Customs Law," in Cottier et al. (eds.), 165–201.

Moles, J. L. 1996, "Herodotus Warns the Athenians," *Papers of the Leeds International Latin Seminar* 9, 259–84.

2002, "Herodotus and Athens," in Bakker, de Jong, and van Wees (eds.), 33–52.

Momigliano, A. 1982, "The Origins of Universal History," Annali della Scuola Normale Superiore di Pisa. *Classe di Lettere e Filosofia* 12, 533–60.

Momigliano, A. and Schiavone, A. (eds.) 1990, *Storia di Roma, Vol. II: L'impero mediterraneo, Pt. I: La repubblica imperiale*, Turin.

Mommsen, T. 1854–1856, *Römische Geschichte*, vols. 1–3, Leipzig and Berlin.

1871–88, *Römisches Staatsrecht*, vols. 1–3, Leipzig.

1885, *Römische Geschichte, Vol. 5: Die Provinzen von Caesar bis Diocletian*, Berlin.

Monard, J. 1999, *Histoire du calendrier gaulois : le calendrier de Coligny*, Paris.

Monson, A. and Scheidel, W. (eds.) 2015, *Fiscal Regimes and the Political Economy of Premodern States*, Cambridge.

Morel, J.-P. 2009, "La céramique à vernis noir et histoire (Review of R. E. Roth, *Styling Romanisation: Pottery and Society in Central Italy*)," *Journal of Roman Archaeology* 22, 477–88.

Morley, N. 2010, *The Roman Empire: Roots of Imperialism*, London and New York, NY.

Morris, I. 1986, "Gift and Commodity in Archaic Greece," *Man* 21, 1–17.

Morstein-Marx, R. 2004, *Mass Oratory and Political Power in the Late Roman Republic*, Cambridge.

Mouritsen, H. 1998, *Italian Unification: A Study in Ancient and Modern Historiography*, London.

2005, "Freedmen and Decurions: Epitaphs and Social History in Imperial Italy," *Journal of Roman Studies* 95, 38–63.

2011, *The Freedman in the Roman World*, Cambridge.

Moyer, I. S. 2011, *Egypt and the Limits of Hellenism*, Cambridge.

Murphy, C. 2007, *Are We Rome? The Fall of an Empire and the Fate of America*, Boston, MA and New York, NY.

Mutschler, F.-H. and Mittag, A. (eds.) 2008, *Conceiving the Empire: China and Rome Compared*, Oxford.

Nachtergael, G. 1977, *Les Galates en Grèce et les Sôtèria de Delphes. Recherches d'histoire et d'épigraphie hellénistiques*, Brussels.

Nappo, D. and Zerbini, A. 2011, "On The Fringe: Trade and Taxation in the Egyptian Eastern Desert," in Hekster and Kaizer (eds.), 61–77.

Neesen, L. 1980, *Untersuchungen zu den direkten Staatsabgaben der römischen Kaiserzeit (27 v. Chr.-284 n. Chr.)*, Bonn.

Nelis, J. 2007, "Constructing a Fascist Identity: Benito Mussolini and the Myth of *Romanità*," *Classical World* 100, 391–415.

Nicolet, C. (ed.) 1983, *Demokratia et aristokratia : à propos de Caius Gracchus: mots grecs et réalités romaines*, Paris.

1984, "Augustus, Government, and the Propertied Classes," in Millar and Segal (eds.), 89–128.

1991, *Space, Geography, and Politics in the Early Roman Empire*, Ann Arbor, MI.

2000, *Censeurs et publicains: économie et fiscalité dans la Rome antique*, Paris.

Nock, A. D. 1933, *Conversion: The Old and the New in Religion from Alexander the Great to Augustine of Hippo*, Oxford.

Noreña, C. F. 2011, *Imperial Ideals in the Roman West: Representation, Circulation, Power*, Cambridge.

2018, "Private Associations and Urban Experience in the Han and Roman Empires," in Beck and Vankeerberghen (eds.).

(ed.) 2018, *A Cultural History of Western Empires: Antiquity*, London.

North, J. A. 1979, "Religious Toleration in Republican Rome," *Proceedings of the Cambridge Philological Society* 25, 85–103.

1981, "The Development of Roman Imperialism," *Journal of Roman Studies* 71, 1–9.

1990, "Democratic Politics in Republican Rome," *Past and Present* 126, 3–21 (reprinted with postscript in Osborne (ed.) 2004, 140–58).

Nutton, V. 1978, "The Beneficial Ideology," in Garnsey and Whittaker (eds.) 209–22.

Öhler, M. (ed.) 2011, *Aposteldekret und antikes Vereinswesen: Gemeinschaft und ihre Ordnung*, Tübingen.

Ogle, V. 2015, *The Global Transformation of Time: 1870–1950*, Cambridge, MA.

Olmsted, G. S. 2001, *A Definitive Reconstructed Text of the Coligny Calendar*, Washington, DC.

Osborne, R. (ed.) 2000, *The Athenian Empire* (4th edn.), London.

(ed.) 2004, *Studies in Ancient Greek and Roman Society*, Cambridge.

Osborne, R. and Cunliffe, B. (eds.) 2005, *Mediterranean Urbanization 800–600 BC*, London.

Osgood, J. 2011, *Claudius Caesar: Image and Power in the Early Roman Empire*, Cambridge.

Ostrow, S. E. 1990, "*The Augustales in the Augustan Scheme*," in Raaflaub and Toher (eds.), 364–79.

Palet, J. M. and Orengo, H. A. 2011, "The Roman Centuriated Landscape: Conception, Genesis, and Development as Inferred from the *Ager Tarraconensis* Case," *American Journal of Archaeology* 115, 383–402.

Panciera, S. 1966, "Il sepolcro ostiense di C. Cartilius Poplicola ed una scheda epigrafica di Gaetano Marini," *Archeologia Classica* 18, 54–63.

Papakonstantinou, Z. (ed.) 2010, *Sport in the Cultures of the Ancient World: New Perspectives*, London and New York, NY.

Patterson, J. R. 2006, *Landscapes and Cities: Rural Settlement and Civic Transformation in Early Imperial Italy*, Oxford.

Pekáry, T. 1968, *Untersuchungen zu den römischen Reichsstrassen*, Bonn.

Pelgrom, J. 2008, "Settlement Organization and Land Distribution in Latin Colonies before the Second Punic War," in de Ligt and Northwood (eds.), 333–72.

Pensabene, P. 2004, "Marmi e classi dirigenti a Ostia tra la tarda repubblica e la prima età augustea," in Gallina Zevi and Humphrey (eds.), 99–107.

Perkins, J. 1995, *The Suffering Self: Pain and Narrative Representation in the Early Christian Era*, London and New York, NY.

Petersen, L. H. 2006, *The Freedman in Roman Art and Art History*, Cambridge.

Phang, S. E. 2001, *The Marriage of Roman Soldiers (13 BC–AD 235): Law and Family in the Imperial Army*, Leiden and Boston, MA.

Pinches, M. (ed.) 1999, *Culture and Privilege in Capitalist Asia*, London and New York, NY.

Pitts, M. and Versluys, M. J. (eds.) 2015, *Globalisation and the Roman World: World History, Connectivity and Material Culture*, Cambridge.

Pobjoy, M. 2006, "Epigraphy and Numismatics," in Rosenstein and Morstein-Marx (eds.), 51–80.

Poccetti, P. 1979, *Nuovi documenti italici (a complemento del Manuale di E. Vetter)*, Pisa.

Pollard, N. 1996, "The Roman Army as 'Total Institution' in the Near East? Dura-Europos as a Case Study," in Kennedy (ed.), 211–27.

2000, *Soldiers, Cities, and Civilians in Roman Syria*, Ann Arbor, MI.

Pollitt, J. J. 1986, *Art in the Hellenistic Age*, Cambridge.

Potter, D. S. 2004, *The Roman Empire at Bay: AD 180–395*, London and New York, NY.

(ed.) 2006, *A Companion to the Roman Empire*, Malden, MA and Oxford.

2013, "The Limits of Power," in Hoyos (ed.), 319–32.

Potter, D. S. and Damon, C. 1999, "The *senatus consultum de Cn. Pisone patre*," *American Journal of Philology* 120, 13–42.

Prag, J. R. W. 2006, "*Cave navem*," *Classical Quarterly* 56, 538–47.

2007, *"Auxilia* and *gymnasia:* A Sicilian Model of Roman Imperialism," *Journal of Roman Studies* 97, 68–100.

2013, "Sicily and Sardinia-Corsica: The First Provinces," in Hoyos (ed.), 53–65.

Prag, J. R. W. and Quinn, J. C. (eds.) 2013, *The Hellenistic West: Rethinking the Ancient Mediterranean,* Cambridge.

Price, S. R. F. 1984, *Rituals and Power: The Roman Imperial Cult in Asia Minor,* Cambridge.

2005, "Local Mythologies in the Greek East," in Howgego, Heuchert, and Burnett (eds.), 115–24.

Prontera, F. (ed.) 1984, *Strabone: contributi allo studio della personalità e dell'opera,* Perugia.

Prosdocimi, A. L. 1989, "Le religioni degli Italici," in Carratelli (ed.), 475–545.

Pucci, G. 2001, "Inscribed *instrumentum* and the Ancient Economy," in Bodel (ed.), 137–52.

Purcell, N. 1983, "The *apparitores:* A Study in Social Mobility," *Papers of the British School at Rome* 51, 125–73.

1990a, "Maps, Lists, Money, Order and Power (Review of C. Nicolet, *L'inventaire du monde: géographie et politique aux origines de l'Empire romain*)," *The Journal of Roman Studies* 80, 178–82.

1990b, "The Creation of Provincial Landscape: The Roman Impact on Cisalpine Gaul," in Blagg and Millett (eds.), 7–29.

1994, "South Italy in the Fourth Century BC," in Lewis, Boardman, Hornblower, and Ostwald (eds.), 381–403.

1995, "On the Sacking of Carthage and Corinth," in Innes, Hine, and Pelling (eds.), 133–48.

2000, "Rome and Italy," in Bowman, Garnsey, and Rathbone (eds.), 405–43.

2005a, "Romans in the Roman World," in Galinsky (ed.), 85–105.

2005b, "Statics and Dynamics: Ancient Mediterranean Urbanism," in Osborne and Cunliffe (eds.), 249–72.

2013, "Rivers and the Geography of Power," *Pallas* 90, 373–87.

Quaß, F. 1993, *Die Honoratiorenschicht in den Städten des griechischen Ostens: Untersuchungen zur politischen und sozialen Entwicklung in hellenistischer und römischer Zeit,* Stuttgart.

Quinn, J. C. 2010, "The Reinvention of Lepcis," *Bollettino de archeologia online* 4, 52–69.

Quinn, J. C. and Wilson, A. 2013, "Capitolia," *Journal of Roman Studies* 103, 117–73.

Raaflaub, K. A. 2009, "Learning from the Enemy: Athenian and Persian 'Instruments of Empire,'" in Ma, Papazarkadas, and Parker (eds.), 89–124.

Raaflaub, K. A. and Toher, M. (eds.) 1990, *Between Republic and Empire: Interpretations of Augustus and His Principate,* Berkeley, CA.

Rathbone, D. W. 1981, "The Development of Agriculture in the *Ager Cosanus* during the Roman Republic: Problems of Evidence and Interpretation," *Journal of Roman Studies* 71, 10–23.

2008, "Nero's Reforms of vectigalia and the Inscription of the lex Portorii Asiae," in Cottier et al. (eds.), 251–78.

Rathbone, D. W. and Alston, R. 2007, "Warfare and the State," in Sabin, van Wees, and Whitby (eds.), vol. 2, 158–97.

Rawson, E. 1975, "Caesar's Heritage: Hellenistic Kings and Their Roman Equals," *Journal of Roman Studies* 65, 148–59.

1987, "*Discrimina ordinum*: The lex Julia Theatralis," *Papers of the British School at Rome* 55, 83–114.

1990, "The Antiquarian Tradition: Spoils and Representations of Foreign Armour," in Eder (ed.), 158–73.

Rea, J. R. 1982, "Lease of a Red Cow Called Thayris," *Journal of Egyptian Archaeology* 68, 277–82.

Rebenich, S. 2009, "Late Antiquity in Modern Eyes," in Rousseau (ed.), 77–92.

Revell, L. 2009, *Roman Imperialism and Local Identities*, Cambridge.

2016, *Ways of Being Roman: Discourses of Identity in the Roman West*, Oxford and Philadelphia, PA.

Reynolds, J. 1988, "Cities," in Braund (ed.), 15–51.

Rich, J. W. 1983, "The Supposed Roman Manpower Shortage of the Later Second Century BC," *Historia* 32, 287–331.

Rich, J. W. and Shipley, G. (eds.) 1993, *War and Society in the Roman World*, London and New York, NY.

Rich, J. W. and Williams, J. H. C. 1999, "*Leges et Ivra P. R. Restitvit*: A New *Aureus* of Octavian and the Settlement of 28–27 BC," *The Numismatic Chronicle* 159, 169–213.

Richardson, J. S. 1979, "Polybius' View of the Roman Empire," *Papers of the British School at Rome* 47, 1–11.

1986, *Hispaniae: Spain and the Development of Roman Imperialism, 218–82 BC*, Cambridge.

1991, "*Imperium romanum*: Empire and the Language of Power," *Journal of Roman Studies* 81, 1–9.

2008, *The Language of Empire: Rome and the Idea of Empire from the Third Century BC to the Second Century AD*, Cambridge.

Richmond, I. A., North, J., and Lintott, A. 2012, "Pomerium," *Oxford Classical Dictionary* (4th edn.) S. Hornblower, A. Spawforth, and E. Eidinow (eds.), Oxford, 1177–78.

Riggs, C. (ed.) 2012, *The Oxford Handbook of Roman Egypt*, Oxford.

Rio, A. (ed.) 2011, *Law, Custom, and Justice in Late Antiquity and the Early Middle Ages: Proceedings of the 2008 Byzantine Colloquium*, London.

Rives, J. B. 1999, "The Decree of Decius and the Religion of Empire," *Journal of Roman Studies* 89, 135–54.

Rix, H. 2002, *Sabellische Texte: die Texte des Oskischen, Umbrischen und Südpikenischen*, Heidelberg.

Rizakis, A. D. 2001, "Les cités péloponnésiennes entre l'époque hellénistique et l'Empire: le paysage économique et social," in Frei-Stolba and Gex (eds.), 75–96.

Robert, L. 1982, "Une vision de Perpétue martyre à Carthage en 203," *Comptes rendus de l'Académie des Inscriptions et Belles-Lettres* 126, 228–76 (reprinted in his *Opera minora selecta* 5 Amsterdam, 1989, 791–839).

Rogers, G. M. 1991, *The Sacred Identity of Ephesos: Foundation Myths of a Roman City*, London and New York, NY.

Root, M. C. 1985, "The Parthenon Frieze and the Apadana Reliefs at Persepolis: Reassessing a Programmatic Relationship," *American Journal of Archaeology* 89, 103–20.

Roselaar, S. T. 2010, *Public Land in the Roman Republic: A Social and Economic History of ager publicus in Italy, 396–89 BC*, Oxford.

(ed.) 2012, *Processes of Integration and Identity Formation in the Roman Republic*, Leiden and Boston, MA.

Rosenstein, N. and Morstein-Marx, R. (eds.) 2006, *A Companion to the Roman Republic*, Malden, MA and Oxford.

Rostovtzeff, M. I. 1926, *The Social and Economic History of the Roman Empire* (2nd edn. rev. by P. M. Fraser, 1957), Oxford.

Roth, J. P. 1999, *The Logistics of the Roman Army at War (264 BC–AD 235)*, Leiden and Boston, MA.

Roth, R. E. 2007, *Styling Romanisation: Pottery and Society in Central Italy*, Cambridge.

2013, "Before Sigillata: Black-Gloss Pottery and Its Cultural Dimensions," in Evans (ed.), 81–96.

Roth, R. E. and Keller, J. (eds.) 2007, *Roman by Integration: Dimensions of Group Identity in Material Culture and Text*, Portsmouth, RI.

Rous, S. A. 2016, Ancient Upcycling: Social Memory and the Reuse of Marble in Athens, PhD diss., Harvard University.

Rousseau, P. (ed.) 2009, *A Companion to Late Antiquity*, Chichester and Malden, MA.

Rousset, D. 2012, "Robert, Louis (1904–1985)," in *The Encyclopedia of Ancient History*, ed. R. S. Bagnall, K. Brodersen, C. B. Champion, A. Erskine and S. R. Huebner, Malden, MA, 5860–1.

Rubin, B. B. 2008, (Re)representing Empire: The Roman Imperial Cult in Asia Minor, 31 BC–AD 68, PhD diss., University of Michigan.

Rüpke, J. 2006a, "Urban Religion and Imperial Expansion: Priesthoods in the lex Ursonensis," in de Blois, Funke. and Hahn (eds.), 11–23.

2006b, "Religion in lex Ursonensis," in Ando and Rüpke (eds.), 34–46.

2006c, "Ennius's *Fasti* in Fulvius's Temple: Greek Rationality and Roman Tradition," *Arethusa* 39, 489–512.

(ed.) 2007, *A Companion to Roman Religion*, Malden, MA and Oxford.

2008, "Kalender- und Festexport im Imperium Romanum," in Rüpke (ed.) 19–32.

(ed.) 2008, *Festrituale in der römischen Kaiserzeit*, Tübingen.

2011, *The Roman Calendar from Numa to Constantine: Time, History, and the Fasti*, tr. D. M. B. Richardson, Chichester and Malden, MA (first published in 1995).

(ed.) 2013, *The Individual in the Religions of the Ancient Mediterranean*, Oxford.

Russo, F. 2012, "The Beginning of the First Punic War and the Concept of Italia," in Roselaar (ed.), 35–50.

Sabin, P., van Wees, H., and Whitby, M. (eds.) 2007, *The Cambridge History of Greek and Roman Warfare*, 2 vols., Cambridge.

Sahlins, M. 1972, *Stone Age Economics*, Chicago, IL and New York, NY.

2004, *Apologies to Thucydides: Understanding History as Culture and Vice Versa*, Chicago, IL.

Saller, R. 1982, *Personal Patronage under the Early Empire*, Cambridge.

2002, "Framing the Debate over Growth in the Ancient Economy," in Scheidel and von Reden (eds.), 251–69.

Salmon, E. T. 1944, *A History of the Roman World from 30 BC to AD 138*, New York, NY.

1967, *Samnium and the Samnites*, Cambridge.

1969, *Roman Colonization under the Republic*, London.

Salomies, O. 1995, "*Some Observations on Consular Dating in Roman Inscriptions of the Empire*," in Solin, Salomies, and Liertz (eds.), 269–92.

(ed.), 2001, *The Greek East in the Roman Context. Proceedings of a Colloquium Organised by the Finnish Institute at Athens (May 1999)*, Helsinki.

Salway, B. 2005, "The Nature and Genesis of the Peutinger Map," *Imago Mundi* 57, 119–35.

2008, "Roman Consuls, Imperial Politics, and Egyptian Papyri: The *Consulates* of 325 and 344 CE," *Journal of Late Antiquity* 1, 278–310.

Samuel, A. E. 1972, *Greek and Roman Chronology: Calendars and Years in Classical Antiquity*, Munich.

Sandwell, I. 2011, "How to Teach *Genesis* 1.1–19: John Chrysostom and Basil of Caesarea on the Creation of the World," *Journal of Early Christian Studies* 19, 539–64.

Schäfer, T. 1989, *Imperii insignia. Sella curulis und fasces: Zur Repräsentation römischer Magistrate*, Mainz.

Scheid, J. 1995, "*Graeco ritu*: A Typically Roman Way of Honoring the Gods," *Harvard Studies in Classical Philology* 97, 15–31.

Scheid, J. and Huet, V. (eds.) 2000, *Autour de la colonne Aurélienne: geste et image sur la colonne de Marc Aurèle à Rome*, Turnhout.

Scheidel, W. 2007, "Marriage, Families, and Survival: Demographic Aspects," in Erdkamp (ed.), 417–34.

(ed.) 2009, *Rome and China: Comparative Perspectives on Ancient World Empires*, Oxford.

2015, "The Early Roman Monarchy," in Monson and Scheidel (eds.), 229–57.

Scheidel, W. and Friesen, S. J. 2009, "The Size of the Economy and the Distribution of Income in the Roman Empire," *Journal of Roman Studies* 99, 61–91.

Scheidel, W. and von Reden, S. (eds.) 2002, *The Ancient Economy*, Edinburgh.

Schörle, K. 2012, "Saharan Trade in Classical Antiquity," in McDougall and Scheele (eds.), 58–72.

Schörner, G. 2011, "Rom jenseits der Grenze: Klientelkönigreiche und der Impact of Empire," in Hekster and Kaizer (eds.), 113–31.

Schürer, E. 1973–1987, *The History of the Jewish People in the Age of Jesus Christ (175 BC–AD 135)*, rev. ed., G. Vermes, F. Millar, M. Black & M. Goodman, 3 vols., Edinburgh.

Schwartz, S. 1990, *Josephus and Judean Politics*, Leiden.

    1995, "Language, Power and Identity in Ancient Palestine," *Past and Present* 148, 3–47.

Schwentzel, C.-G. 2010, "La propagande de Vaballath et Zénobie d'après le témoignage des monnaies et tessères," *Rivista italiana di numismatica e scienze affini* 111, 157–72.

Scott, J. C. 1985, *Weapons of the Weak: Everyday Forms of Peasant Resistance*, New Haven, CT.

Scott, S. and Webster, J. (eds.) 2003, *Roman Imperialism and Provincial Art*, Cambridge.

Sear, F. 2006, *Roman Theatres: An Architectural Study*, Oxford.

Settis, S., Gabba, E., Capogrossi Colognesi, L. et al. (eds.) 1983, *Misurare la terra: centuriazione e coloni nel mondo romano*, Modena.

Severy, B. 2003, *Augustus and the Family at the Birth of the Roman Empire*, New York, NY and London.

Sewell, J. 2010, *The Formation of Roman Urbanism, 338–200 BC: Between Contemporary Foreign Influence and Roman Tradition*, Portsmouth, RI.

    2014, "Gellius, Philip II and a Proposed End to the 'Model-Replica' Debate," in Stek and Pelgrom (eds.), 125–39.

Seyrig, H. 1950, "Antiquités syriennes," *Syria* 27, 5–56.

Shapiro, H. A. (ed.) 2007, *The Cambridge Companion to Archaic Greece*, Cambridge.

Shaw, B. D. 1983, "Soldiers and Society: The Army in Numidia," *Opus* 2, 133–59.

    1984, "Bandits in the Roman Empire," *Past and Present* 105, 3–52 [rev. ed., with addendum on recent research in Osborne (ed.), 326–74].

    1992, "Under Russian Eyes (Review of M. A. Wes, *Michael Rostovtzeff, Historian in Exile: Russian Roots in an American Context* and M. I. Rostovtseff, *Histoire économique et sociale de l'"Empire romain* [tr. O. Demange])," *Journal of Roman Studies* 82, 216–28.

    1993, "The Passion of Perpetua," *Past and Present* 139, 3–45.

    2001, *Spartacus and the Slave Wars: A Brief History with Documents*, Boston, MA and New York, NY.

    2003, "Judicial Nightmares and Christian Memory," *Journal of Early Christian Studies* 11, 533–63.

Sherk, R. K. 1969, *Roman Documents from the Greek East: Senatus consulta and epistulae to the Age of Augustus*, Baltimore, MD.

1984, *Rome and the Greek East to the Death of Augustus*, Cambridge.
Sherwin-White, A. N. 1973, *The Roman Citizenship* (2nd edn.), Oxford.
1982, "The *lex Repetundarum* and the Political Ideas of Gaius Gracchus," *Journal of Roman Studies* 72, 18–31.
Sherwin-White, S. and Kuhrt, A. 1993, *From Samarkhand to Sardis: A New Approach to the Seleucid Empire*, Berkeley, CA.
Simpson, C. J. 1977, "The Date of Dedication of the Temple of Mars Ultor," *Journal of Roman Studies* 67, 91–4.
Sion-Jenkis, K. 2009, "La perception du pouvoir impérial en Asie Mineure à l'époque Julio-Claudienne: l'exemple d'Aphrodisias," in Callagerin and Réchin (eds.), 69–95.
Sisani, S. 2014, "Qua aratrum ductum est. La colonizzazione romana come chiave interpretativa della Roma delle origini," in Stek and Pelgrom (eds.), 357–404.
Skinner, J. E. 2012, *The Invention of Greek Ethnography: From Homer to Herodotus*, Oxford.
Smallwood, E. M. 1976, *The Jews under Roman Rule: From Pompey to Diocletian*, Leiden.
Smarczyk, B. 1990, *Untersuchungen zur Religionspolitik und politischen Propaganda Athens im Delisch-Attischen Seebund*, Munich.
Smith, C. and Yarrow, L. M. (eds.) 2012, *Imperialism, Cultural Politics, and Polybius*, Oxford.
Smith, R. J. 1991, *Fortune-Tellers and Philosophers: Divination in Traditional Chinese Society*, Boulder.
Smith, R. R. 1987, "The Imperial Reliefs from the Sebasteion at Aphrodisias," *Journal of Roman Studies* 77, 88–138.
1998, "Cultural Choice and Political Identity in Honorific Portrait Statues in the Greek East in the Second Century AD," *Journal of Roman Studies* 88, 56–93.
Solin, H., Salomies, O., and Liertz, U.-M. (eds.) 1995, *Acta colloquii epigraphici Latini (Helsinki, Sept. 1991)*, Helsinki.
Speidel, M. A. 1992, "Roman Army Pay Scales," *Journal of Roman Studies* 82, 87–106.
2007, "Rekruten für ferne Provinzen: Der Papyrus ChLA X 422 und die kaiserliche Rekrutierungszentrale," *Zeitschrift für Papyrologie und Epigraphik* 163, 281–95.
Speidel, M. P. 1978, *The Religion of Iuppiter Dolichenus in the Roman Army*, Leiden.
Spencer, D. 2002, *The Roman Alexander: Reading a Cultural Myth*, Exeter.
Squarciapino, M. F. 1958, "I rilievi della tomba di Cartilio Poplicola," in Squarciapino (ed.), 191–207.
(ed.) 1958, *Scavi di Ostia, Vol. 3: Le necropoli, Pt. I: Le tombe di età repubblicana e augustea*, Rome.
St. John, R. 2011, *Line in the Sand: A History of the Western U.S.–Mexico Border*, Princeton, NJ.

Stadter, P. A. and van der Stockt, L. (ed.) 2002, *Sage and Emperor: Plutarch, Greek Intellectuals, and Roman Power in the Time of Trajan (98–117 AD)*, Leuven.

Stanton, D. C. and Stewart, A. J. (eds.) 1995, *Feminisms in the Academy*, Ann Arbor, MI.

Starr, C.J., Jr. 1952, "The Perfect Democracy of the Roman Empire," *American Historical Review* 58, 1–16.

Steel, C. E. W. 2001, *Cicero, Rhetoric, and Empire*, Oxford.

Stein-Hölkeskamp, E. and Hölkeskamp, K.-J. (eds.) 2006, *Erinnerungsorte der Antike: Die römische Welt*, Munich.

Stek, T. D. 2013, "Material Culture, Italic Identities and the Romanization of Italy," in Evans (ed.), 337–53.

Stek, T. D. and Pelgrom, J. (eds.) 2014, *Roman Republican Colonization: New Perspectives from Archaeology and Ancient History*, Rome.

Stern, S. 2012, *Calendars in Antiquity: Empires, States, and Societies*, Oxford.

Stoll, O. 2001, *Zwischen Integration und Abgrenzung: Die Religion des römischen Heeres im Nahen Osten. Studien zum Verhältnis von Armee und Zivilbevölkerung im römischen Syrien und den Nachbargebieten*, St. Katharinen.

  2007, "The Religions of the Armies," in Erdkamp (ed.), 451–76.

Stone, D. L. 2013, "The Archaeology of Africa in the Roman Republic," in Evans (ed.), 505–21.

Storchi Marino, A. (ed.) 1995, *L'incidenza dell'antico. Studi in memoria di Ettore Lepore, Vol. 1: Atti del Convegno Internazionale, Anacapri, marzo 1991*, Naples.

Strobel, K. 2007, "Vom marginalen Grenzraum zum Kernraum Europas: Das römische Heer als Motor der Neustrukturierung historischer Landschaften und Wirtschaftsräume," in de Blois and lo Cascio (eds.), 207–37.

Subrahmanyam, S. and Bayly, C. A. 1988, "Portfolio Capitalists and the Political Economy of Early Modern India," *Indian Economic and Social History Review* 25, 401–24.

Swain, S. and Edwards, M. J. (eds.) 2004, *Approaching Late Antiquity: The Transformation from Early to Late Empire*, Oxford.

Syme, R. 1939, *The Roman Revolution*, Oxford.

Talbert, R. J. 2004, "Rome's Provinces as Framework for World-View," in de Ligt, Hemelrijk, and Singor (eds.), 21–37.

  2012, "Roads Not Featured: A Roman Failure to Communicate?," in Alcock, Bodel and Talbert (eds.), 235–54.

Tan, J. 2015, "The Roman Republic," in Scheidel and Monson (eds.), 208–28.

  2017, *Power and Public Finance at Rome, 264–49 BCE*, Oxford.

Thonemann, P. J. 2004, "The Date of Lucullus' Quaestorship," *Zeitschrift für Papyrologie und Epigraphik* 149: 80–2.

Thorne, J. 2007, "Battle, Tactics, and the Emergence of the Limites in the West," in Erdkamp (ed.), 218–34.

Thornton, J. 2013, "Polybius in Context: The Political Dimension of the Histories," in Gibson and Harrison (eds.), 213–29.

Tomlin, R. S. O. 1988, "The Curse Tablets," in Cunliffe (ed.), 59–277.

Torelli, M. 1999, *Tota Italia: Essays in the Cultural Formation of Roman Italy*, Oxford.

Treves, P. 1953, *Il mito di Alessandro e la Roma d'Augusto*, Milan.

Tuplin, C. J. 1985, "Imperial Tyranny: Some Reflections on a Classical Greek Political Metaphor," in Cartledge and Harvey (eds.), 348–75.

Twitchett, D. and Loewe, M. (eds.) 1986, *The Cambridge History of China, Vol. 1: The Ch"in and Han Empires, 221 BC–AD 220*, Cambridge.

Urso, G. (ed.) 2010, *Cesare: precursore o visionario?: atti del convegno internazionale, Cividale del Friuli, 17–19 settembre 2009*, Pisa.

Van Bremen, R. 1993, "Women and Wealth," in Cameron and Kuhrt (eds.), 223–42.

1996, *The Limits of Participation: Women and Civic Life in the Greek East in the Hellenistic and Roman Periods*, Amsterdam.

Van den Hout, M. P. J. (ed.) 1988, *M. Cornelii Frontonis Epistulae. Schedis tam editis quam ineditis Edmundi Hauleris usus iterum edidit*, Leipzig.

Van Dommelen, P. and Knapp A. B. (eds.) 2010, *Material Connections: Mobility, Materiality and Mediterranean Identities*, London and New York, NY.

Van Nijf, O. M. 1997, *The Civic World of Professional Associations in the Roman East*, Amsterdam.

2008, "The Social World of Tax Farmers and their Personnel," in Cottier et al. (eds.), 279–311.

Vanacker, W. and Zuiderhoek, A. (eds.) 2017, *Imperial Identities in the Roman World*, London and New York, NY.

Vance, N. 1997, *The Victorians and Ancient Rome*, Oxford and Cambridge, MA.

Varto, E. (ed.) 2018, *Brill's Companion to Classics and Early Anthropology*, Leiden and Boston.

Vasunia, P. 2011, "The Comparative Study of Empires (Review of W. Scheidel [ed.], *Rome and China: Comparative Perspectives on Ancient World Empires*; I. Morris and W. Scheidel [eds.], *The Dynamics of Ancient Empires: State Power from Assyria to Byzantium*; F.-H. Mutschler and A. Mittag [eds.], *Conceiving the Empire: China and Rome Compared* and V. Smil, *Why America Is Not a New Rome*)," *Journal of Roman Studies* 101, 222–37.

2013, *The Classics and Colonial India*, Oxford.

Versluys, M. J. 2014, "Understanding Objects in Motion. An Archaeological Dialogue on Romanization," *Archaeological Dialogues* 21, 1–20.

Vervaet, F. and Ñaco del Hoyo, T. 2007, "War in Outer Space: Nature and Impact of the Roman War Effort in Spain, 218/217–197 BCE," in de Blois and lo Cascio (eds.), 21–46.

Veyne, P. 1992, *Bread and Circuses: Historical Sociology and Political Pluralism*, London.

Visser, R. 1992, "Fascist Doctrine and the Cult of the *Romanità*," *Journal of Contemporary History* 27, 5–22.

Von Reden, S. 2010, *Money in Classical Antiquity*, Cambridge.

Vout, C. 2007, *Power and Eroticism in Imperial Rome*, Cambridge.

Walbank, F. W. 1957–1979, *A Historical Commentary on Polybius*, 3 vols., Oxford.

1972, *Polybius*, Berkeley, CA.

1974, "Polybius between Greece and Rome," in Gabba (ed.), 3–38.

1985, *Selected Papers: Studies in Greek and Roman History and Historiography*, Cambridge.

Wallace-Hadrill, A. 1982, "*Civilis princeps*: Between Citizen and King," *Journal of Roman Studies* 72, 32–48.

1986, "Image and Authority in the Coinage of Augustus," *Journal of Roman Studies* 76, 66–87.

1987, "Time for Augustus: Ovid, Augustus and the Fasti," in Whitby, Hardie, and Whitby (eds.), 221–30.

1989a (ed.), *Patronage in Ancient Society*, London.

1989b, "Rome's Cultural Revolution (Review of P. Zanker, *The Power of Images in the Age of Augustus* [tr. A. Shapiro])," *Journal of Roman Studies* 79, 157–64.

1998, "To Be Roman, Go Greek: Thoughts on Hellenization at Rome," *Bulletin of the Institute of Classical Studies* 42, 79–91.

2005, "*Mutatas formas*. The Augustan Transformation of Roman Knowledge," in Galinsky (ed.), 55–84.

2008, *Rome's Cultural Revolution*, Cambridge.

Ward-Perkins, B. 2005, *The Fall of Rome and the End of Civilization*, Oxford.

Webster, J. and Cooper, N. (eds.) 1996, *Roman Imperialism: Post-Colonial Perspectives. Proceedings of a Symposium Held at Leicester University in November 1994*, Leicester.

Weiler, G. 2007, "Römisches Militär und die Gründung niedergermanischer Städte," in de Blois and lo Cascio (eds.), 371–90.

Weißenberger, M. 2002, "Das Imperium Romanum in den Proömien dreier griechischer Historiker: Polybios, Dionysios von Halikarnassos und Appian," *Rheinisches Museum für Philologie* 145, 262–81.

Welch, K. (ed.) 2015, *Appian's Roman History: Empire and Civil War*, Swansea.

Welch, K. E. 2007, *The Roman Amphitheatre: From Its Origins to the Colosseum*, Cambridge.

Wesch-Klein, G. 1999, "Equites Romani und Euergetismus," in Demougin, Devijver, and Raepsaet-Charlier (eds.), 301–19.

Wheeler, E. L. 2007, "The Army and the Limes in the East," in Erdkamp (ed.), 235–66.

Whitby, M., Hardie, P., and Whitby, M. (eds.) 1987, *Homo Viator: Classical Essays for John Bramble*, Bristol and Oak Park IL.

White, R. 1991, *The Middle Ground: Indians, Empires, and Republics in the Great Lakes Region, 1650–1815*, Cambridge.

Whitehead, J. 1993, "The Cena Trimalchionis and Biographical Narrative in Roman Middle-Class Art," in Holliday (ed.), 299–325.

Whitmarsh, T. (ed.) 2010, *Local Knowledge and Microidentities in the Imperial Greek World*, Cambridge.

Whittaker, C. R. 1994, *Frontiers of the Roman Empire: A Social and Economic Study*, Baltimore, MD.

1997, "Imperialism and Culture: The Roman Initiative," in Mattingly (ed.), 143–63.

2004, *Rome and Its Frontiers: The Dynamics of Empire*, London and New York, NY.

Wiedemann, T. E. J. 1992, *Emperors and Gladiators*, London and New York, NY.

Wilhelm, A. 1914, "Urkunden aus Messene," *Jahreshefte des Österreichischen Archäologischen Instituts in Wien* 17, 1–120.

Williams, J. 2005, "Coinage and Identity in Pre-Conquest Britain: 50 BC–AD 50," in Howgego, Heuchert, and Burnett (eds.), 69–78.

Wilmott, T. (ed.) 2009, *Hadrian's Wall: Archaeological Research by English Heritage 1976–2000*, Swindon.

Wilson, A. 2002, "Machines, Power and the Ancient Economy," *Journal of Roman Studies* 92, 1–32.

2004, "Tuscan Landscapes: Surveying the Albegna Valley (Review of A. Carandini and F. Cambi [eds.], *Paesaggi d'Etruria. Valle dell'Albegna, Valle d'Oro, Valle del Chiarone, Valle del Tafone: progetto di ricerca italo-britannico seguito allo scavo di Settefinestre*)," *Journal of Roman Archaeology* 17, 569–76.

Wilson, R. J. A. 2006, "What's New in Roman Baden-Württemberg? (Review of Archäologischen Landesmuseum Baden-Württemberg [ed.], *Imperium Romanum. Roms Provinzen an Neckar, Rhein und Donau*; Badischen Landesmuseum Karlsruhe [ed.], *Imperium Romanum. Römer, Christen, Alamannen: Die Spätantike am Oberrhein*, and D. Planck [ed.], *Die Römer in Baden-Württemberg, Römerstätten und Museen von Aalen bis Zwiefalten*)," *Journal of Roman Studies* 96, 198–212.

Winkler, J. 1980, "Lollianos and the Desperadoes," *Journal of Hellenic Studies* 100, 155–81.

Winter, I. J. 1995, "Homer's Phoenicians: History, Ethnography, or Literary Trope? (A Perspective on Early Orientalism)," in Carter and Morris (eds.), 247–71.

Wiseman, T. P. 1970, "Roman Republican Road-Building," *Papers of the British School at Rome* 38, 122–52.

1994, "The Senate and the Populares, 69–60 BC," in Crook, Lintott, and Rawson (eds.), 327–67.

Witcher, R. E. 2000, "Globalisation and Roman Imperialism: Perspectives on Identities in Roman Italy," in Herring and Lomas (eds.), 213–25.

Woolf, G. 1990, "Food, Poverty and Patronage: The Significance of the Epigraphy of the Roman Alimentary Schemes in Early Imperial Italy," *Papers of the British School at Rome* 58, 197–228.

1993, "Roman Peace," in Rich and Shipley (eds.), 171–94.

1994, "Becoming Roman, Staying Greek: Culture, Identity and the Civilizing Process in the Roman East," *Proceedings of the Cambridge Philological Society* 40, 116–43.

1996, "The Uses of Forgetfulness in Roman Gaul," in Gehrke and Möller (eds.), 361–81.

1998, *Becoming Roman: The Origins of Provincial Civilization in Gaul,* Cambridge.

2000, "Urbanization and its Discontents in Early Roman Gaul," in Fentress (ed.), 115–31.

2003, "Seeing Apollo in Roman Gaul and Germany," in Scott and Webster (eds.), 139–52.

2011, *Tales of the Barbarians: Ethnography and Empire in the Roman West,* Chichester and Malden, MA.

2012, *Rome: An Empire's Story,* Oxford.

2014, "Romanization 2.0 and Its Alternatives," *Archaeological Dialogues* 21, 45–50.

Yadin, Y., Greenfield, J. C., Yardeni, A., and Levine, B. A. (eds.) 2002, *The Documents from the Bar-Kokhba Period in the Cave of Letters: Hebrew, Aramaic and Nabatean-Aramaic Papyri,* 2 vols., Jerusalem.

Yarrow, L. M. 2006, "Lucius Mummius and the Spoils of War," *Scripta Classica Israelica* 25, 57–70.

Ying, L. 2004, "Ruler of the Treasure Country: The Image of the Roman Empire in Chinese Society from the First to the Fourth Centuries AD," *Latomus* 63, 327–39.

Zanker, P. 1988, *The Power of Images in the Age of Augustus,* tr. A. Shapiro, Ann Arbor, MI.

(ed.) 1976, *Hellenismus in Mittelitalien: Kolloquium in Göttingen vom 5. bis 9. Juni 1974,* 2 vols., Göttingen.

Ziolkowski, A. 1992, *The Temples of Mid-Republican Rome and Their Historical and Topographical Context,* Rome.

1993, "Urbs direpta or How the Romans Sacked Cities," in Rich and Shipley (eds.), 69–91.

Zuiderhoek, A. 2009, *The Politics of Munificence in the Roman Empire: Citizens, Elites and Benefactors in Asia Minor,* Cambridge.

# Index